Conversations with Maxine Hong Kingston

Literary Conversations Series

Peggy Whitman Prenshaw
General Editor

D1378458

University of California, Berkeley. Photo by Jane Scherr, 1996

Conversations
with Maxine Hong Kingston

Edited by
Paul Skenazy and Tera Martin

University Press of Mississippi
Jackson

Books by Maxine Hong Kingston

The Woman Warrior: Memoirs of a Girlhood Among Ghosts (New York: Knopf, 1976).
China Men (New York: Knopf, 1980).
Hawai'i One Summer, 1978 (San Francisco: Meadow Press, 1987).
Tripmaster Monkey: His Fake Book (New York: Knopf, 1989).

Copyright © 1998 by University Press of Mississippi
All rights reserved
Manufactured in the United States of America

01   00   99   98   4   3   2   1

The paper in this book meets the guidelines for permanence and durability of the Committee on Production Guidelines for Book Longevity of the Council on Library Resources.

Library of Congress Cataloging-in-Publication Data

Kingston, Maxine Hong.
    Conversations with Maxine Hong Kingston / edited by Paul Skenazy and Tera Martin.
        p.   cm. — (Literary conversations series)
    Includes index.
    ISBN 1-57806-058-3 (cloth : alk. paper). — ISBN 1-57806-059-1 (paper : alk. paper)
    1. Kingston, Maxine Hong—Interviews.   2. Women and literature—United States—History—20th century.   3. Authors, American—20th century—Interviews.   4. Chinese Americans in literature.
5. Chinese Americans—Interviews.   I. Skenazy, Paul.   II. Martin, Tera.   III. Title.   IV. Series.
    PS3561.I52Z466   1998
    973'.04951'0092—dc21
    [B]   98-6741
                                                                    CIP

British Library Cataloging-in-Publication Data available

Contents

Introduction

Maxine Ting Ting Hong Kingston has published three books: two memoirs, *The Woman Warrior: Memoirs of a Girlhood Among Ghosts* (1976) and *China Men* (1980), and a novel, *Tripmaster Monkey: His Fake Book* (1989). These books have earned her a number of honors and awards, among them a National Book Critics Circle Award in nonfiction, an American Book Award, and a National Humanities Medal. In 1980, she was declared a "Living Treasure of Hawaii" by an Hawaiian Buddhist sect, an honor usually reserved for someone twice her then age of 39.

More important than these official recognitions, however, is the cultural position she has assumed as a Chinese American. It is estimated that her work is the most anthologized of any living American writer, and that she is read by more American college students than any other living author. Students, particularly Asian American women, look to her as a model, find themselves in her tales, seek her out with sycophantic regularity. She has opened the way to a whole generation of Asian American writers who have found a national audience for the first time; standing for many, poet Marilyn Chin confessed to Kingston during her interview that reading *The Woman Warrior* "really made a difference in my life. . . . I think it gave us permission to go on. . . . My whole family was in that book." (Chin) By the late 1980s, as Kingston notes in her interview with William Satake Blauvelt, her voice had so stamped itself on the publishing industry as *the* Asian American consciousness that some young writers complained to her that they were getting "a generic Maxine Hong Kingston rejection letter" from publishers looking for Kingston imitations: "the publishers reject [these writers], but on top of that, they advise them to read my work." (Blauvelt) Struggling against stereotypes, she had become something of a type herself.

All this from someone who describes herself as a child who was unable to answer questions in school, who failed kindergarten, who was given an IQ score of 0 and condemned to the corner of the classroom for her so-called stupidity, and whose mother cut her tongue to improve her "pressed-duck voice."[1] But even as she struggled to speak, Maxine Hong Kingston knew she wanted to write; as she told Kay Bonetti, "In a way, I've never been silent. . . . While I've had problems speaking, I've always been a writer. There was always the wanting to tell the stories of the people." (Bonetti) For her, she explains to Karen Horton, writing is like a habit: "I have to eat, I have to breathe, I have to write." (Horton)

Kingston's great contribution to American literature has been to tell us story after story of her family and forebears as they've encountered the adventures, pleasures, and disappointments of their migration from China to the "Gold Mountain" of America. Working back to the early Chinese immigrations of the late nineteenth century and forward to her own struggles to make meaning of her life during the 1940s, 1950s, and 1960s, Kingston has given voice to a marginalized community: to the women—her mother and aunts—in *The Woman Warrior*, and to the men—her father, grandfathers, uncles and brothers—in *China Men*.

Her achievement, as she notes at the beginning of *The Woman Warrior*, was to "name the unspeakable," to violate a series of cultural injunctions and introduce us to a nameless Chinese American girl growing to womanhood in Stockton, California (5). The very first sentence of *The Woman Warrior*— " 'You must not tell anyone,' my mother said, 'what I am about to tell you.' "—announced that Kingston's memoir would break silence, undo a legacy of secrecy, and betray her mother's warnings by communicating the story of her "no name aunt" to the world (3). Throughout these interviews, Kingston movingly, and jokingly, returns to this moment when she challenged long-standing familial, and cultural, confinements and opened her family's practices to observation, examination, and reinterpretation. Sometimes, she will playfully admit her culpability, and accept her role as a transgressor; as often, she will lightly evade blame by rationalizing that she *wrote* rather than *told* the story (and so did not literally defy her mother). Eventually, as in the interviews with Donna Perry and Eric James Schroeder, she proudly recognizes how her own revelations, and reevaluations, of the often secret rites inside her community echo the openings of books like *The Color Purple* by Alice Walker and *The Bluest Eye* by Toni Morrison—other ethnic women writers whose works at once defy and seek to renew the woman's position within their cultural traditions.

---

[1] Maxine Hong Kingston, *The Woman Warrior: Memoirs of a Girlhood Among Ghosts* (New York: Knopf, 1976), 192. Subsequent page references to *The Woman Warrior* come from this edition.

As she makes clear throughout these interviews, Kingston's project in *The Woman Warrior* is to remake the world that has made her. She struggles to repossess, to appropriate, her inheritance as a Chinese American—her individual one as a girl growing to maturity in a culture that has historically enslaved and belittled women, and her communal one as part of a culture whose stories have been banished from the record of American life. Against this legacy, she argues, reimagines, alters, revises. She takes lessons in modest behavior and suppression like the tale of her "no name aunt" and reconstructs them, seeking what she calls "ancestral help" from her condemned progenitors. She recognizes how even as she was raised on myths designed to demean, she was also provided with tools of liberation, like the legends of Fa Mu Lan, a woman warrior, and Ts'ai Yen, an exiled and imprisoned poet. She puts her inheritance to the test of present need, sifting to discover what in it is useful and to challenge what is not; to pay homage to ancestors but resist blind conformity to their faiths.

In the process, Kingston discovers new forms of narrative within her inherited tradition of "talk-story." She creates a malleable tale-telling frame where stories become a site of self-questioning. Revealing the mixed meanings inherent in her inheritances, Kingston takes adages and customs meant to denigrate and turns them back on themselves. Stories of oppression become stories of defiance; tales of enslavement are reshaped into dreams of freedom. Appropriating the past rather than merely absorbing it, she reminds readers that legacies can be created as well as acquiesced to: we might, at least partially, reimagine the past, and so provide unimagined possibilities for the future. It is this achievement that has made her a magnet for so many women who find their own struggles mirrored in hers. As she looks back with Shelley Fisher Fishkin at *The Woman Warrior*'s continued popularity, she jokingly realizes that she's written sophisticated "how-to" books: " 'How to Live,' . . . 'How Not to Give Up,' 'How to Understand One Another,' 'How to Cut Through Silences,' . . . 'How to Keep the Family Together.' " (Fishkin)

These how-to's are, in fact, subjects Kingston returns to again and again under the questioning of reporters, critics, and students. She emphasizes the dual and contradictory inheritances she has as a Chinese American woman taught subservience as well as heroism: through the women in the form of talk-story, and through the men in the adventures they encountered as travelers to Hawaii, California, and New York. In recounting these traditions, Kingston provides readers with access into a world, or series of worlds, both familiar and strange—at once an essential part of American life and one long excluded from the public conversation. As Kingston frequently notes in these interviews, she struggles constantly with the problem of how to write about Chinese Americans to audiences that often know little of their traditions, less of their customs, and almost nothing of their language. She explains the difficulties this way to Timothy Pfaff: "The mainstream culture doesn't know the history of Chinese Americans. . . . That ignorance makes a tension for me." (Pfaff) She tells Paul Skenazy that since most American readers know so little about Chinese American culture, "I easily could have tried to explain everything, but then there would have been too much exposition."(Skenazy, "Coming Home") Instead, Kingston develops several distinct strategies that she uses at different times in her writings, and which she explains in detail in these interviews: her insertion of asides about her own research; her references to dictionary definitions of Chinese terms; her recapitulation of many Chinese myths even if in somewhat altered form; and, in *China Men*, her insertion of a chapter on the exclusionary acts that controlled Asian immigration and settlement in this country for nearly a century.

Part of her work, then, has been to serve as what she calls a "translator"—an intermediary between Chinese American history and mainstream assumptions, between Chinese folk tales and American popular culture, and between her parents' experiences and her own youth. These efforts at translation are cultural and linguistic, actual and metaphorical. Kingston frequently refers back to the particular pressures she felt as a writer early in her career, attempting to develop a language, and a form of storytelling, that might adequately suggest the Chinese American world she found around her, where old traditions came to her with an American accent. She explains to Marilyn Chin that when she wrote *The Woman Warrior* and *China Men*, "I was trying to find an American language that would translate the speech of the people who are living their lives with the Chinese language. They carry on their adventures and their emotional life and everything in Chinese. I had to find a way to translate all that into a graceful American language." (Chin) To Timothy Pfaff, she worries about her orthographic skills trying to represent "people who speak a dialect of Cantonese called Say Yup. . . . I'm specifically interested in how the Chinese American dialect is spoken in the California Valley." (Pfaff)

In her struggle to represent her own, and her family's, history, Kingston also demands recognition for the Chinese American community's role in American life. Talking to William Satake Blauvelt, she recalls that as early as the age of fifteen, she published her first essay, entitled "I Am an American," in *American Girl* magazine. (Blauvelt) Writing of her grandfathers, she explains to Marilyn Chin, she offers a portrait of nineteenth-century America, where Chinese labor helped to "bind the country together with steel, the bands of steel that are the railroads." (Chin) She insists that Americans recognize the importance of Asian immigrants in the development of the nation, and she offers her works as a corrective to the historical record—an effort, as she puts it to Arturo Islas, to "claim America." She tells him, "I am saying, 'No, we're not outsiders, we belong here, this is our country, this is our history, and we are a part of America. We are a part of American history. If it weren't for us, America would be a different place.' " (Islas) And in presenting this corrective to the historical record, Kingston wants also to suggest an artistic methodology: an entrance into the past through storytelling, mythology and imagination. Her model for *China Men*, she explains, is William Carlos Williams' *In the American Grain*; as she notes speaking to Timothy Pfaff, "Williams has told American history poetically and, it seems to me, truly. In a way, I feel that I have continued that book." (Pfaff)

Insistent as she is about her role as an intermediary between cultures, Kingston is equally emphatic that her life not be read ethnographically. Early in *The Woman Warrior*, she asks rhetorically, "Chinese Americans, when you try to understand what things in you are Chinese, how do you separate what is peculiar to childhood, to poverty, insanities, one family, your mother who marked your growing with stories, from what is Chinese? What is Chinese tradition and what is the movies?" (5–6)

Her answers to these questions, though various, work to resist simple categorization. Even as she tells Timothy Pfaff that she can use the word "we" as a Chinese American and knows she speaks for more than herself, she also insists that it is too easy for people to turn her into a cultural voice, and that her work is most important as she is most distinct. (Pfaff) To Arturo Islas she explains that when she asked her sister to rank the uniqueness of their family in relation to other Chinese Americans on a scale of 1 (representative) to 10 (odd), her sister's answer was that they were an 8. (Islas) However often she hears from others that she has represented their lives in recording her own, Kingston underlines to interviewer after interviewer that her particular experiences were marked by her particular family, its literacy, its rural peasant background in China, her mother's talk-stories, her father's training as a poet, and the small if intimate Chinese American community in Stockton. All of these forces, she insists, make her memoirs uniquely her own. But as she realizes, the issues of representativeness will not be solved until there are more books by more Asian Americans; as she explains to Paul Skenazy, "If there were lots of books about us then every book wouldn't have to carry the burden of being representative. Then everyone would see that since there's such a variety in the way that we write, there must be a variety in our people." (Skenazy, "Kingston at the University")

But the fact that Kingston has acquired an enormous following, that her books were best sellers, and that she is the most frequently taught Chinese American in United States universities at the present time means that her comments carry special weight. Her prominence has not only led to misreadings and stereotyping by white audiences eager to turn her into a cultural spokeswoman, but to some fierce disagreements within the Chinese American community about Kingston's approach to her material. Again and again in these interviews, Kingston is forced to respond to the critical remarks of her Chinese American detractors. Three kinds of challenges dominate. First, her critics note what Kingston herself is quick to point out, that her books do not reflect the experiences of a majority of the Chinese American community. Second, they argue that she distorts or is ignorant about the Chinese mythologies she uses in her talk-story legends, particularly the stories of Fa Mu Lan and Ts'ai Yen. Third, she is accused of feminizing and emasculating the Chinese American male community; her fame, these critics argue, comes from the support of white feminists who have conspired with the New York publishers to encourage the work of a few ethnic women while excluding the writings of many Chinese American men. To these three accusations, a fourth was added with the publication of *Tripmaster Monkey*: that the novel was a satiric attack, a deliberate *roman à clef* based on the life of Frank Chin, a Chinese American playwright of note and one of Kingston's most frequent, and virulent, critics.

Kingston's responses to these arguments vary from explanation to annoyance. She freely admits her idiosyncratic childhood, and also talks frequently about the calculated emphases in her portraits of Chinese Americans—her stress on their playfulness and raucousness, for example, as a counterweight to the stereotypes of the joyless Asian always at work. As she notes talking to Paula Rabinowitz, Marilyn Chin and Neila Seshachari, the charges of manipulation by a feminist cabal echo similar accusations leveled at other well-known ethnic women writers like Alice Walker by African American males. Linking the argument to issues of physical violence within minority communities, she tells Marilyn Chin that the man in these circumstances "has it all wrong, who the enemy is" and so strikes out at women rather than at the broader atmosphere of racism that is responsible. (Chin) The challenges to *Tripmaster Monkey* cause her more direct consternation, because they shift the critical ground from consideration of the novel's success as a representation of a man struggling to find his way to right action in the 1960s into a literary revenge scenario. She is quick to point out that though there might be resemblances to Chin's life in the book, these come not from an effort to satirize any individual but from shared historical experiences: Chin and Kingston were students at Berkeley in these years, and many of the experiences in *Tripmaster Monkey* were based on her own life, her husband's and those of friends. She notes how several Chinese American men have embraced their resemblance to Wittman Ah Sing, the protagonist, and she insists to William Satake Blauvelt that she doesn't believe "in revenge. I see [*Tripmaster Monkey*] as a kind of big love letter." (Blauvelt)

Her manipulation of traditional Chinese legends is a more interesting and complex issue, and has produced some of her most valuable self-critical comments about her intentions as a writer. For Kingston, memory provides a guide to what remains valuable about the past; as she tells Paula Rabinowitz, "The artist's memory winnows out; it edits for what is important and significant." (Rabinowitz) Because of that, she is less interested in what the myths were in China than in what they have become in America; as she tells Timothy Pfaff: "We have to do more than record myth. . . . The way I keep the old Chinese myths alive is by telling them in a new American way." (Pfaff) To Kay Bonetti, she explains that "mythology and stories and rituals change to give you strength under present circumstances. Either that, or they die." Thus Kingston feels free, as she tells Bonetti, to change the myths: "I change them a lot. . . . I have no intention of just recording myths. I mean, I'm not an archivist." (Bonetti) And so, for example, when she integrates a male story of words carved on a man's back with the legend of Fa Mu Lan, a female warrior, her decision is calculated: "I gave a man's myth to a woman because it's part of the feminist war that's going on in *The Woman Warrior*, to take the men's stories away from them and give the strength of that story to a woman. I see that as an aggressive storytelling act, and also it's part of my own freedom to play with the myth." (Bonetti)

So once again, as with her revisions of the story of her "no name aunt," Kingston insists on her right, and need, to appropriate the tales of her growing. By remaking the past, she cunningly usurps forms meant for socialization and recreates them as the shape of her resistance. Her commitment is to rejuvenation and reinterpretation of the inherited myths: to recognizing their sustaining importance, and redesigning them as appropriate vehicles for her American life. The mythology of *Tripmaster Monkey*, for example, derives from the connection she discovers between the irreverence of 1960s America and the Monkey King's role in Chinese culture as a trickster. She tells Paula Rabinowitz, Marilyn Chin, and Jody Hoy how she appropriates American precursors—novels like *The Scarlet Letter*, Gertrude Stein book titles, the plot structure of "I Love Lucy" episodes, Walt Whitman's poetry—and combines them with her own stories. She notes how she alters European tales like the story of Robinson Crusoe, which came to her as talk-story through her mother, to fit her need in *China Men* to emphasize issues of fatherhood. She talks about how in both *The Woman Warrior* and *China Men* she shifts the relationship of myth and everyday reality to accommodate her different sense of how that relationship developed for women and men in America: integrated and supportive for women; divided and disengaged for men. And, in many of the interviews, she not only explains her revision practices as a writer but exemplifies them as well, when she answers a question with new details about the myths, demonstrating how she continues to worry a story, to discover more in it, and to wonder why she left certain portions out of her books.

At least as important as what these interviews reveal about Kingston's intentions, however, is what they offer as a map of the development of a writer eager to both reclaim and rectify a legacy that encouraged her silence. Speaking to college students, she admits that she couldn't write as a child in Chinese, that it was only at the age of 8 or 9 "when I learned English that I started writing down the stories. . . . Oh, I just thought it was a miracle. . . . And I just kept writing from there." (Skenazy, "Kingston at the University") She recounts her early hopes that she might be a painter rather than a writer. She discusses her slow development of skills and discipline; her devious mental maneuvers to give herself permission to write without self-censorship; her growing realization that form itself might provide revelation and reconciliation. She insists to Timothy Pfaff that "Most literary forms are not artificial. They reflect patterns of the human heart," and to a university audience she explains her process in more detail: "I could be as ungrateful and ugly as I wanted to. I could put down forbidden emotions and thoughts. But then the next thing that happened was that the form of a short story . . . guides you to confronting all kinds of things, . . . and then it guides you toward resolution." (Pfaff; Skenazy, "Kingston at the University") As she tells Shelley Fisher Fishkin, "There's a redemption that takes place in art." (Fishkin)

As a writer, Maxine Hong Kingston has based much of her work on talk-story: the tales of fantastic adventure, memory, dream, and everyday accident and happenstance she heard as a child in her home, especially from her mother. It should be no surprise, then, that Kingston herself is a wonderful storyteller in person, able to season a conversation with anecdotes and reminiscences that link her acute aesthetic and political ideas to the mire and wonder of the commonplace. The interviews collected in this volume are filled with instances of this sort, suggesting the relish with which Kingston enters discussions of her family, her culture, her work, her world, and her ambitions as an artist.

The interviews span almost twenty years, from 1977, shortly after the publication of *The Woman Warrior*, to 1996. They represent about two-thirds of the interviews we were able to discover, and show Kingston discussing her work with the press, students, critics, and other readers. They are concentrated in the period from 1980 to the early 1990s and cluster around a few moments: the early 1980s, immediately after the publication of *China Men*; 1986, when Kingston was nearing completion of *Tripmaster Monkey* and met with critics anxious to discuss her first two books within the emerging fields of ethnic women's writing and autobiography; 1989, when the publication of *Tripmaster Monkey* allowed Kingston to travel extensively and accept several invitations to teach at universities around the United States; and in the mid-1990s, when she talks of the fire that destroyed her manuscript, looks back to the workshops on peace and reconciliation she has been conducting for Vietnam veterans, and projects forward to her new novel, tentatively titled *The Fifth Book of Peace*.

The main issues, or obsessions, of Kingston's career are evident from the very first, and are reiterated frequently from interview to interview: the question of the fictional versus autobiographical content of the companion volumes, *The Woman Warrior* and *China Men*; the place of recollection and invention in her stories; the roles of intuition and research in Kingston's process of writing; the relative importance of aesthetic and political concerns in her sense of herself as a writer; her feminism in relation to her Chinese American inheritance as a woman. In these first interviews, she gradually fills in details of her family's experiences: their background in their small villages in China; the particular features of the Chinese American community in Stockton; the effects of growing up in a bilingual home; her talk-story inheritance; her distinction between the "imaginary China" she was trying to create in her books and the actual political nation; her passion for writing;

and her desire to claim a place for herself in the traditional canon and for
Chinese Americans in the national historical narrative. She moves in expan-
sive ways from these subjects to others: her gradual discoveries about how to
transmute family stories into public, artistic tales; the influence of other writers as varied as Nathaniel Hawthorne, Gertrude Stein, Virginia Woolf, Walt
Whitman and Jade Snow Wong; her feeling of alliance with the work in
cultural excavation of contemporaries like Toni Morrison, Alice Walker, and
Leslie Marmon Silko; her experiences living in Hawaii and returning home
to California.

In the interviews that begin in the mid-1980s, Kingston returns frequently
to her observations as she traveled in China for the first time and had the
opportunity to compare the reality of the country with her imaginative repre-
sentations of it in her first two books. By the time she was at work on *Tripmaster Monkey*, Kingston could look back at her first two works and reopen
discussion of the different pleasures and problems of writing fiction and
memoir. The novel also brought her new questions from her interviewers:
about her decision to focus her book on a male protagonist; about the role of
the female narrative voice; about the relationship between American individ-
ualism and community; and about her interest in issues of pacifism that would
result in her work with Vietnam veterans. And through all the interviews,
there is Kingston's love of a good story, her wonderful outbursts when she
would disengage from a question and launch into an illuminating tale, or
offer an extended meditation on art or mythology, war or the imagination.

Reading these interviews in chronological sequence provides the opportunity to see the variations in Kingston's responses to similar questions. Partly
through facing the same concerns again and again, Kingston reaches fuller
and more intense formulations of her ideas or provides new contexts in which
to consider them. In her first interviews with Gary Kubota and Karen Horton,
for example, Kingston was reticent to talk about *The Woman Warrior* as
autobiography. She admitted to Kubota that "the stories within the book are
based mostly on my past experiences as a child," but focused on the "fictional techniques" that for her defined the book as fiction. (Kubota) In the
detailed and thoughtful interview with Timothy Pfaff in 1980, *The Woman
Warrior* and *China Men* continue to be called "novels," even as they were
being published as nonfiction. (Pfaff) By 1986, however, no doubt under the
pressure of her discoveries as she worked on *Tripmaster Monkey*, she offers
a different and more complex commentary to Kay Bonetti and Paula Rabinowitz. To Bonetti, she explains that she has "begun to understand" that she's

written "a new kind of biography, . . . the biographies of imaginative people. I tell the imaginative lives and the dreams and the fictions of real people. These are the stories of storytellers, and so I tell you what their dreams are and what stories they tell." (Bonetti) And to Paula Rabinowitz, she offers a similar suggestion for reclassification of her first books: "I invented new literary structures to contain multiversions and to tell the true lives of non-fiction people who are storytellers. . . . After going back and forth on my classification for a couple of years, I've decided that I am writing . . . about real people, all of whom have minds that love to invent fictions. I am writing the biography of their imaginations." (Rabinowitz) Kingston continues to play with this issue of classification in many of the interviews, one time emphasizing the different freedoms and constraints each kind of writing provides, at another noticing how her focus on dreams, imagination and the inner life correspond to her own family's traditions and the belief systems of many minority communities, at still another telling Donna Perry that "I never categorize my work. It all feels like one long flow, and the process is not that different." (Perry)

One sees similar expansion and self-revision throughout this book, as Kingston tries out ideas in front of interviewers. She argues with her convoluted syntax in *The Woman Warrior*, suggesting its source in her own evasive efforts to confront difficult subjects from her childhood; sometimes she is proud of the style as a device for forcing readers to struggle with their own confusions, at other points she is equally proud that she had moved in *China Men* to a simpler, more direct language. She develops a theory to explain her shifts in narrative voice from book to book, the self-focused interiority of *The Woman Warrior* giving way to the more formal and observant position as a female narrator of male lives in *China Men*, and that in turn preparing her for a stance as a chiding yet forgiving female goddess-voice of Kuan Yin in *Tripmaster Monkey*. After her trip to China, Kingston talks about things she wished she had known about the villages of her parents, adds wonderful asides about some of the less prominent figures in her memoirs, and offers altered versions of the myths she used.

These shifts in position and idea are more than just afterthoughts: they suggest a consciousness that never rests content, that is always seeking to understand herself in new contexts, new relationships. In her books, one rarely encounters a finality that is not qualified, framed by doubt, enmeshed in uncertainty. In these interviews too, one senses a writer who refuses to simplify, who insists on elaborating, embroidering, and wondering. If there is any faith that survives the self-questioning it is Kingston's confidence in the powers of the imagination, given form in words; in the hands of the artist, she constantly suggests, language might move the heart, and alter the world. And it is as she speaks of imagination that Kingston reveals how her aesthetics and politics are inseparable. She recounts with pride how her imagination leads her from chaos to form, from confusion to truth; how it provides an accurate depiction of a China she had never known; how it prepared her to notice a whistling arrow in a Chinese museum. She tells Shelley Fisher Fishkin that "words can get through all kinds of barriers," and insists that the first step in creating a peaceful world is imagining the possibility. (Fishkin) Her faith wavers at times. She tells Kay Bonetti that "in my stories the pen is always problematical. It's always on the verge of not winning. But I think maybe the frustration I feel is that writers have the power to change the world only a little bit at a time. We conquer a reader at a time. We change the atmosphere of the world, and we change moods here and there, whereas the people who have the guns and the bombs have so much direct power. . . . If only the word had as much power." (Bonetti) But she returns frequently to the idea that it is the writer's task, and privilege, to reimagine the present and so provide new alternatives for the future. As she explains with pride to Paul Skenazy, by emphasizing the dignity of the words "china . . . men" in the title of her book, she was able to remove the pejorative slur from the term and "straighten up the language a little bit. . . . I feel a lot of triumph in just that one word." (Skenazy, "Coming Home")

As is the practice in the Literary Conversations series, the interviews in this volume are presented in chronological order according to the dates on which they were conducted; these dates are provided in the headnotes as precisely as was possible. With the exceptions mentioned below, the interviews are presented in their entirety, as originally published. Book titles have been regularized into italics. Typographical errors and obvious factual mistakes (an inaccurate allusion to a book title, for example) have been silently corrected. We have shortened some of the introductions to the interviews by eliminating repeated references to the titles of Kingston's own publications; any other material in the introductions—comments on Kingston's appearance or manner, her preoccupations, her language, her speaking voice, her home— have been retained.

Some of the interviews in this volume occur in two versions; in each case we have provided the more inclusive one. Timothy Pfaff's *New York Times*

Book Review discussion with Kingston includes material missing from his article developed from the same interview and published in *Horizon*. The published version of Arturo Islas's interview, included in the volume *Women Writers of the West Coast*, deletes some of the original interview material and transforms the question-and-answer format to a magazine style, thereby truncating some of Kingston's intricate responses; instead, we've used a typed transcription of the original interview provided by Islas to the editors. Likewise Paul Skenazy's "Coming Home" is based on the transcriptions of his conversations with Kingston and not on the published newspaper article. Kay Bonetti chose to alter the transcript of her radio interview with Kingston by editing some of her questions. In addition, the longer interview "Kingston at the University" is published for the first time; as the headnote describes in more detail, it represents a compilation of Kingston's work with several classes at the University of California, Santa Cruz, in November 1989.

We want to thank a number of people for their help in compiling this manuscript. First, there is Ms. Kingston herself, who has supported the idea of such a compilation from the outset and has provided such fine material for us to work with. Second, our thanks to the interviewers and publishers, who have been generous with their permissions to reprint material. More locally, we want to thank Kenji M. Treanor, who generously helped with research on early interviews with Kingston in Hawaii; Maureen Kawaoka, who thoughtfully sent important materials on Kingston from Berkeley; the Editing Center at the University of California, which provided needed help in transcription; Betsy Wootten, who offered valuable administrative assistance; and Mindy Yaninek, who scrupulously recorded nearly illegible corrections at crucial stages. And finally, we thank Seetha Srinivasan and Anne Stascavage, who encouraged us throughout and provided needed guidance about all aspects of the volume.

One of Maxine Hong Kingston's continued preoccupations, apparent in all her comments, written and in conversation, is that people be encouraged to discover their own voices, so they might add their stories to the public dialogue. In this spirit, we'd like to dedicate this book to those who remain silent, or silenced. We hope that Ms. Kingston's comments on her struggles to find her voice, and to realize forms appropriate to her experiences, will help inspire others to create their own talk-stories, their own translations of life into language.

Chronology

1940   Maxine Ting Ting Hong is born on October 27 in Stockton, California to Chinese immigrants Tom and Ying Lan Hong. Her father was a scholar, manager of a gambling house and a laundry worker. Her mother practiced medicine and midwifery, was a field hand and laundry worker. The eldest of six children, Maxine was named by her father for a blond woman lucky at the gambling tables.

1954–58   Attends Edison High School in Stockton, California

1955   Publishes her first essay, entitled "I Am an American," in *American Girl* magazine

1958   Writes an article about the Chinese New Year for a Stockton newspaper and wins a journalism scholarship to the University of California, Berkeley

1958–62   Attends the University of California, Berkeley as an undergraduate and works for the student newspaper, the *Daily Californian*

1962   Graduates with an A.B. in English from University of California, Berkeley; on 23 November marries Earll Kingston, an actor whom she met while at UCB. They live in Berkeley.

1964   Their son, Joseph Lawrence Chung Mei, is born.

1964–65   Returns to UC Berkeley in order to earn a teaching certificate; works as a student teacher at Oakland Technical High School.

1965–67   Works as a teacher of English and Mathematics at Sunset High School in Hayward, California; is active in the free speech movement and anti-Vietnam War protests.

1967   Moves to Hawaii with Earll and Joseph; teaches English at Kahuku High School.

1968   Teaches at Kahaluu Drop-In School, Kahaluu, Hawaii

1969   Teaches English as a Second Language at Honolulu Business College and Language Arts at Kailua High School

1970–77   Teaches Language Arts at Mid-Pacific Institute, Honolulu

1973   Publishes "Literature for a Scientific Age: Lorenz' *King Solomon's Ring*" in the January edition of *English Journal*

1975   Contributes to *Your Reading: A Booklist for Junior High Students*, published by the National Council of Teachers of English

1976   Publishes *The Woman Warrior: Memoirs of a Girlhood Among Ghosts* in July and wins the National Book Critics Circle Award in nonfiction

1977   Wins a National Education Association Award and the *Mademoiselle* Magazine Award for *The Woman Warrior*; publishes "Duck Boy," a short story, in the 12 June 1977 edition of *New York Times Magazine*.

1977–81   Visiting Professor of English, University of Hawaii, Honolulu

1978   Wins the Anisfield-Wolf Race Relations Award; publishes "Reservations about China" in the October issue of *Ms.* magazine and "San Francisco's Chinatown: A View from the Other Side of Arnold Genthe's Camera" in the December edition of *American Heritage*.

1979   *Time* rates *The Woman Warrior* as one of the top ten nonfiction works of the decade

1980   Publishes *China Men*; it is named to the American Library Association Notable Books List and wins the National Book Award for nonfiction. A Honolulu Buddhist sect names Kingston a "Living Treasure of Hawaii" in a ceremony at the Hoopa Hongwanji Temple. She becomes increasingly active in the anti-draft movement in Hawaii and receives a National Endowment for the Arts Writing Fellowship. Publishes "The Coming Book," an essay, included in the collection *The Writer on Her Work*, edited by Janet Sternburg and "How Are You? I Am Fine, Thank You. And You?" in *The State of the Language*, edited by Christopher Ricks.

1981   *China Men* is awarded the American Book Award. It is also a nominee for the National Book Critics Circle Award and a runner-up for the Pulitzer Prize. Kingston wins the Stockton Arts Commission Award, the Asian-Pacific Women's Network Woman of the Year Award, and a Guggenheim Fellowship. The Bancroft Library at the University of California, Berkeley begins to consolidate manuscripts for one of its special collections—the Maxine Hong Kingston Papers.

1982   Tours Japan, Australia, Indonesia, Malaysia, and Hong Kong on a trip sponsored by the United States International Communications Agency and the Adelaide Arts Festival; publishes "Cultural Misreadings by American Reviewers" in *Asian and Western Writers in Dialogue: New Cultural Identities*, edited by Guy Amirthanayagam.

1983   Wins the Hawaii Award for Literature; publishes "A Writer's Notebook from the Far East" in the January edition of *Ms.* magazine and "Imagined Life" in the Fall 1983 issue of the *Michigan Quarterly Review*.

1984   In October, takes an extended trip through China, her first, with a group of seven other writers (Allen Ginsberg, Gary Snyder, Francine du Plessix Gray, Leslie Marmon Silko, William Least Heat Moon, Toni Morrison, Harrison Salisbury), co-sponsored by UCLA and the Chinese Writers Association; moves with Earll from their home in Oahu, Hawaii to Los Angeles. Their son, Joseph, remains in Hawaii.

1985   Wins the California Council for Humanities Award and publishes "Postscript on Process" in *The Bedford Reader*, edited by X. J. Kennedy and Dorothy M. Kennedy

1986   Thelma McAndless Distinguished Professor in the Humanities at Eastern Michigan University

1987   Publishes *Hawai'i One Summer, 1978*, a collection of twelve prose sketches, including original woodblock prints by Deng Ming-Dao, in a limited edition of 200 copies; publishes *Through the Black Curtain*, an essay on her writing process, for The Friends of the Bancroft Library; moves with Earll to the Rockridge district of Oakland, California.

1988   Receives an Honorary Doctoral Degree from Eastern Michigan University; publishes "A Chinese Garland" in the September issue of *North American Review* and "Rupert Garcia: Dancing Between Realms" in the October issue of *Mother Jones* magazine.

1989   Publishes *Tripmaster Monkey: His Fake Book*, her first novel, which wins the P.E.N. USA West Award in fiction; visits the University of California, Santa Cruz for one week in November as a

UC Regents Lecturer; wins the California Governor's Award for the Arts; publishes "Students of Tiananmen: Braving a Way of Peace" in the 14 July issue of the *Honolulu Advertiser* and "The Novel's Next Step" in the December edition of *Mother Jones* magazine. *The Woman Warrior* continues to be listed as a best-seller on the trade-paperback lists.

1990   Returns to her alma mater, the University of California, Berkeley, as a Chancellor's Distinguished Professor in the English Department; wins the Brandeis University National Women's Commission Major Book Collection Award and the American Academy and Institute of Arts and Letters Award in Literature; receives an Honorary Doctorate degree from Colby College; publishes "Violence and Non-Violence in China, 1989" in the Winter 1990 edition of the *Michigan Quarterly Review*. Joan Saffa and Stephen Talbot produce "Maxine Hong Kingston: Talking Story" for KQED, San Francisco and CrossCurrent Media.

1991   Receives Honorary Doctorate degrees from Brandeis University and the University of Massachusetts; named the Martha Heasley Cox lecturer at San Jose State University. The Modern Language Association publishes *Approaches to Teaching Maxine Hong Kingston's The Woman Warrior*, edited by Shirley Geok-lin Lim, to which Kingston contributes an essay entitled "Personal Statement." In September, her father, Tom, dies in Stockton. One month later, the Kingstons' home in the Rockridge district of Oakland, California burns in the Oakland Hills firestorm. All of Kingston's manuscripts, including her work-in-progress, *The Fourth Book of Peace*, are destroyed. In local newspapers and at the annual meeting of the Modern Language Association in December, Kingston issues a call for help in reconstructing and recreating a new manuscript, to be called *The Fifth Book of Peace*.

1992   Wins the Lila Wallace Reader's Digest Writing Award and uses its prize money to begin funding writing workshops with Vietnam veterans; inducted into the American Academy of Arts and Sciences and receives an Honorary Doctoral degree from Starr King School for the Ministry.

1993   Takes a leave of absence from teaching at UC Berkeley; holds a series of on-going workshops entitled "A Time to Be: Reflective Writing, Mindfulness, and the War: A Day for Veterans and Their Families" through the Community for Mindful Living in Berkeley, California; writes the Forward, along with Thich Nhat Hanh, to Sister Chân Không's *Learning True Love: How I Learned and Practiced Social Change in Vietnam*; publishes "Precepts for the Twentieth Century," an essay, in Thich Nhat Hanh's *For a Future to be Possible: Commentaries on the Five Wonderful Precepts.*

1994   "The Woman Warrior" is produced and performed by the Berkeley Repertory Theatre from May through July at the Zellerbach Playhouse. The Huntington Theatre Company in Boston, Massachusetts produces the same play in September and October. Kingston acts as the guest conductor for a benefit concert of the Berkeley Symphony; publishes "A Letter to Garrett Hongo Upon the Publication of *The Open Boat*" in the *Amerasia Journal.*

1995   Moderates a reading of U.S. and Vietnamese novelists and poets as part of an April conference entitled "Vietnam Legacies: Twenty Years Later," held at the University of California, Davis. "The Woman Warrior" is produced by the Center Theater Group of Los Angeles at the Ahmanson Theater. Publishes excerpts from her writing journals in *The Writer's Notebook*, edited by Howard Junker.

1997   Resumes teaching at UC Berkeley; in June, is one of the featured speakers, along with the Dalai Lama of Tibet, Alice Walker, and Dolores Huerta, at "Peacemaking: The Power of Nonviolence," a three-day conference held in San Francisco. In September, President Clinton awards Kingston a 1997 National Humanities Medal.

1998   In March, the Bay Area Book Reviewers Association awards Kingston its Cody Award for Lifetime Achievement.

Conversations with Maxine Hong Kingston

Maxine Hong Kingston: Something Comes from Outside Onto the Paper

Gary Kubota / 1977

From *Hawaii Observer*, 28 July 1977, pp. 27–28.

For the past ten years, the 33-year-old Kingston has lived on Oahu along with her husband Earll, an actor, and her son Joseph. Their present home is a teacher's cottage in Manoa on the campus of Mid-Pacific Institute, where she has taught English to high school students. The Kingstons plan to find another house, however, since this coming year she will teach literature and creative writing at the University of Hawaii.

Although I wanted to find out what Kingston, as a Chinese American woman, thought of her role as a writer, I generally tried to keep the interview free-flowing to allow the author to speak on topics that most interested her.

Kingston: Well, what shall we talk about?

Observer: Let's start with the book jacket. It says here that *The Woman Warrior* is your first book.

Kingston: It's my first published book. I've written others. I started writing when I was nine and remember the incident quite clearly. I was sitting in a class and all of a sudden this poem came to me. I wrote 25 verses in something like a trance. I don't recall what the class was about. Later, I wrote prose.

Observer: Did writing prose come naturally?

Kingston: Yes. When I was in high school, I didn't know about different forms of writing. I always wrote in my story form and got away with it. I never understood what teachers meant when they assigned us term papers. Once our class was assigned to write about produces of California. I wrote a story about these hoboes who were hitchhiking around California and who visited cities and towns that specialized in different produce. I was more interested in the hoboes than the products.

Observer: That must have presented some problems.

Kingston: It did. I don't think I understood the essay form till my senior year in college. I got some really bad grades during the transition.

1

Observer: How long did it take for you to write *The Woman Warrior*?

Kingston: Two years. I thought of it as a novel when I mailed it out to the publishers. I felt it had to be defined in that form because of the fictional techniques I used in the story.

Observer: What happened?

Kingston: I was told by my editors that most first books that are fiction don't usually sell out their first printing and that critics are hesitant to review a young writer's first published novel. In nonfiction, everyone feels they have a grasp on the story. Critics review it and people can more readily identify with the characters.

Observer: Are you saying the book is not autobiographical?

Kingston: In some ways, it is. I might have felt the same emotions as the main character, the girl, at moments in my life. But when I wrote the book, I certainly didn't feel that way anymore. I remember my editor calling me up one day after the book had been published and telling me it was too bad the book had not been classified as fiction, because then I stood a good chance of winning the award in that category.

Observer: Did you do any research before writing the book?

Kingston: I don't do research when I write. I believe there's some creative source in people, and if they can tap it, they don't need to do research. The stories within the book are based mostly on my past experiences as a child living with my parents in Stockton, California. They operated a laundry in the downtown area, and while growing up, I was constantly listening to them and my relatives talk-story. Their recollections of myths, fables and Chinese history turned out to be amazingly accurate. After the book was published, several people pointed out the presence of these stories in anthropology and art books. It seems that our family had an oral tradition that was really accurate.

Observer: What in particular made you want to become a writer?

Kingston: Oh, I don't know. Actually, sometimes I think writing has nothing to do with me and that I shouldn't take credit for it. I feel that something comes from outside through me onto the typewritten paper. Often, I sit at the typewriter and compose stuff I didn't even know I knew. It happens all the time. It's not like I've decided what I'm going to write.

Observer: Some aspects of the book seem to naturally attract a certain audience. It's ethnic, from a feminist viewpoint and somewhat politically anti-establishment. Do you identify yourself with any social movements?

Kingston: Artistically, no. I feel that my writing simply happens to be that way. It's an accident that it's about Chinese and that it's about women. I happen to have been born that way, so it's the easiest way for me to write. Politically and socially, however, I look at myself as being very much a feminist. Growing up as I did as a kid, I don't see how I could not have been a feminist. In Chinese culture, people always talk about how girls are bad. When you hear that, right away it makes you radical like anything.

Observer: Under what category would you place your book?

Kingston: I feel I've written a political and artistic work. It's important for me to show that both are possible. I've always felt that it's easy to fall into propagandizing when one does political writing. It can also be very poor writing. It's important for me to show that racial or feminist writing doesn't have to sound like polemics. It can dramatize events and make them brighter.

Observer: Has that been one of the major problems you've had to overcome as a writer?

Kingston: No. I think my main problem is discipline. Writing is a very painful act. I try to start writing in the mornings, but I fool around and put it off to wash dishes or sharpen my pencils. I'm pretty regular on writing every day, but sometimes I start late and end up finishing in the afternoons. Of course, supporting yourself while you write can present problems.

Observer: I've heard a number of writers say it's difficult to write in Hawaii because of the easy climate.

Kingston: I think that's an excuse for not writing. I know I can write anywhere—even at the beach.

Observer: What made you and your family settle in Hawaii?

Kingston: Actually, we planned to stop here on our way to live in the Far East. This was about ten years ago during the Vietnam War when my husband and I were active in demonstrations at Berkeley. Things were getting really rough there, and we felt discouraged because, despite the protests, the war continued. A lot of our friends were also getting burned out on drugs. The tension was hard to deal with, and we thought it might be good to see what living in a different area was like. Berkeley was exciting then. People living there used to ask, "Is there life after Berkeley?" Their conclusion was no. Many students felt that the revolution was imminent. But when we finally left, we found that the situation was not the same in the rest of the world. Of course, Hawaii had its own problems, and with the presence of the military here, the Vietnam War was even more real on these Islands.

Observer: Getting back to your book—has it been financially successful?

Kingston: It's in its seventh printing in hardback. I really don't know the exact number of copies that have been sold. I've also had four or five offers to turn the book into a film, but I've put off any decision since I have zero knowledge about the movie business. I've written to some people for advice. One thing I do know, however, is that I don't want any haoles with taped eyelids playing roles as Chinese.

Observer: Has the recognition given your first book put pressure upon further writing?

Kingston: No. Right now I'm working on a second book. I made up my mind long ago that it didn't matter if my work was never published. At least my writing would still be there in manuscript form. Another realization I've had during my work is the fact that I can't stop writing. Maybe people who can stop are lucky—at least then the obsession is gone.

Honolulu Interview: Maxine Hong Kingston

Karen Horton / 1979

From *Honolulu*, December 1979, pp. 49–56. Reprinted by permission of the interviewer.

With her actor-husband Earll busy auditioning for New York stage plays, Hawaii author Maxine Hong Kingston is currently ensconced in a West End apartment for the final months of editing her second novel, *The Gold Mountain Heroes*. It's the companion book to her highly acclaimed *The Woman Warrior: Memoirs of a Girlhood Among Ghosts*, which won the 1976 National Book Critics Circle Award for general nonfiction and thrust her into the forefront of America's feminist writers. *The Woman Warrior*, although not autobiographical, was about a Chinese American girl growing up in California's Central Valley, the daughter of peasant immigrants from southern China, which Kingston is. The book was a mesh of fantasy, fiction and fact, borrowing from the legends of the homeland and their influence on a contemporary woman. The new book is about men, about heroes, in the same way the other one was about women. The Cantonese referred to America as Gold Mountain and Kingston writes about her various heroes in the settings of Hawaii, California and New York.

Honolulu writer Karen Horton initially interviewed Kingston in her Manoa home, then followed up with telephone conversations with the author in New York.

Kingston explained she always knew she wanted to write from the age of 9—or maybe it was 8. She's uncertain, just as she's uncertain of how old she is—36 or 38. While her Chinese counterparts in Stockton may have dreamed of growing up to be wives or mothers or nurses or teachers forever, it was always Kingston's dream, even an assumption—an acceptance—that she would be a writer. She wrote poems and she wrote books as a young girl, finally clearing the cans and whatever out of a family storeroom to make space for her papers and pencils, her typewriter and notes.

Her editor at Alfred A. Knopf Publishing Co. in New York, Charles Elliott, has an absolute admiration of Kingston. In a telephone conversation, Elliott noted that by the time he got *The Woman Warrior* manuscript, it needed very little editing. But Kingston is not the prima donna who rants and raves when an editor suggests changes. She likes tough editors. Although Elliott does not communicate toughness over the telephone, Kingston immensely admires him and that means he's tough. He admits to early concern over her public presence after publication of the book (a mere 5,000 hardcover, first printing) and the subsequent stampede of publicity wrought by John Leonard, then *New York Times* book review section editor. His review glowed with praise for the book. Word spread and it's been literary history ever since.

"I'd sent John a copy of the book and he would have gotten around to it eventually," Elliott recalls. "Apparently, someone at the *Times* read it before he did, viewed it as exceptional and immediately brought it to his attention."

Elliott is very good at telling Maxine Hong Kingston stories—with a great deal of fondness—one of them being when she came to New York from Honolulu during cold weather. "She had to borrow a coat from a friend," Elliott says. "She came into the office wearing a coat that reached down to the ground and a stocking cap that stood straight up. She looked like a bag lady. But she wasn't at all self-conscious."

The Woman Warrior subsequently sold some 40,000 copies hardcover and was tapped for the Book Critics award. Then Kingston was scheduled to appear with the other award-winners at a dinner and Elliott confesses how he was extremely nervous about his new author's grip on the situation.

"She was the last of the four main speakers, the previous being John Gardner, Elizabeth Bishop and Bruno Bettelheim," he says. "She arrived wearing a dress that came down all the way to the ground and wearing a lei of flowers that were very fragrant. I don't remember what they were.

"She was so short that she couldn't see over the rostrum and had to bend the microphone over the side to speak. I remember thinking, 'Oh, no!' She started off with this little tiny voice and before I could believe it, she had it right under absolute control with everyone nearly weeping.

"She told the audience that she had been writing for 30 years but never knew she was a writer. 'Now you have told me I am a writer,' she said. She was wonderful. The woman is exceptional.

"Now," he says, "if I can just get the newest manuscript out of her hands."

Honolulu: When will Mr. Elliott get his manuscript?

Kingston: Charles wants to bring it out in the spring, and I'm almost finished with the book. It feels like the last draft. I'm not sure how many I've done. I've lost count. I've been editing over 25 pages a day here in New York, six hours each day. That's a lot of pages, which makes me feel the book is being finished. I think the book will be 450 pages long.

Honolulu: Do you think it will outsell *The Woman Warrior*?

Kingston: I don't know if it's going to do better. I can't tell. A lot of the writing in that other book was such a blur to me. The new book will appeal to probably the same people as before. *The Woman Warrior* was liked by men. I think many men, the man-in-the-street, bought it for wives or daughters or girlfriends. I could tell because when I was autographing books, they acted as if they were buying it for a woman. I have the feeling with the new book, men will buy it for themselves. It is written with a man's point of view. There are hardly any women in it. It is about men.

Honolulu: Were there any writers in your family?

Kingston: My father writes poetry. But the family, most of the people, were not writers. They were readers. They were literate. I think that's very important in that most people in China were illiterate. My family was special. They could read and they read poetry. The last time I was home, my parents were singing some poems and they were by an important writer. My brother said, "Oh, I just thought they sang village ditties." But it was like they know village songs, but they also know the classics. So I feel I come from a tradition of literate people, even though they weren't writers.

Honolulu: You graduated from Cal. You were the oldest of six children and your father owned a laundry. Did the family experience financial hardship?

Kingston: I didn't work much during school because the family saved ahead of time. My parents saved a lot. But I remember the agonizing feeling of wanting to get out of school and work. I wanted to go to Berkeley ever since I was a child. It never occurred to me to go anywhere else. I guess it all started with a field trip from Edison High School in Stockton.

Honolulu: How does the Chinese community in Stockton differ from that in Honolulu?

Kingston: The Chinese community in Stockton is much tighter. It's smaller and a lot of the people come from the same village—Sun Woi. The *sun* means new and *woi* is the same as *hui* in Hawaii. It's a very stable community. People lived there all of their lives and even the next generation, my age, stayed there. People really knew each other. I think the Chinese community in Hawaii is more diverse. I don't know much about the Chinese community in Hawaii. They come from another village, Chung San, I believe. And they seem to be of various economic backgrounds, whereas in Stockton we're all about the same. It was more of a rural background. People there would work in the fields even if they lived in the city. There is more of a closeness to nature that way. In Hawaii, as you know, it's not like that. Hawaii feels more urban to me.

Honolulu: How have your Stockton compatriots viewed your fame?

Kingston: I was just there last summer. You know, I have a lot of friends who don't read. Lots of people heard that I write or they always knew that I wrote. I was writing in high school and grammar school and people knew it so it's like what I'm doing now is what I've always been doing. I know lots of English-speaking people who don't read and I know lots of Chinese-speaking people who don't speak English and so the people I know who read, oh I don't know. They're people. I guess what I'm saying is that I have lots of friends who don't read and I feel just as close to them and it's kind of nice in a way because then they just like me for my character. I don't hold it against them if they don't read my writing. In fact, I feel very bad when, quite often people come up to me or they are introduced to me, and they apologize for not having read my work. I feel terrible. You see, I've been a teacher for so many years and I feel exactly like students coming up to me, telling me why they didn't do the assignment. I don't like to hear that from other people. I don't want to impose this trip on them of feeling like I gave them an assignment and they didn't do it. Also I find that people who can't or don't read are very interesting people. They have their own very imaginative kinds of minds that I guess aren't governed by reason. So they do all kinds of interesting things that I can write about.

Honolulu: With all your China-oriented writing, when will you go there?

Kingston: I wanted to finish these two books first. It's about my imaginary China that I write. I didn't want to go until I finished because if I did, I might have had a very different idea. The older generation feels it's a very terrible place. If any of us go, something bad will happen to us. We will get killed or something. In my family, just about all the men were killed in the revolution. The other fear is that we'll be thought of as Communist sympathizers if we go and if there is a McCarthy type witchhunt, we will be thrown in relocation camps. There is a whole weight of history involved here. In Hawaii, it seems

so different. There are so many people going to China on vacations! But not
so in Stockton. They feel very relieved at having escaped. And they are also
getting so many immigrants from Hong Kong who are so glad to be there.
This curse is a very middle class attitude I picked up from my family. Travel
means desperately running from country to country. The idea of touring is
very foreign to them.

Honolulu: What brought you to Honolulu?

Kingston: Earll had been teaching English at Berkeley High in California
and I'd been teaching at Sunset High in Hayward. We had been here for a
vacation once before and liked it a lot. But we had been doing a lot of protest-
ing in the Bay Area of the Vietnam War and started thinking of leaving the
Mainland. We thought that to go to some other place would be like getting
away from the war. Only, Hawaii was more like the war because it was closer
to Vietnam and because of all the military activities. We also wanted to get
away from all the violence in Berkeley. And everyone we knew there was on
drugs.

Honolulu: You once expressed the belief that writing is not enough to
express political activity. You'd done much in the way of political writing,
including anti-war, when you and Earll left California in 1967 and came to
Hawaii. What are you doing now?

Kingston: I feel there should be more time for everything. All of this has
to be done. But it takes a whole life to organize and demonstrate and it takes
another whole life to get writing done. The problem is making the day stretch
from one point to another. There are so many anti-nuclear demonstrations in
New York. Almost everyday there is something. I'm thinking of speaking at
an anti-nuclear rally in New York and I'm definitely committed to speak at
an Asian American feminists' fundraiser. It is a large movement here on the
East Coast and I think it's nonexistent in Hawaii. I may get involved with
Susan Brownmiller's anti-pornography efforts here. She is taking people on
tours of Times Square and showing them the anti-women effects of pornogra-
phy. Up until now, I've been mainly active in opposing the draft bill.

Honolulu: How is staying in New York affecting your routine?

Kingston: I've managed to establish a routine here, but it boils down to
trying not to see so many people. I haven't gone to anything here because
I'm waiting until the book is done. I've had several weeks of really hard
work. After that, I start touring. But the writing is the same. It's the life that's

very different. I don't think I understand New York. Many times I've been walking on the street with a friend who will say, "Look, oh, how beautiful that is" and I look and I feel really bad because I can't figure out what's so beautiful. Hawaii's beauty to me is the trees and the ocean. I think they mean something else in New York and I feel terrible. But there are so many people from Hawaii here. We were at a party last night where at least a dozen were from Hawaii and they're all in the theater. They are all so good. Hawaii people have a wonderful reputation in New York. And most people I meet here are actors. They are just different anyway. And they are so wonderful because they take such chances with their lives. While I love young people, I like to talk to people my own age. I feel very lucky when we get together and there are middle-aged people and they still have their art, their writing, their acting. That's exciting. Like there is still life and the business of time and taking that away from them has not stopped them from being youthful.

Honolulu: Would your prefer to continue working in New York?

Kingston: We may come back to New York, but we haven't made a clear-cut decision. My son likes Hawaii very much. It's his home. Even though Earll and I don't have Hawaiian blood, I can see that Joseph is a Hawaiian person. He's made up his mind that's where he wants to live so we'll probably remain there until he graduates from high school. He likes surfing. He likes Hawaii best. I can see where, in the future, there will be more work in New York. But people here are as provincial as they are in Honolulu. No one seems to realize that you can jump in a plane and be somewhere else in a matter of hours. This is especially the case with theater people. They feel you have to live in New York. I feel more mobile than most people. It is easy to rent your house out. You don't have to live in one place.

Honolulu: You wrote *The Woman Warrior* in Honolulu. Obviously, the setting agreed with you.

Kingston: Hawaii is a wonderful place to work. It is conducive to creativity. The visual things, the sensory impressions are strong in Hawaii. And you need that to make you aware of the sensory experiences that go into the writing. That doesn't mean that I write what I see around me. The sense of being more alive is very important to creating. The quiet in Hawaii, well, that makes me able to think. It keeps your intuitions open and that's important. But now that I'm in New York . . . well, we drove up to New England the other day and saw the fall leaves. It was wonderful. Now I know where all those pictures of bluebirds and robins came from in the *Dick and Jane* books.

Honolulu: A friend once described *Woman Warrior* as convoluted.

Kingston: Oh, I'm very proud of being convoluted. I try to be convoluted. Life is convoluted. I know there are some people who have a certain expectation of a linear kind of story where everything is explained to them and it goes at a slower pace and it's more of an accessible, popular kind of writing style. If they expect that, then they can't get into a more complicated book. I think that people like that miss out on something because they are not willing to work harder.

Honolulu: Were you surprised by the acclaim the book received?

Kingston: No, I wasn't. I think I was sort of matter-of-fact about it. Maybe it's because I'm older. Maybe if I were in my 20s, I would be surprised and react to it more violently. I think it made a big difference having a lot of acclaim in my 30s. I'm 36. Or is it 38? How old am I? But I think when you are older, you're sort of set in the way you react to the world. I think I'm pretty much formed. I don't think it's important getting all that attention. Just every once in awhile, it hits me.

Honolulu: Did the attention make you nervous about this next book?

Kingston: Quite often, you see critics go after the second book and they say, "Oh, they're up to their same tricks again," but it doesn't seem to influence my writing. One friend said I seemed to be a more confident person, but I don't see that. I don't see where it's changed me. I wasn't nervous about the writing and the attention doesn't seem to have influenced me. But I did have to get an unlisted telephone. The people who were calling! They want things and sometimes I'm not sure what they want. And, well, I guess my work hits people at various emotional levels and some very unstable people also get affected and I got some obscene phone calls. But then I get a lot of really nice people who want me to do something for them or do something for me. But it all gets in the way of writing.

Honolulu: How do you prepare to write a book?

Kingston: It's already there. I don't think I need research. I want to write about something you can't find in research. Research can only, oh, I guess, confirm some of the small details, like what kinds of clothes these people wore and you can see the big historical things that happened. But what I want to say, I can't find through research. There's a feeling that I have, or there are feelings, the way people are in certain circumstances. I feel that it comes from the heightened moments in all our lives when we are really aware of what it feels like to be a person or what life is all about. You don't feel it too often, but every once in awhile you feel it. I want to put that feeling into writing or I want to write words so that when somebody reads it, they can have that feeling. And all the details are only components to get to this feeling. It's sort of a heightened awareness so that you know what it means to be human.

Honolulu: How much influence does self-confidence have on your writing?

Kingston: There have been bad days, but I've never felt that I should give it up. Mostly because it's like a habit. I have to eat, I have to breathe, I have to write. I'm very satisfied working with myself, too. But there's no question of stopping. My husband lately says, "You say this, then every day you moan and groan and say it's no good," and I guess I shouldn't subject him to that. I think that every time I say it, it's really true and it's the first time I've said it. I write upstairs in our home in Honolulu. It's my room. So I just go up there and it's very hard to get up the stairs. I'm not neat and clean. But that's like confidence and no-confidence. Some days, I'm really neat and clean and some days it's really just chaos. But in a way, maybe this is just to comfort myself, because some days when it's really bad, it's good for you, too. As long as you feel that it's bad, you keep working on it. And you feel it's bad because you kind of have a vision of what it should be and so you strive and work and re-work. But when you feel good, maybe it's very deceptive, because then you don't re-work.

Honolulu: So how do you get anything done?
Kingston: By doing it and by doing it.

Honolulu: Does Maxine Hong Kingston have hobbies?
Kingston: I used to sew and paint but I gave them up when they started to feel too much like writing. I read, but that sounds like the same thing, too. I like to walk. I like to sit at the beach. I like to see people. That's the main thing. Sitting and talking to people when I have the time.

Honolulu: How has your son reacted to all this?
Kingston: Aside from the fact he was not too pleased with being referred to as my "small son" on the first book jacket, Joseph is doing fine. He's 16 and this will be the longest we've ever been away from him. So I'm going through this terrible mother thing. He calls me up, or rather I call him in Honolulu—he never calls us—and says, "I haven't eaten in three days," or

he's got a dent in his car and then I think, oh, he had a close call. And then it's something to do with his studies. I don't know whether he's making it up, but it's just awful. I keep hoping this is actually good for him. But I'm wondering if some day he won't do a strange thing like tell everyone about the time his parents abandoned him and went to New York. We'll just have to wait and see.

Honolulu: Finally, have you figured out your true age?
Kingston: Yes. It's 38. The years go by too quickly to keep track.

Talk with Mrs. Kingston

Timothy Pfaff / 1980

From *New York Times Book Review*, 15 June 1980, pp. 1, 24–26.

"What I am doing in this new book is claiming America," declares Maxine Hong Kingston. "That seems to be the common strain that runs through all the characters. In story after story Chinese American people are claiming America, which goes all the way from one character saying that a Chinese explorer found this place before Leif Ericsson did to another one buying a house here. Buying a house is a way of saying that America—and not China—is his country."

Long snakes of galley proofs line the walls of the living room and small dining room of the Honolulu home she and her husband Earll, an actor, bought in 1978. "We never really made a decision to stay here," she notes, though they have lived on the island of Oahu with their son Joseph for the last 12 years. But the deal on the new house was clinched when they discovered an office upstairs, "the very writer's garret of your imagination." Their New England-style house looks good-naturedly incongruous in its setting. Five kinds of ginger bloom in the yard, which ends at a precipitous mountain slope lush with vegetation. Directly inside the front door is a place for leaving snowboots.

Her eyes sometimes wander to the proofs on the nearby table, but the barefoot author seems at ease, relieved that this siege of writing is at an end—and delighted by perhaps the most unusual honor of her career. A few days after the final revisions of *China Men*, Mrs. Kingston became a Living Treasure of Hawaii. A Honolulu Buddhist sect honored her—primarily for *The Woman Warrior*, her eloquent account of growing up Chinese American—during a chant- and incense-filled ceremony at Hoopa Hongwanji Temple. "Hawaii has all kinds of traditions and ceremonies that are not immediately apparent," Mrs. Kingston says. "I didn't know about this one until I was made a part of it. This tradition comes from ancient China via modern Japan. In the same way that we designate paintings and monuments and mountains as treasures, they designate certain people as Living Treasures."

At 39, Mrs. Kingston is unusually young to be so honored ("in Japan you have to be at least 80"); she is also the first Chinese American Living Treasure. "During the ceremony, the Buddhist priests talked about their own experience of coming to Hawaii and wanting to be a part of its culture," she recalls. "They decided that one way was to honor some of Hawaii's treasures. It makes me feel really good to be honored by them. It feels as if the islands are saying, 'You can be a part of Hawaii too.' I think this is a hard place to belong to."

Her musical voice, which can elongate, accent and repeat words tellingly, has a vigor that works in curious counterpoint to the ceaseless, hypnotic bird songs outside. She starts at a volume just above the birds ("I still think of my speaking voice as inadequate"), but talk of *China Men* soon elicits confident, protracted statements.

Mrs. Kingston insists that she approaches other writers' work as a "fan" and seldom can see that someone else's writing has influenced hers. One book that is a major influence ("I wish I had written it") is William Carlos Williams's *In the American Grain*. "Williams retold the American myth, which I think is exactly the right way to write American history. His book starts with Leif Ericsson and ends with Abraham Lincoln, but his Lincoln is a woman, a feminine force in American history. He's like an old nurse, tending to his soldiers; it's as if he were the mother of our country. Williams has told American history poetically and, it seems to me, truly. In a way, I feel that I have continued that book. The dates are even right. The earliest episode in my book is about 1850, which is roughly where Williams left off."

As scrupulous with historical detail as she is free with plot, she nevertheless is confronted with a problem. "The mainstream culture doesn't know the history of Chinese Americans, which has been written and written well. That ignorance makes a tension for me, and in the new book I just couldn't take it anymore. So all of a sudden, right in the middle of the stories, plunk—there is an eight-page section of pure history. It starts with the Gold Rush and then goes right through the various exclusion acts, year by year. There are no characters in it. It really affects the shape of the book, and it might look quite clumsy. But on the other hand, maybe it will affect the shape of the novel in the future. Now maybe another Chinese American writer won't have to write that history."

China Men claims America in a more literal sense as well. Its stories are set in New York, California, and Hawaii (as in *The Woman Warrior*, portions of it are also set in China, which the author has yet to visit). It is less a California book than its predecessor was, even though it, too, derives much

of its substance from Mrs. Kingston's experience of Stockton, the city in
California's San Joaquin Valley where she was born and raised.

The New York sections rely extensively on stories her parents told of their
time together there, just after her mother arrived at Ellis Island in 1939.
"They told me wonderful things about New York, and I have always had a
sense that they had a very good time there. I wrote from stories I remembered, because I knew if I asked them again, they would just tell another
version. Besides, I feel that what is remembered is very important. The mind
selects out images and facts that have a certain significance. If I remember
something that someone told me 20 years ago, then the story has lasted in
that form for a very long time. I'm more interested in things that have survived in time than I am in how people are feeling recently.

"When I was in New York last fall to work on *China Men* with my editor,
I was trying to feel more at home there, so I started digging up anything I
could help me connect with the city. I suddenly realized that although I was
born in California, I was conceived in New York—so I went around telling
everybody that I was a New Yorker," she laughs.

Mrs. Kingston thinks of her two novels as "one big book. I was writing
them more or less simultaneously. The final chapter in *China Men* began as
a short story that I was working on before I even started *The Woman Warrior*.
But the writing is different in the new book. The style is much simpler—and
I think better. I was wrestling with the language in the first book, so the
sentences are sometimes quite convoluted. After I wrote that book, I had a
strong desire to write simple sentences. I wanted to see if I could use language that is simple and clear and still have a complicated content."

In *China Men* Mrs. Kingston tells the men's stories, sagas of Chinese men
who came to America and Chinese American men who created a new life
here. "There are great-grandfathers from the last century," she says, "and
then men from all the successive generations, down to a contemporary character I simply call 'the brother,' who is a kind of combination of my three
brothers. There also are a lot of uncles in the stories, but these are not all
blood relatives. What I am doing is putting many kinds of stories and people
right next to one another, as they are in real life. Each character is viewed
from the vantage point of the others.

"I have a father character who comes up in various guises throughout the
book. He is really only one character, but I call him different things, like 'the
legal father,' 'the illegal father,' 'the father from China' and 'the American

father.' In the course of the book, I have him coming into this country in five different ways. I'm very proud of that."

Like Cheever's Bullet Park and Faulkner's Yoknapatawpha County, Mrs. Kingston's Stockton is a literary microcosm—though in her case it is more a language than a place. "I write about a group of people who speak a dialect of Cantonese called Say Yup," she explains. "Say Yup is also the name of a region in China, actually four districts. The dialect is a common language, spoken by people many of whom historically have been illiterate and many of whom are still illiterate today.

"Working in that dialect has posed some problems for me, especially in the area of orthography. The Romanized spelling in Cantonese words has been worked out to some degree, but that is not true of Say Yup. And even if it were, it would not reflect the way that it is spoken: with an American accent. I'm specifically interested in how the Chinese American dialect is spoken in the California Valley. For proper names, I have made my own orthography. When I write dialogue for people who are speaking Chinese, I say the words to myself in Chinese and then write them in English, hoping to capture some of the sounds and rhythms and power of Say Yup."

Mrs. Kingston's knowledge of Chinese American men derives principally from Stockton's Chinese community ("which is not a geographically distinct place; there isn't even one whole block that is Chinese"), where her family owned and operated a laundry. "In a way, I grew up in a big nest," she says. "There were always other people around, including a lot of old men who didn't have families of their own. We had 'our old men' the same way other families had theirs. They did magic tricks and sang songs and ran errands and babysat. They're all gone now. Even though I suspect that the whole system is breaking down, I still have a very strong sense that there will always be someone to take care of me."

The opening section of *China Men* makes it abundantly clear that Mrs. Kingston is still writing from a feminist perspective. What was it like, then, to focus her attention on the men and their stories? "When I was working on *The Woman Warrior*," she replies without hesitation, "I thought that there would be a big difference between the men and the women. I thought that in the process of writing the new book I would learn something new about how men think. I feel that I've gone as deeply into men's psyches as I can, and I don't find them that different. I care about men—at least individual men—as much as I care about women, and I do have three brothers, which helps. Up to this point, I haven't written about lover-type men. I don't know why, but right now, that's not in the writing. Besides, it's been done well by other people."

Although women do not figure prominently as characters in *China Men*, Mrs. Kingston notes, "There still are women who take the role of storyteller. The women are not center-stage, but without the female storyteller, I couldn't have gotten into some of the stories. A great many of the men's stories were ones I originally heard from women.

"In a way, *The Woman Warrior* was a selfish book. I was always imposing my viewpoint on the stories. In *China Men* the person who 'talks-story' is not so intrusive. I bring myself in and out of the stories, but in effect, I'm more distant. The more I was able to understand my characters, the more I was able to write from their point of view and the less interested I was in relating how I felt about them."

If her feelings *about* her characters matter less, her feeling *for* characters matters as much as ever. "The kind of writing I do is an emotional process as well as an artistic one. The form of what I write forces me through a series of emotions. When I confront an ugly situation or a hateful person in my writing, I try to present the case as I see and feel it. If I'm writing well, by the end I have come to a resolution, a kind of love for a character based on my experience of the way that person sees the world. There's something wonderful about a form that lets you go from conflict to climax to resolution and then come out with a different feeling than you began with. Most literary forms are not artificial. They reflect patterns of the human heart."

Her attitudes about myth have undergone changes as well. "I have come to feel that the myths that have been handed down from the past are not something that we should be working toward, so I try to deal with them quickly—get them over with—and then return to a realistic kind of present. This time I'm leaving it to my readers to figure out how the myths and the modern stories connect. Like me, and I'm assuming like other people, the characters in the book have to figure out how what they've been told connects—or doesn't connect—with what they experience."

Mrs. Kingston has been criticized for tampering with the Chinese myths. "We have to do more than record myth," she counters. "That's just more ancestor worship. The way I keep the old Chinese myths alive is by telling them in a new American way. I can't help feeling that people who accuse me of misrepresenting the myths are looking at the past in a sentimental kind of way. It's so *easy* to look into the past," she says vehemently. "It's harder to look into the present and come to terms with what it means to be alive today."

Since the publication of *The Woman Warrior*, she has had to wrestle with questions about her place in the community of Asian American writers and about the degree to which her books represent the Chinese American experience as a whole. Now she can answer in her hard-won new style, simply and directly. "The one thing about which I am absolutely sure," she says, "is that I am a Chinese American woman. That feeling affects my writing in a particular way: I know that what I have to say is what a Chinese American person is thinking. I don't have to go out and make a survey; I don't have to get a committee of my peers to correct my work. I see writing as a very solitary thing that I have to do by myself, and polish by myself. It's a very free activity: I can think whatever I want and write in whatever way I want. When I get it into as perfect a state as I can, then I show it to people."

Mrs. Kingston is a tremendously disciplined writer—"like an accountant" with her time. By an enviable combination of her disposition and Hawaii's accommodating climate, she says matter-of-factly, "I can write anywhere—inside, outside, even at the beach." Her working habits reflect her attitude toward writing: that it is an integral part of living and as natural and necessary as eating.

"I have two methods of working. One of them involves tapping the sources of creativity, that part of the self that for me includes a higher vision of what is going on in life. I don't have a controlled way of going about that. I might be anywhere when it comes, and I could end up writing all over the floor or up the walls and not know what is going on. It's like having a fit.

"That either comes or it doesn't come. The second method is following a trail made by words themselves—by sitting down and writing, writing crazy, writing anything, fast. The words induce the vision. That rush, that outpouring—that vision or high or whatever it is—doesn't last very long. A lot of writing gets done in a very short time, but it's not very good writing. Often it turns out to be just a reminder about how something felt. It has to be reworked. Most of my time goes into that rewriting, which I have much more control over. I come back to the original material, think about it rationally, rewrite it and reshape it." She estimates that *China Men* went through "at least eight drafts," including galley proof revisions so extensive that the entire book had to be reset in type.

Like *The Woman Warrior, China Men* ends on a martial note. In the first book, the battle was mythical; in the second, it is the Vietnam War. "But that's not as exciting as it sounds," the author cautions. "It's not about blood or hand-to-hand combat; it's about the tedium of having to live in barracks and follow orders. I guess I'm afraid that people want to go to war right now. And I look at my writing to see where it's going, and it keeps going toward war. When I was writing about Vietnam, and therefore thinking a lot about the military, all these bills to bring back the draft suddenly appeared in Congress. I felt this tension—that I couldn't just write about it, even though I still think that writing is my best weapon. I felt I had to do something about it."

As a result, Mrs. Kingston has become active in the anti-draft movement in Hawaii. "It's as if my writing spilled over into real life, and I felt I had to act. It's not that I enjoy it. Anti-draft work intrudes on my life, so I just put my resentment right back into the struggle. I don't like going to meetings or carrying signs, but I feel that it is my duty."

Does the future hold another battle with words for the woman warrior? "Now that this book is done, I'm going to take a little time off and act like a regular person. I've told all my childhood stories that I wanted to tell, and I don't have any more stories accumulated. Now I have nothing, but I feel good about that, too. I feel like I am looking out over an ocean. It's a blank ocean, and the sky is empty too. I'm watching to see what comes up over the horizon, and that is going to be the next book. I'm going to make something out of nothing, which is the greatest creativity. And I'm willing to wait a long time."

Interview with Maxine Hong Kingston

Arturo Islas with Marilyn Yalom / 1980

An edited version of this interview first appeared in *Women Writers of the West Coast: Speaking of Their Lives and Careers*, ed. Marilyn Yalom (Santa Barbara: Capra Press, 1983), pp. 11–19. This longer transcript is reprinted by permission of Islas's estate and Capra Press.

This interview took place in Berkeley, California on October 1, 1980.

Islas: As the author of two highly successful books that spring from your personal ethnic background—*The Woman Warrior* and *China Men*—do you see yourself as representative of the Chinese American community?

Kingston: That is a very difficult problem because there is an expectation among readers and critics that I should represent the race. And then there are the white people who pick up the work and say, "She must be just like the rest of them." I don't like hearing non-Chinese people say to a Chinese person, "Well now I know about you because I have read Maxine Hong Kingston's books." Each artist has a unique voice. Many readers don't understand that. The problem of how "representative" one is will only be solved when we have many more Chinese American writers. Then readers will see how diverse our people are. Black writers have already surmounted the problem.

Islas: Are there any other Chinese American writers who do see themselves as representatives?

Kingston: Yes, there are writers who set out to represent the rest of us; they end up with tourist manuals—chamber-of-commerce public relations whitewash. What I look forward to is the time when many of us are published and then we will be able to see the range of personalities and the range of viewpoints, of visions, of what it is to be a Chinese American.

I have asked my sisters, "On a range of 1 to 10, how odd do you think we were? How odd was our upbringing?" My sister said it was 8. That means pretty odd, which is saying that we are not very representative.

Don't forget that I am writing about one little village in the South of China and already in that little village they were not representative of all of the great, big China. And then those few people came to America and went to Stockton. A Stockton Chinese is not the same as a San Francisco Chinese. I know that if I write about some very particular custom, some people will say, "Yes, it is one of the customs that we have," and other people will say, "No, we don't have that custom at all." The question of being representative is very interesting but it is also very bothersome.

The only way to get any work done—without polling everybody, as in a statistical study in sociology—is to give your own peculiar vision; because that's what's interesting, the way one person sees the world. It's up to other people to ask themselves whether they think like that or not. And if they don't think like you, that should be very exciting to them. They would read about something that they are completely unfamiliar with . . . I was just in Hong Kong and I loved seeing Chinese who were different from myself. To think of the possibility of another way of being Chinese or being a human being is much more exciting than to see someone just like me.

Islas: I agree with you; however, we live in a world in which your books really are the only ones published by a major American press that open up the Chinese American community to the rest of the country and to the world, and it is inevitable that you are going to be looked upon as a national representative.

Kingston: You do take on some of the responsibility for the race.

Islas: Was there any central event for either *The Woman Warrior* or *China Men* that served as the genesis of their origin?

Kingston: I don't think there was a single precipitating event. My writing is an ongoing function just like breathing or eating. I started writing as a child—I'd write down anything and these two books are just part of the things I wrote down. I have this ongoing habit of writing things down. Anything. And then some of it falls into place, as in these two books.

Islas: Did you show your work to other people while you were writing it or did you keep it to yourself?

Kingston: I kept it to myself, just as I basically keep things to myself, in general.

Islas: What about the history of the publication of these books? Were you ever told there was no audience for them?

Kingston: No, I was never told anything like that. I think it was very easy for me to publish them.

First I tried to find an agent, and the reason I did that was that I thought I didn't know the market well enough. If I was turned down by a major publisher, I wouldn't know the names of minor ones. So my idea was that if I found an agent, an agent would find a small press for me, even an English press or a Hong Kong press or maybe Canadian.

I thought that if the major presses all rejected my work, then the next step would be a small press. But I didn't realize that New York agents don't know the small presses. So when I found an agent, he looked immediately at the large presses and sold it almost right off.

Islas: How long had you been writing *The Woman Warrior* before you came to the point of showing it to an agent?

Kingston: Two years, two and a half years, but that is a deceptively short time. I was writing these books as a child, but I didn't have the ability or the maturity.

A kid doesn't yet have the vocabulary, though I had the feelings. I had a lot of feelings, and a lot of stories. In some sense you could say that I was working on these books for 20 or 30 years, but in another sense I wrote them just a few years ago.

Islas: Were you surprised at the immediate reception?

Kingston: Yes, sometimes I am surprised. Other times I just think, "Well, of course" because one thing that keeps you going as a writer are the fantasies of that big-selling book. But I was surprised when these two books were both on the best-seller list at the same time. And that really surprised me because it never occurred to me that that could happen.

Islas: What was your family's reaction to your books? I assume that they have read both of them; there is such a strong sense of family in your work.

Kingston: I have a pretty large family, so there is a range of reactions. In the case of my parents, they don't speak English and they don't read English, so they don't have an accurate sense of what I have written. My brothers and sisters are the people whom I feel closest to; they are most like me. And their reactions are very satisfying, because they can talk about my work in a way that makes sense to me. Like, they'll remember an event that I write about and they'll think what I wrote is very funny. That is satisfying because a lot of people don't understand the humor of my work. I guess when people come to ethnic writing, they have such reverence for it or are so scared that they don't want to laugh. But my brothers and sisters say, "Oh, this is really funny." And they'll remember the event and say, "Oh, that is the way I remember it." Usually, they remember it the same way. Although sometimes there's disagreement, like one brother said, "Oh, that wasn't opium the men were smoking," and my other brother said, "Oh yes it was. That *was* opium." And I like that difference in seeing because it could have been either way; one remembered it one way and one the other. That gives me two stories for one event.

Islas: And no one is saying to you, "Oh Maxine how could you have told all of these family secrets?"

Kingston: There are some cousins who feel that way. For example, there is an aunt who felt, "How could you be so nasty!" But I felt she was unfair; that kind of reaction usually comes from the people who didn't finish the book. They read the beginning and they don't understand that things are resolved by the end. And I think there is a lot of resolution—the mother and daughter come out OK, you know. But it is at a price of a lifetime of struggle, and I think that a few of my cousins don't understand that, and they get to the hard part and stop reading.

Islas: What about the fact that you are a woman and a Chinese woman and that you are a writer? Are you in some sense like your "no name woman"—a traitor to the village or the clan?

Kingston: Well, for people who know me, it is a very normal thing that I would write these books but I have had criticism from people who don't know me. They're critics or strangers or scholars . . . Chinese American males who, I guess, use my work for their own political purposes. In a way, I don't connect with that kind of criticism in that I don't think they are talking about me or my work. Some people have said that the white male press or publishing industry will publish women, but they'll castrate male writers, and they say this is why we don't have a major male novelist among Asian Americans. That has been a charge against me, as if somehow I was in collusion with the white publishers in America.

Islas: When you sit down to write, do you have a special audience in mind? Do you ask yourself, who is going to read this and what are they going to think about it?

Kingston: I am really a megalomaniac because I think of everybody. Everybody living today and people in the future, that's my audience, for generations. So I don't have just a Chinese American audience in mind.

Islas: When you give readings, do you feel different if you have a Chinese American audience or a non-Chinese audience?

Kingston: I treat them pretty much the same. It probably comes from years of teaching where you have kids who can't read in the same classroom with geniuses. They are all in the same room and each one is your student. You must teach so that it means something to every student, so that you are valuable as a teacher to each one of those kids.

Islas: How many years did you teach?

Kingston: Oh, about 14 or 15 years.

Islas: Where? On the West Coast?

Kingston: Some here and some in Hawaii. Mostly in Hawaii.

Islas: You say somewhere that your books are about claiming America. Does that mean assimilation of American values?

Kingston: No, I mean that it's a response to the legislation and racism that says we of Chinese origin do not belong here in America. It's a response to the kind of assumption that I came from Vietnam or that I came from another place—when I say I am a native American with all the rights of an American, I am saying, "No, we're not outsiders, we belong here, this is our country, this is our history, and we are a part of America. We are a part of American history. If it weren't for us, America would be a different place." When I write I also claim America in a literary way, in an artistic way. When people claim countries, it's usually thought of as conquering them in war. I'm claiming America in a pacifist way, in an artistic way.

Islas: The pen is mightier than the sword, or at least as mighty. You have mentioned in another interview the same idea about claiming America, and said that William Carlos Williams' *In the American Grain* was some sort of inspiration for you, if not an influence. Are there other writers, male or female, whose work inspired you or had an effect on your writing?

Kingston: I read a lot of poetry. I keep up, as much as possible, with modern American poetry and I think that I'm very influenced by its rhythms. I like Walt Whitman, and I read all of Yeats a couple of months ago.

Islas: Who else? John Ashbery? James Merrill, Elizabeth Bishop?

Kingston: Yes, yes, and I've read Galway Kinnell and Carolyn Kizer and Bob Hass, and some of the people who are sort of like poets but are prose writers like Grace Paley and Cynthia Ozick.

Islas: You've mentioned quite a number of women. Do you find yourself at this point in your life reading mostly women writers?

Kingston: No, it doesn't matter, although I have been reading Virginia Woolf too. I don't know whether I'm influenced by her but I read *Orlando* over and over again because I enjoy what she does with language and time. I notice I do some of the same tricks with time like the China Men who have lived for hundreds of years, just like Orlando lived for hundreds of years, and their history goes on and on. So I guess I must be influenced by her. *China Men* has six modern stories framed by about twelve myths; the readers have to work out the connections on their own.

Islas: What about the whole question of feminism? Do you consider yourself a feminist?

Kingston: I have always been a feminist but feminism is just one modern political stance, like being an ethnic writer. One has to have an even larger vision which encompasses all that. I don't think my writing would limit itself to whatever is politically useful.

Islas: What about your present work in progress?

Kingston: I'm not doing anything right now. I decided after I finished *China Men* to take some time off. Just to see what happens in the subconscious because I've been working for seven years on these two books. You go into the subconscious by not writing and then you make it normal consciousness by writing. Then you rewrite until you are working almost mechanically: the grammar and the structure all mental and rational. But now comes the time for not doing any writing. I mean to get far into the subconscious, where there are not word sequences.

Islas: So you've not even a plan?

Kingston: No. May I ask you a question? You said you had learned a lot about ethnic writing by reading my work and I was wondering what you meant?

Islas: What I meant was how you are able to portray a culture in such a way that it is more general than just portraying a specific culture. You have such wonderful material, portraits and sketches and fantasies coming from your background, and it's instructive to read you and to see how you tap those sources: that they are you, that you are Chinese, and that you make it accessible to the rest of us who are not familiar with that world at all. Even though you say you were not trying to be representative, I know I can't go to

Chinatown now in quite the same way I used to go because I've read your works. Now I look in a different way. I see things I had ignored or been indifferent toward.

Kingston: I see what you mean. It reminds me that one of the problems in writing the books was to figure out what to do with the language. So many of the people are not speaking English or they speak it with an accent. They use Chinese words, and they aren't just speaking Chinese-Chinese. They're asking Chinese with an American change in the language, and also they are speaking the dialect of one little village. So what are you going to do to give readers a sense of this language without just repeating it because then nobody will understand it? That's an example of the artistic problems you encounter when you deal with a culture that has not been adequately portrayed before. I'm also writing about poor people in another subculture. Are poor people representative? And all the mythology in *China Men* is of the small tradition of China, what the Chinese call the small tradition, not the great literary traditions, but those of lower-class people. When I write, I think of them in the language of the peasants of this one village, and that language has not been written down. I write about illiterate people whose language has not even been Romanized. So it's a matter of starting with a language that has no writing and yet writing about people who talk-story in that language.

Islas: Can you talk about the namings? How many names do Chinese people have?

Kingston: Well, as an example, there are some grandfathers in *China Men* who obviously must have a name just like everybody else, like the names that their parents gave them, but I call them "great-grandfather" and "great-great-grandfather," because that's what I actually call them, that's what they were known by in the family. Also, it was the custom for children *not* to know the name of their parents and grandparents. I decided to go ahead and use the name "grandfather" because I thought that all of us see them as ancestors, the grandfathers and great-grandfathers who are like mythical characters of the past golden age. Those people would have died before we were born or in our childhood—we saw them as big and we were little. We know their stories as great stories—they are almost like people we read about in books or in mythology. They are far from us, and so I decided that it was all right just to call them "great-grandfather" because they become the great-grandfather of us all. Also, they become the great-grandfathers of our country in that sense of claiming America. I didn't go into it in much detail but many

Chinese had a baby name given by parents; when they grew up, they chose an adult name, one appropriate to an ability or a feat. People often changed a name to celebrate a change in life. Then, of course, most who came to the U.S. have an American name. Chinese are also good at nicknames. Naming tells the world who you are. It also gives a new American identity—and don't forget the paper names for immigration.

Islas: As you said in another interview, very few people know Chinese history or Chinese American history. In the middle of *China Men* you even have to insert Chinese American history and forget about your characters, as a way of educating the rest of us.

Kingston: But this is true for Chinese Americans as well as for non-Chinese Americans. People don't seem to understand what I am doing; for example, a sinologist (Chinese scholar) might review my book and not even mention that I don't spell the words right. I don't spell them the way you would find them in a Cantonese dictionary or in a Mandarin dictionary because I decided to spell them in a new way, because Americans would speak this new way. A sinologist should say, "Hey, she's got it all wrong," but they don't seem to notice.

I was sort of disturbed when I read the review in the *New York Review of Books* where the critic said that I was trying to connect my family and Chinese Americans to the great high tradition of China by writing its myths; these people tell the peasant myths to each other, they pass them on and derive their strength from them. They also derive their doubts by comparing themselves to heroes of the past. I know all of these great heroes and they're not helping me in my American life. These myths are integrated into the peasant's life and into American Chinese life. And also, myths change from one telling to another. It really bothered me that that wasn't getting through.

Islas: Are there other Chinese American writers who are doing something similar?

Kingston: Actually there are quite a few. They just haven't gotten the big publicity which I have, and I think that it's important that we remember that I am not an exception. I'm not the only one who can use the language. And there are new writers publishing all the time. There is a new mystery writer named Tony Chin; he wrote a book called *Port Arthur Chicken*. Laurence Yep has published at least six books—children's books and science fiction. There is a playwright named David Hwang; he's written a play called *FOB* which is a wonderful play. Working independently, we came to many of the same images. He had two characters, who were having a food race; they were putting hot sauces on their food. They were seeing who could eat this hot sauce the fastest and the two of them were shoving hot food into their mouths. I had a food race in *China Men* too and I thought while watching David's play: "That's right. We are right." Chinese are so interested in food, and he saw it and I saw it, and it means that we both are authentic. Just a little detail like that. . . .

Islas: Is he an East Coast Chinese American?
Kingston: I don't know very much about him.

Islas: Would you describe yourself as a West Coast Chinese American?
Kingston: Yes, I am very West Coast. I really feel West Coast, like Central California Valley, as distinguished from San Francisco. I don't identify with San Francisco. Stockton, Sacramento, Fresno, all of the Valley in the north— Steinbeck's land—which reminds me. I read *Cannery Row* very carefully. I wanted to see how he did some things. At the end of *Cannery Row* there is a party and somebody recites a poem and it doesn't stop the dramatic action. I studied how he did that because I wanted to quote some songs and poems without stopping the drama.

Islas: Well, I guess I've covered most of the questions I had in my mind. Marilyn, do you want to ask any questions?

Yalom: Yes! I've been using *The Woman Warrior* in one of my classes and I'd like to ask a couple of questions that my students ask me. One thing they respond to is the thin edge that exists in your work between madness and myth. For example, there is the character of the aunt, Moon Orchid, who comes from Mainland China. There it's explicit—she goes mad in America. You were speaking earlier about humor, and she is so funny! We can't help but laugh, but it is also tragic. I wonder if you could comment on the aunt. Does she go crazy because she is outside of her own context? Was that really situational, having to do with trying to adapt to a new culture?

Kingston: I think that was exactly what I was saying with that story. I was contrasting her to her sister, Brave Orchid, who is in some way so insensitive, but it took that hardness for her to survive in America. Moon Orchid is soft, feminine, and she goes mad. I think that people of various cultures go mad in specific ways. One of the symptoms is that she says the Mexicans are after her, and then the rest of the family say, "Well, how do you know, because you don't speak English?" But she was claiming that she could hear these people plotting about her life. Language is important to our sanity. *You have to be able to tell your story, you have to be able to make up stories or you go mad.* Part of sanity is to be able to understand the language of other people, and also I think that even when people aren't mad, sometimes when you hear two people speaking in another language—you get a little bit of paranoia. "Are they saying something about me?" And we sane people feel like that! So, when she goes over the edge, that same tendency is exaggerated, and I am sort of hinting that perhaps if she spoke the language, it might have saved her a little bit. I think she is not the only person who went mad in that way. There are other people in life that this happens to. A psychiatrist phoned me after that book was published and said that it was like a very carefully written case history of some of the syndromes he had seen. In the last few years, there has been a lot of work done with refugees because of the Southeast Asian situation, but when I wrote it about 1975 there wouldn't have been a psychiatrist who could have looked at Moon Orchid and said, "Oh she's going through refugee syndrome."

Yalom: The relationship that you just spoke about between madness and having a language that one can use to communicate with, that comes through certainly in the early part of the book when you speak about your own difficulty in finding a voice. And one of the other questions that the students ask is, "Did she really go through a period in which she just didn't speak to anyone?"

Kingston: Oh, yes. That question has to do with fantasy life and the so-called real life. I feel that everyone has a blurred area, which is a border between their imagination and what actually happens, and I am very interested in that border. So, yes, I went through a time when I did not talk to people.

Yalom: About how old were you at that point?

Kingston: Oh you know, it comes and goes. It's still happening to me but not so severely. And also, I'm all right now but I do know people who never came out of it.

Yalom: The little speechless girl in the book, is she a double for you in some way?

Kingston: She is, but then also she is based on somebody I know, and she is a recluse today in that Victorian-woman sense. Even today, she is that closed off. Now I'm talking about people who grew up in the 1940s and

1950s. When I wrote that story, I thought: I am writing about my generation of Chinese Americans. But I am very startled when I now speak at colleges, and people in the audience, educators, psychologists, teachers, come up and tell me that they are working with people like that right now. Children who are going through this right now, and I am very surprised that this is an ongoing problem with people who are trying to figure out what to do when the home culture is different from the public culture. I guess what happens to some people is that they are just shocked into silence.

Yalom: You spoke earlier to Arturo about the resolutions that take place at the end of *The Woman Warrior* and I thought immediately of the resolution that takes place between the mother and daughter. You, the narrator, seem to become the inheritor of the oral tradition, which becomes a written tradition, and it's all tied up with your finding your voice, which is your mother's voice, surprisingly enough.

Kingston: And writing it down. . . .

Yalom: Is your mother able to recognize the role that you have assumed which was similar to her role?

Kingston: I don't know because part of the tension in my writing is that the oral tradition is very different from the written, and I see the oral tradition as being very alive, very immediate. It has the impact of command; it has the impact of directly influencing action. Also the oral stories change. A story changes from telling to telling. It changes according to the needs of the listener, according to the needs of the day, according to the interest of the time, and the story can be different from day to day. So what happens when you write it down? Writing is so static. The story will remain as printed for the next two hundred years and it's not going to change. That really bothers me, because what would really be neat would be for the words to change on the page every time, but they can't. *So the way I tried to solve this problem was to keep ambiguity in the writing all the time.*

Yalom: That ambiguity is what is most disturbing to students.

Kingston: I know. They want you to come to class and tell them, "Yes, I was that silent girl," or they want me to say, "Yes, I have this aunt, Moon Orchid." They want that. But what I want is to see the stories change. Maybe Moon Orchid is like this today, but tomorrow I'm going to tell you something else that she did. I try to keep the stories with that extra little doubt in them. I throw it in. I can't help it, it seems to be part of every story. Oh, I've got to tell you an anecdote. Did you know that in some Asian cities—I know this happened in Singapore, but probably less so now—there are storytellers who walk into a restaurant and they will come to your table and tell you a story, and then, just before the climax, they'll stop telling the story until you pay them. And after you pay them, they tell you the ending! The more money you pay, the better the ending! I feel so bad sometimes thinking of this great oral tradition, and along comes somebody like me who writes it down. People go to the library and pull out a book and say, "Here's the authentic story." It's not! That was only the odd person who came along, like Homer, and wrote it down. It's the same thing with the Chinese. Most of the tradition was oral and then someone came along and wrote it down.

Islas: That's a wonderful note to end on.

An Interview with
Maxine Hong Kingston
Kay Bonetti / 1986

This is a print version, edited by Kay Bonetti, of an interview conducted in May of 1986 at the author's home in Los Angeles, where she was living with her husband Earll, an actor. It is available on audiocassette from The American Audio Prose Library, PO Box 842, Columbia, MO 65205. 1-800-447-2275. Free catalog of recordings of readings by and interviews with 132 contemporary authors available on request. © 1986 American Audio Prose Library. All rights reserved.

MHK: After college I thought that I was a painter because I always see pictures, and I see visions before the words come, and it's always a secondary step to find the words. So at one time I thought that I could go directly from picture to picture because when I write I want the readers to see the pictures. So why not forget the words and just paint pictures? I did that for a year until I realized that I had already put in twenty years of apprenticeship with words, and that in order to be as good a painter as I was already a writer, I would need to paint for another twenty years. So I quit doing that and continued writing.

KB: It seems to me that one of the central metaphors, especially in *The Woman Warrior*, is the story of your childhood drawings. When you drew your silence in the first three years of school and could not speak, out of shyness and fear and not knowing English, you drew these wonderful pictures and then covered them all in black paint, and that was the curtain. You imagined that that was the curtain that was going to come up and reveal the scene under it. And of course your teachers thought you had a learning disability?

MHK: They thought I was trying to destroy the pictures, I think.

KB: Do you feel that the curtains were analogous to your parents' silences, and your not knowing much about China? And was your writing an attempt, through art, to raise the curtain and reveal the drama of your heritage and everything behind it?

MHK: Yes, and I also think that there is just something about life that's like the theater. Somewhere in there I talk about looking at mountains, like

33

the mountains in Hawaii, and I keep thinking that they're going to open and the face of God is going to be on the other side. There's something in life that's a curtain, and I keep trying to raise it and I know there's more on the other side. I mean, I don't see it as a sad image at all, but as anticipation.

KB: Exactly. And then there's the curtain of the clouds in *The Woman Warrior* vision, when the Woman Warrior is taken, led by the bird.

MHK: Oh, she goes through the clouds.

KB: She goes through the clouds into another world, then she can see back through the gourd into the "real world," and it's like there's the physical world and then there's the world of the imagination.

MHK: I guess I walk around all the time thinking that imminently, something is going to happen that will reveal what's really going on. I think I've spent a lot of my life trying to figure out what's really going on.

KB: Well, certainly that's what *Woman Warrior* and *China Men* are about—reclaiming history, reclaiming heritage, and finding out for yourself what's going on. When did you decide to break the silence, to start laying to rest the ghosts and to work on the material that ended up being *The Woman Warrior*?

MHK: In a way, I've never been silent. I suppose oral expression is so different from writing, it's almost like a different language. While I've had problems speaking, I've always been a writer. There was always the wanting to tell the stories of the people coming. I remember writing *China Men* stories when I was 8, or 9, 10 years old, but I didn't have the vocabulary and the form because I was just a kid. The emotions and the stories I had already, but not the craft. I tried telling the *China Men* stories like Jason and the Argonauts, because I read that as a kid, where they were using epic hexameter meter, and so I tried to tell the story of the China Men as Jason and the quest for the Golden Fleece, using the hexameter rhythms and epic form. I suppose for decades I kept telling the same stories again and again, but each time I told it I had a better vocabulary and better craft.

KB: In *Woman Warrior*, with the opening scene the "No Name Woman," and at the end there, we get this feeling of revelation, that you are going to break silence in revealing this story of being Chinese and being female.

MHK: I guess that that story comes from my mother actually ordering me not to tell it.

KB: Right, the first lines of the book are "You are not to tell this to anyone."

MHK: But the wonderful thing about writing is that you weasel your way around it, because you can think to yourself, "Okay, I'm just gonna write it down. I'm not going to publish it. I'm not going to show it to anybody." Or you can say, "I'm not telling it. I'm writing it." Then, step by step, you break the silence because there are all these intermediary decisions you can make. At a certain point, by the time I'd written it down, it didn't seem like such a big deal to get it printed.

KB: In *The Woman Warrior* you say that "Even now China wraps double binds around my feet," and I wondered if that was still true for you or if these two books brought liberation for you and resolution of any kind of the tensions?

MHK: I no longer feel double binds around my feet. I feel like a very peaceful, healthy person and I don't know why. I don't think it's because I wrote the books. It would seem that writing books would get all kinds of neuroses straightened out because of the intense examination, but I don't see the direct relation to my own psychology. I have a feeling that it's just time; it makes you tired of hassling.

KB: I take it then from what you're saying that writing in general for you is a joyful, rejoicing celebratory process.

MHK: Oh, yes, but it's everything. I think that when you're a born writer—I feel like I'm a born writer—then when you're celebrating, you put it into words, and when you're mourning, you put it into words. There's this desire always to find the words for life and for the invisible and for the visible and for the imagination.

KB: What about the structure of the two books. I've heard that you wrote both of them really together, and in fact that the last section in *China Men*, "A Brother in Vietnam," was really the first thing that you wrote that ended up as these two companion volumes. Is that true?

MHK: Yes. A lot of *China Men* I was writing simultaneously with *The Woman Warrior*. I saw this as a big novel about men and women, and going from ancient feudal times up to the Vietnam War and past that. The books seemed to fall into place as two separate books because the power in *The Woman Warrior* has so much to do with a feminist vision and feminist anger, and so it became a coherent work without the men's stories. The men's stories were sort of undercutting the women's stories, so it fell into two books, and I think that reflects the history of Chinese American people, where the women were excluded from immigrating to the United States, where men set out on these great journeys.

KB: Sojourns.

MHK: Yes, and so the men and the women live their lives and their adventures separately, so it worked out very well, as two books, historically and thematically.

KB: Thematically, it seems that *The Woman Warrior* is a much more personal book. It's much more a book about yourself, and the women in it seem to be much more, truly, the women that you name and say they are, your aunts, your mother, whereas *China Men*, the "On Discovery" and "On Fathers" sections, set up the idea that the men in there are more archetypal, or their stories stand for many China men.

MHK: Well, the way I saw it, too, was that *The Woman Warrior* is this story of a young person, a young woman, and being young, she is still creating herself, and she is usually a first-person narrator. She only knows herself as she knows women, and she has very little sympathy or interest in knowing what men are like. I think that *China Men* is a story of a mature, grown person who is able to look at the opposite sex and to know them for themselves. At the beginning of *China Men* when I tell the myth about the man who goes to the Land of Women, and then he gets his feet broken, he becomes a woman, in a way I'm saying that I am a woman going into the Land of Men and what will become of me. I become the kind of woman that loves men, and I can tell their story without judging them, or showing just their relation to myself. So I see these books as a growth from a young woman to an adult woman, and to be a good grown woman means that one is able to tell the story of men.

KB: At what point did you take on or realize, as you were working, the metaphor of yourself as writer, as woman warrior, and also, as the poet, Ts'ai Yen, at the end, in the Barbarian Reed section?

MHK: I don't know that I ever really identify myself completely with the woman warrior. My editor said to name the book *The Woman Warrior*, and I guess about a year later said, "Oh, well you know that that's you," and my reaction was very negative. I don't feel that she's me.

KB: As writer, though, the figure of Hong Kingston as writer?

MHK: No, it's always an ideal that I have not reached. Also, I don't really like warriors. I wish I had not had a metaphor of a warrior person who uses weapons and goes to war. I think that there's always a doubt about war as a way of solving things, so throughout, I keep trying to say, isn't there another—

KB: Well, it's like the war of words, though, because the god of war and the god of literature go with the woman warrior in the story as you tell it.

MHK: And in my stories the pen is always problematical. It's always on the verge of not winning. But I think maybe the frustration I feel is that writers have the power to change the world only a little bit at a time. We conquer a reader at a time. We change the atmosphere of the world, and we change moods here and there, whereas the people who have the guns and the bombs have so much direct power. We're using images and moods against the bombs. If only the word had as much power.

KB: I'm very interested in what you would choose to call *The Woman Warrior* and *China Men*. Are you bothered, or do you concern yourself with distinctions between fiction and nonfiction? The book has been received, as you know of course, as memoir, autobiography, all kinds of things.

MHK: It doesn't bother me, but it's bothered a lot of other people. There have been quite a few scholarly articles done on it. In England, when the books first came out, the critics only wrote on genre, and they couldn't seem to come to terms with any of the characters or the stories. They just wanted to figure out first what genre it was. At first, I didn't know what to call them. It would have been all right to call them novels, I think. On the other hand, lately, I've begun to understand, maybe it's because I'm working on a novel right now, a fiction, I see that what I've written are a new kind of biography. They're different from biographies that have come before because they are the biographies of imaginative people. I tell the imaginative lives and the dreams and the fictions of real people. These are the stories of storytellers, and so instead of telling the dates when people are born and where they're born, I tell you what their dreams are and what stories they tell. So what I've written are biographies of imaginative people, and this is culturally correct, because this is the way my people are, my family. People come together and they tell each other their lives, and they make up the stories of their lives. Some of the stories they tell to immigration officials, and some are heroic stories to make themselves look better. So it's part of the Chinese American culture, to make fictive lives. As a writer, I'm just part of that. These are real people in my books, and to depict them as accurately as I can, I tell what they make up about themselves.

KB: So in some cases, in other words, these really are the stories that you were told.
MHK: Yes.

KB: By your parents?
MHK: Yes.

KB: And uncles and grandparents?
MHK: Yes. But all the storytellers have a freedom to change the stories, and I hear people tell the same stories about themselves, and they will tell three or four different versions of how they came to America—like my father.

KB: You mean those were all his versions?
MHK: They're all of the same man, and so if he has the freedom to tell four stories about himself, then I have the freedom, as a writer, to give my versions, too.

KB: Because I really wanted to ask you, do you know how your father really came over here? Do you know what the real truth is?
MHK: As I listen to each story, since they are told so well, each one is true. And again, this is reflecting our culture, because many Chinese American people have an immigration story and a birth story and a fire and earthquake story.

KB: How would you describe your style, do you think?
MHK: It's the way I talk. It's the way I hear people around me talk. I try to be influenced by actual language, and I work very hard to tune my ears so that I can hear language as it is spoken by real people. Now, I've been very fortunate in that the people around me speak Chinese and English, and then they have this Chinese with an English accent, no, English with a Chinese accent, and this new vocabulary that they make up that's English but it's got all this influence from Chinese language, and I try to get that power and music in my writing. So sometimes I've said things in Chinese and typed in English in order to capture the rhythms. So I suppose my style has something to do with a Chinese American voice.

KB: I also read someplace that you were strongly attached to William Carlos Williams' *In the American Grain*.

MHK: I want to put two books on the list of most attached to, OK? One of them is *In the American Grain* because he tells the story of America as myth. He starts with the Vikings and he ends at the Civil War with Abraham Lincoln as a woman who is walking through the fields with his/her shawl and looking at the fallen soldiers, and I thought that that was the truest book of American history I had ever read. And he did it mythically, and I wanted to do American history in that same way, especially for *China Men*, and I was so lucky because he ended at the Civil War and I pick up at the Civil War when the Chinese Americans came, and I showed how the Chinese made the bands of steel, which is a railroad, and they banded the country back together again. That is the way I want to think about American history, about history, in that mythic, true way. The other book that I really love is *Orlando*, by Virginia Woolf, and I think it's interesting again, here's the story of a man/woman, a person who could be a man and a woman, a person who could live for hundreds of years. Those two books made me free to write about people that are 150 years old and I don't have to be constrained by death or dates, and I can be free of being a man or a woman. People can be a man and then they can be a woman, and then, for the next hundred years, they can be something else.

KB: Your work is full of rebirths, reincarnations, stories, and often, cross-gender.

MHK: More often than I thought. I was really surprised when people pointed that out to me. I didn't notice that.

KB: I wanted to ask if you think your affinity with William Carlos Williams is in any way connected to his affinity, along with his friend and his colleague, Ezra Pound, with the Chinese?

MHK: Oh, probably. I have been very excited by Ezra Pound's work with Chinese. People don't realize how much of Chinese culture is part of American culture. I mean, all those transcendentalists at the beginning of American writing.

KB: Nineteenth-century Romanticism as the Eastern influence?

MHK: Yes, and all of the Beatniks, all the people that are writing people out of Buddhism and out of the ideograms. It's always been part of America.

KB: In your use of myths, I wanted to ask about the ideogram. Have you retold them to create your own ideograms in *China Men*?

MHK: No, I don't create any, they're all actual—

KB:—They're all actual myths. But have you changed them in any way, though?

MHK: Oh, the myths. I thought you meant the ideograms. Oh, yes, the myths I change. I change them a lot, and I've been criticized for that by traditionalists because they don't understand that I have no intention of just recording myths. I mean, I'm not an archivist. I want to give you an example of myths that I've changed. When the woman warrior has the words carved on her back, that's actually a man's story. It's about a man named Yüch Fei who had the vow carved on his back by his mother. Now, I took that and gave that to a woman. I gave a man's myth to a woman because it's part of the feminist war that's going on in *The Woman Warrior*, to take the men's stories away from them and give the strength of that story to a woman. I see that as an aggressive storytelling act, and also it's part of my own freedom to play with the myth, and I do feel that the myths have to be changed and played with all the time, or they die. The problem with doing all that is that these myths are not known to most of my readers. So I had to figure out a way to inform people and at the same time play around with them. I think at that point I just decided not to tell anybody the original stories, and then tell them how I played around with them, because I just wanted to get on with the story, and I just figured, well, let the scholars figure it out later, but they've actually attacked me for not sticking with the story.

KB: What about the story of Fa Mu Lan. Was there really that story of the swordswoman?

MHK: Yes, it's a chant that goes back to the days of the Tartars, when the Tartars attacked China, and it's a chant that has lived to this day in all Asian countries.

KB: How do you think it fits in with the picture of the way women are, their role, in China? Is this wish fulfillment, that this is the secret in the women's quarters?

MHK: Yes, or hope. Hope and a heroic myth that they might live up to. But also, it's historical. I mean there were lots of women that were, that did many things, that were scholars and that were warriors, so it's not just a dream. It's an act of history, and it interests me, which ones of these chants and stories survive in America. That one has come to us intact, I think, to the United States. So people here are able to chant it. It interests me, like, which things die away, and which things come with us and remain. I now think of these as American myths because that's where I heard them, and that's the people that tell them. So it's not as important what this has to do with China as what it has to do with America. Why are we singing those woman warrior myths now?

KB: This is very philosophical material we're talking about here, because what is truth? I, myself, have always been, coming from a written culture, rather suspicious of oral history because I know I have a very good memory, but I get things wrong, from my own childhood, and my mother corrects me a lot.

MHK: Well, I am suspicious of oral history too, and this is why I will tell four or five versions of a story, and I ask that question: which one is true? But then I also ask: which one of these stories is most useful? And the important stories are what people are doing right now. What are the adventures we're having right now?

KB: In *China Men* in particular, you have the little sections, where you, like Pound, paint little ideograms out of myth that then juxtapose against the longer pieces. Were you conscious of that as a technique?

MHK: Oh, yes. I was very careful selecting the myths that come between. I guess I think of them as the real stories, and then there's the myth. There's myths between the stories. I think *China Men* is like a six-layer cake and the myths are like icing, and the rest are like the cake.

KB: But they illuminate each other in juxtaposition.

MHK: Yes, I want people, for example, to read the mythic story of a pacifist, and then the next story is "The Brother in Vietnam," and I want us to think, well, what good is it to go to Vietnam with that myth hanging in back of you? Does it help this person survive in Vietnam? Does it help him not to fight, or what? And I just keep that myth ahead of you so that you think about what the morals are. But I don't, in *China Men*, tell you what the myth and the reality have to do with one another.

KB: What are some of the things you got from your parents through the love and anger, the love/hate ambivalence, that you're now very grateful to them for?

MHK: Oh, they have a life-force that is so passionate and dramatic and strong. They can do drama before your very eyes, and I don't see people like that all the time. I used to think everybody was like that, and another thing too, is they truly love literature. All my life they sang Li Po and Tu Fu, and I didn't know that. My brother said, "Oh, I thought those were village ditties."

So I was raised on all this classical Chinese poetry, plus the chants, like the chant of Fa Mu Lan, and I grew up with those rhythms, and now I realize how rare that is. Not everybody had that. As a writer, these were priceless gifts that they just strew in their path and I was just in the way, picking it up. Then, I don't realize it at the time that I'm writing this, but of course, their religion is all the stronger because it is so flexible. Like the stories, the traditions are always different. They don't explain it because tomorrow they may change it, and this is what's kept them vital, and also what makes them so American, because they're making it up as they go along, and that's their strength. I guess Chinese American people are always talking about what's traditional. Should you keep it or should you toss it, you know. And this is sort of my answer. It never was a tradition to keep everything the same.

KB: And that's your answer to the traditionalists who criticize your work?

MHK: Yes, that mythology and stories and rituals change to give you strength under present circumstances. Either that, or they die. Oh, I want to tell you, I was at a New Year's thing in Riverside, at a public school. There was this kindergarten teacher who had her kids make a dragon and so all the kids were under the dragon, and then they kept talking about our dragon, and then the little dragon gets all made out of crepe paper and all kinds of stuff, little boxes and bags over their heads, and you couldn't really see the kids' faces, but you could see their little feet, you know, and their black feet and white feet and brown feet, and I thought, "That is an American dragon." And that means that it's here. The traditions are here, and they have been changed, and the dragon is alive. Now if we kept saying, "It's got to be done the way they did it in China," then it's all over. Not only for the dragon, but for people.

KB: When the books came out, you had not yet gotten to go to China.

MHK: Yes, and in a way that was purposeful because I wanted to record the myth of China, and I didn't want to confuse that with the reality of China.

KB: I wonder what your thoughts are about the China of now? The post-revolutionary China, because both books have occasional statements about it and both of them show understandable ambivalence. Parts of your family and relations were killed, but as you pointed out, they obviously treat women better, too—there are tradeoffs. What are your thoughts about that at this point?

MHK: Well, it's difficult to have a line on China because China itself has changed so much. When we went, it was not too much after the end of the Cultural Revolution and the Gang of Four, so there's been such turmoil and so much that's unknown. The stories that have come out of China have been so confusing, too, but our trip there was just wonderful because I got to see the sights of the places that I wrote about.

KB: You got to go to your ancestral village?

MHK: Yes. In some ways I was so gratified because I saw what I had described, and it felt like I was coming home because I had described it right. Not only that, but it gave me a faith in talk-story because they had described it pretty much the way it looked. But also, there were things that I wish that I had seen earlier so that I could have written it more accurately.

KB: Such as?

MHK: I saw the Hong family temple, and it's right next to the well where the aunt jumped in. I brought pictures back of the well and of the temple, and then my mother said, "Oh you know, the guys used to stand around the temple on the steps and they used to make comments at the girls that are drawing the water, trying to get them flustered so they'd drop their earthenware jars, and then the men would laugh." And then I thought, "God, I wish I'd known that. That would have been perfect to put into the 'No Name Woman' section," and it's so typical of men and women all over the world, you know, guys standing on the steps making remarks.

KB: Cracks at women.

MHK: Yes, yes. And then that temple has a ramp, you know, a cement ramp going up, because during the Cultural Revolution they turned it into a tractor shed, and I think it's still a tractor shed. It's not torn down. So, looking at things like that, it was just so amazing. I could see parts of my stories that were missing that I could put in, but not anything substantial would change. So that made me feel good.

KB: The astonishing strength and the courage and the tradition that you reveal in both of those books about your family! You speak of the Cantonese as being these very adventuresome types, wildly imaginative and prone to revolutionary thought. Were most of the Chinese who came to this country from certain areas where they were prone to wander?

MHK: Oh, yes, yes. Most of the people in the U.S. are Cantonese, and so almost all of us come from the same region in the Pearl River Delta, and they're the people that started the peasant uprisings and the revolutions in

China. Sun Yat Sen was a Cantonese, and so they're the people with the imagination to make up the Gold Mountain and then to go and find it.

KB: I was just astonished at the amount of trafficking in the nineteenth century. I mean, they went back and forth.
MHK: They commuted.

KB: They commuted.
MHK: Yes, that amazed me too. They would do like three or four trips to the West during a lifetime. Since being to China, a feeling that I have now, too, is how lonely it is in America. I mean, not just how lonely it was when my mother came, but how lonely it is now. I see those villages and streets with a party going on all the time, and all those families living in one room, and if you felt like socializing some more you could just step out in the street and there's all the sidewalk cafes and the street vendors and the food. Everyone together dressed in blue like an ocean. I just felt so at one and harmonious with many people. And then in contrast, the people in the United States seem very lonely and very individual. There seems to be an exuberance there. Life and optimism about building a new country. It always surprises me that they keep talking about building a new country when they're so old.

KB: Did you find relatives when you were there, in your home village?
MHK: Oh, yes. It was really wonderful to be able to talk to people who talk like me.

KB: You did find out there was a Chinese language that's like the one you speak?
MHK: Yes, just like it. In fact this whole trip to China was linguistically very amazing because we started traveling from the north, and the further south we went the more I could understand them. By the time we got to Canton I gave a speech, and then by the time we got to the villages I could understand them and they could understand me. Everybody ought to have a journey like that. It was just great.

KB: That's a very important thing we haven't talked about, and that is about the reception among the Chinese of your books. What was it?
MHK: Oh, my books have been translated in Hong Kong and Taiwan and the People's Republic. They've been pirated.

KB: What does that mean?
MHK: That means that they just steal them and sell them and translate

them without permission and without consultation. So there's been some very bad pirated translations. But, the People's Republic is working very hard on my books and the Language Institute translated the two books into the national standard language, and the wonderful thing that happened was that they sent the books to the south, to Canton, and some scholars read them, the translations, and said that they would have to be retranslated because it was obvious from reading the English that I was writing in Cantonese. That I meant my people to be speaking Cantonese. And they could pick up those rhythms in the English language. So they retranslated it into Cantonese. That makes me feel really happy about my own writing, but it also makes me feel good that China isn't putting everything into the national standard dialect and that they're going to support the colorful minorities.

KB: You're a Chinese American woman, you're married to an Occidental man, and you have a son. How are you raising your son in relationship to your Chinese relationship and in response to the tensions and all the ambivalences that you've documented?

MHK: Oh, we raised our son in Honolulu, so I think that solved everything, because he was among people who are very much like himself, a lot of Asian Americans, but they are part of the Polynesians. But actually, as a whole, I don't know how much influence any parent has on any kid. I would have really liked to have raised him as a reader, as a more scholarly person, but he's become a Hawaiian. That's what he is now. He's a Hawaiian, and his culture is Hawaiian music and he has Hawaiian families that are like his families. I also see, still though, the Asian influence, or the affinity with ghosts, although the Polynesians have their own shapes of ghosts and spirits. In Hawaii, he could see his own ghosts and spirits, and of course they come out of the land, so they're Hawaiian in shape, so our son has become very much that, a Hawaiian person. I think that incorporates being a Chinese person.

KB: What is it to be a Hawaiian person, though?

MHK: Oh, that's a person who feels that he is a son of the earth, a son of the land. He hears music and he can play the music. And the music comes from a people who have not lost a tribal identity. A genius of being a Chinese American person is the ability to make community. In Hawaii there's a sense of community, and that my son has.

KB: Our lives, after all, are our own. I mean they are the lives that we are given and we live them, and so when somebody says was your life experience unique, who can say? It was our life, right? I wonder, though, if with other Chinese children in your generation, was the fact that your parents were really old enough to be your grandparents when you were born important and significant?

MHK: I think there's quite a few people of my generation that are like me with parents that, well, maybe the mother immigrated quite late—I've seen a Ph.D. dissertation that documented five women that had, they had the exact same background as me, where the parents were separated for fifteen years or so, where they had their kids when the mother was forty, and the psychological profile seemed to be very similar. There's a lot of people who've told me that I've written their diaries. On the other hand, there have also been people who say that what I've written is nothing like them, Chinese American people who say this is not the way Chinese American people are. That we don't have stories; we don't have superstitions. But I think that that usually comes from people maybe from another generation, or they come from another part of China, or maybe they were wealthy people. So I get all kinds of reaction.

KB: What are you working on now?

MHK: It's a novel. It's about a young man in 1963, and he lives on Jackson Street, which is between North Beach and it's part of Chinatown. He goes to all the coffee shops and jazz places and also, he lives in Chinatown. He's just a little bit too young to be a Beatnik, but the hippies haven't come yet. He's a fifth or sixth generation Chinese American, and doesn't have the support of the myths that are in the other two books. So he's very alienated, but that's part of the style of the times, too, so I just tell about what happens to him as he wanders around in 1963.

KB: When do you think it will be done, do you know?
MHK: Maybe December?

KB: Oh, it's getting close.
MHK: Yes. I have two more chapters.

KB: Well, good. Thank you for taking so long to visit with us today.
MHK: Thank you.

To Be Able to See the Tao

Jody Hoy / 1986

From *The Power to Dream: Interviews with Women in the Creative Arts* (New York: Global City Press, 1995), pp. 120–47. Reprinted by permission of the interviewer.

I was introduced to Maxine Hong Kingston by Loralee MacPike, a mutual friend. When I met Maxine on a trip to Hawaii, I invited her to lunch at the Waimea Tea House in Honolulu. At 5′½″ I towered over her! Maxine must be around 4′8″. She looks fragile and delicate like the flowers that surrounded her that day, but she is immensely strong and wise. She brings to mind the Native American saying, "Women hold up half the sky." When I met her she had long, lustrous, black hair with a single, broad streak of gray in it. By the time we did the interview several years later, her hair was just as beautiful, but almost completely gray.

Maxine and her actor husband Earll had moved from Hawaii to the mainland, where I interviewed her in a rented home in Southern California. Maxine's combination of clarity, humor, whimsy, intelligence and passion were most exciting. She has an exquisite mind. Subsequently I heard her speak at UC Irvine, UC Santa Cruz, and eventually on my own campus, where she was the 1990 Commencement Speaker. She is so petite that a special box had to be built for her to stand on so the students could see her over the podium!

Some of my more conservative Orange County colleagues probably regretted that students could see and hear her, as she began by saying this was her first commencement address, and then went on to tell them that when she graduated from UC Berkeley she hadn't been able to find a job. Eventually she got a job doing drudge work in an office, from which she escaped by writing novels in the restroom. Personally, I loved her candor.

In public, Maxine speaks with the same small voice she describes as belonging to the main character in *The Woman Warrior:* yet the voice says things of amazing eloquence, power and passion. There is a parallel between the small woman with her enormous power and the small voice with its powerful message. In person Maxine is gentle, warm and full of pixy humor. Maxine the writer is ferocious, sensual, inventive, funny and shocking—a literary trickster, to borrow one of her own images.

Currently she lives in California with her husband Earll. Their son is a musician and lives in Hawaii.

Jody: I read somewhere that *The Woman Warrior* was not your choice of a title. Is that true, and if so, what was the original title?

Maxine: Yes, that's true, my original title was *Gold Mountain Stories.* The publishers didn't like a title that sounds like a collection of short stories; they never like to publish collections of short stories. I wasn't that happy with either of those titles, I think that calling that book *The Woman Warrior* emphasizes "warrior." I'm not really telling the story of war, I want to be a pacifist. So I keep hoping we will all take the woman warrior in another sense, that there are other ways to fight wars than with swords.

Jody: I took it to mean someone of courage and strength. Isn't "no name aunt" a warrior in her silence, in the fact that she never revealed the name of the man who got her pregnant, and that she took the baby with her—given the choices she had? Fa Mu Lan and Brave Orchid are warriors in that sense too, and Moon Orchid is a kind of failed warrior, isn't she? I saw Moon Orchid as on a journey which she cannot complete. Then too, there is the character who is yourself as a child. Why did you choose to write about these particular women?

Maxine: I think there are more. There is the woman who is captured at the end and taken into the desert, and she comes back with the songs. Then there's the woman who appears briefly and dies during the Japanese bombing.

Jody: The crazy woman?

Maxine: Yes. The people said, "Oh, she looks like a spy, she must be a spy for the Japanese," and they stoned her to death. And somewhere there's a pair of sisters who are wives of a warrior. When I was writing about these women I didn't think of them as warriors, I saw some of them as people who didn't know how to fight, or who were outdated. Also, they were living at a time when their abilities were not useful. My feminine women I killed off. Even Moon Orchid, who knows how to dress right. She's feminine in this sense.

Jody: In the sense of role?

Maxine: Yes, literally role. We've had three workshops for a play or a movie of *The Woman Warrior.* During the casting there were no end of women who can do Moon Orchid, or any of the failed women. But it's really hard to find anybody to do Brave Orchid. I think this shows that in 1986 the feminine, bound-foot, dainty type is with us. But where is the peasant woman with the big feet who is fierce and strong and of the earth, and yet beautiful? There aren't any, there isn't anyone out there. It's very sad what's happening to us now. Why aren't there actresses to choose from to play the powerful woman?

Jody: The story of "no name aunt" is a terrible introduction to menstruation: talk about a curse!

Maxine: Isn't that awful?

Jody: You labeled it "a story to grow up with." You said that whenever your mother wanted to warn you about life she would tell you one of these stories. How did you receive such stories? Did they frighten you a lot? Did you experience them as truth? Did you identify with them? How could anybody grow up normal, being told stories like that? They are so powerful, they touch every woman's fear. What was your response as a young person, hearing a story like that?

Maxine: Joyce Chopra told me when she read that story it reminded her that some Jewish mothers, when the daughter starts to menstruate, slap her face. And I thought, my God, I would feel the same way as if I had had my face slapped. Now, picture a hard slap . . . I don't picture a ritualistic little tap. I was so mad at my mother for telling me a cruel tale for the joy of the telling. I told her it wasn't a true story, yet part of me was really interested in hearing the story. I don't know that I'm all that normal; I also have that joy of telling. My mother and I are both artists. My fascination in the story is saving it: I've been given this thing that I'm going to write down . . . a gift. It's merely a story. I've thought: there never was such a woman. But as I got older I saw that the stories seemed to check out, they're probably true. I bet that story is true.

I used to spend a lot of years being very angry. I think that anger was a basic emotion for me for about twenty years—I thought anger was just the way you feel. Maybe when I was writing "No Name Woman" I got more complex and began to see this woman as a romantic figure, a person who was capable of going outside her culture sexually, as very daring, vengeful. Then also there was a battle against silence in that story: my mother told me not to tell anybody. There was an artistic battle of what can be told and written and what is unwritable.

Jody: Meridel le Sueur, the Minnesota writer, interviewed her grandmother, who said, "I've lived all my life trying to suppress these stories of what happened to me, and now you're going to write them." And she did, and they were sexual stories too: how her grandmother had been married off into rape and had children when she was very young and didn't know what sex was or where babies came from. Meridel wrote it all down.

Maxine: I think maybe I'm not crazy because I wrote the unspeakable out. I spent a lot of years trying to break the silence and may have failed. I was about thirty-five when I wrote *The Woman Warrior*—that's sort of old for a first publication. I have met women who have told me that they had great stories but decided not to write them. I can picture myself in those women's places very easily. A way I could write it was to write very convoluted stories that set up the possibility that nothing happened at all. I often say, "Well, maybe it didn't happen." I suggested there was maybe love, or that she wasn't responsible, it was just rape, which is a saving story too: "Wait, I didn't have anything to do with it, it was forced on me." This complicated way of writing allows me to write.

Jody: What about exclusion as a theme, exclusion from Western culture as an Asian, exclusion from Chinese culture as a woman: is this part of the impetus to write? What permits you to do the big deeds, write the big books? Where does the creative drive come from, and is exclusion a part of that?

Maxine: Exclusion plays right into the hands of the American writer. There have been amazing coincidences of exclusion, so that I become a person who is able to look at everything from an interesting perspective. The alienated, individualistic writer or hero or heroine is a tradition in American literature. I take that stance very easily: I don't worry whether my voice is "our" voice. Even though I have a peculiar voice I'm able to speak to everyone from my stance of exile, as outsider, and then I can make my way in. I like the way Anaïs Nin often talked about being a spy; one can be invisible and spy on everybody.

In America, typically writers are isolated geographically from one another: Arthur Miller in New York, Hemingway in Florida, Faulkner in Mississippi, Steinbeck in Central California, Gary Snyder in the California mountains and Kerouac on the road . . . and so forth. There are all these voices calling out to one another across a vast continent. Writers, though, in this country keep trying to have a community. I've always envied Ginsberg his getting beatniks together, and Ken Kesey who bussed the Merry Pranksters, and Anaïs Nin with Henry Miller and Lawrence Durrell. But when I look at those groups more realistically, community seems like their dream only.

If you looked at how many times people actually met, they didn't see each other that often. The community was a dream they wrote about, that they imagined. I would like a community, not just for writers, but for everyone. I would love to be able to speak about my tribe doing this or that. I'd like to say "we women," but community has yet to be invented.

Jody: Is there perhaps a different kind of community, a community of writers going back in time who move through you and provide a different kind of support?

Maxine: Yes, I do feel that. There are writers both living and dead—we don't have to physically live in the same commune, we are doing something together. On the other hand, I also feel the isolation: I am doing something all by myself that nobody else is doing, and maybe nobody will ever read it—and it's all right.

Jody: To what degree have you had to work alone? I mean this in an ontological, not a literal sense. You described your husband as your most sensitive reader; you said he feeds you (that's your own image), that he has fed you in that sense. But what about the actual work of being a writer and having to do it all alone?

Maxine: I remember saying that my husband read my work at the end. This means that there were five, six years by myself, and he reads after the work has been perfected.

Jody: Isn't that aloneness characteristic of all artists? There is also such an isolated quality in Americans which is not true of Europeans, and which is balanced by a dream or a communal fantasy in our culture, as you've said.

Maxine: That's right, and isolation's not true of Asians either. Artists always take to extremes what everybody else is doing. I don't think it's just the American writer; I think Americans are alone. There's the ideal of the individual, and also we are physically very apart. I saw it clearly when we were in Asia, how life can be a party all the time: all you had to do was go out in the streets, these narrow streets, and everybody else was sitting in the street eating. Any time you feel like it you can go outside and have company. Also in the house—you have so many people living in small quarters. They don't seem to think they're small rooms, it's just being with your people. I felt so sad because I realized my parents left that village, and tribal life, to come to a country where they were, they are, so alone. But they aren't the only ones who are alone; everybody in America is lonely. We have to make these appointments in our books way ahead of time and drive for miles to get together. There isn't a community, there isn't just walking out in the street and being with your people. When you walk out in the street you're out there with strangers. So when writers speak with the alienated single voice, they are speaking for other single voices all across this country. What we have to do is make the communities, and that's really far off now. People join the army in order to be in a community and they have this wonderful, high experience of going to war together.

Jody: Do you believe in the possibility of social and spiritual change? And are your books written with that in mind?

Maxine: I am not exactly sure how the spirit and the world are connected, but there have been times when I have believed somehow that we create the world by our way of seeing and knowing. Literature has some way of changing atmosphere and changing mind—and then mind creates the world. However, there are also times when there is chaos in the world that is so powerful, and the world's weapons have gotten so strong . . . What are we going to do about the bomb? I don't know what the people with right politics and gentle weapons such as words can do. I remember during the Vietnam War Allen Ginsberg declared an end to the war on PBS, and he did it poetically. Do you remember when they tried to levitate the Pentagon? I asked him about that and he said they hadn't done it right. He said they used the wrong syllables, they were doing "om," but "om" goes around and in again. They should have said "ah," and then it would have levitated. Even if we're going to lose we're still going to have to use the words. We still have to keep saying "om" and "ah" and all those other words, because as soon as we pick up a gun, we lose. So, we're already on the right path to keep writing, and ahing, and oming . . .

Jody: In your books you move from the biological family to the extended family to the cultural family to the mythological family, and all those are connected. Are you speaking for a larger family at the same time as you are speaking for yourself?

Maxine: Yes, and as I have the dream of a larger family, I also criticize the small family, because there's an idea abroad in the world that Chinese really have these terrific families and that's why we do so well. But when I portray the family I show the terrible problems, fights, wars within the family—even mother and daughter who love each other so much and yet have wars that tear them apart—and families fighting families. And then the fathers go across the ocean, not just because they want a better life, but because they can't stand their families. And what do they look for? They

look for another family. One of the talents that's needed today is the talent
to make a community. Everywhere you go, like school, "How am I going to
find my friends? How am I going to find a community?" If that talent isn't
in us, then there's loneliness forever. Also, there may be something just
wrong with nuclear families. Maybe we shouldn't have them, because maybe
they stop us from finding our larger human family.

Jody: That sounds like my son's struggle in high school to find his community.

Maxine: Those awful, sick communities in high school, that's one of the
worst places! That's why kids have gangs, because there's all that romance
about the brotherhood. I feel grateful that my son's friends didn't become a
gang.

Jody: Why did you leave Hawaii?

Maxine: Earll is an actor and he wanted to do some auditioning here.

Jody: Was that hard?

Maxine: To leave Hawaii? Yes, because that means leaving our son. He's
decided he's really a Hawaiian now. I know he became a Hawaiian because
Hawaiians have a sense of the community and the tribe, which has become
his, along with the music and the mythology.

Jody: I sense that you'll go back.

Maxine: We're going back this summer.

Jody: Several times in *China Men* you describe your father's arrival in
America, and each time the story is different. It made me think of film, the
way film can tell a story and change it over and over again in a way which is
very hard to do in literature. I had never read anything like that before.

Maxine: No, I think of film as a plot. My flexibility with versions came
from talk-story, the way I actually heard my mother and their friends telling
about how they came to America and what happened. Each time they told a
story, they told it differently. The stories change according to personalities,
occasions and listeners.

Jody: There is a circularity in the books and also in the recreation of
myths, which you reenter and change.

Maxine: Yes, that is what I was doing. I have to assert myself as a storyteller too, so I also claim a right to change myths, to have my versions. It's a
powerful assertion, because all of the storytellers I listened to are older peo-

ple, and as a listener I was a child, or a woman, or somebody who hadn't lived adventures. And a writer does not come from a talk-story tradition, but from a literary tradition. To write in a culture where most readers do not have a background of Chinese or even of Chinese mythology, or even of Chinese American history, I felt I had to educate the reader at the same time that I was playing around with these stories. I got really mad at critics who said, "She really messed these stories, this wasn't the way they're supposed to be told, this isn't the traditional story." And all along I was asserting the right not to tell a traditional story. I'm not an anthropologist or a historian: I wanted the right to play around with the stories.

Jody: In the article *"China Men, Song of Solomon* and *Ceremony,"* Paula Rabinowitz commented on the importance of the mythos, legends and stories that surrounded your early years, and the recreation of the elements of dream and folklore, repetition, fantasy and circularity in your works. Could you comment on that?

Maxine: Yes, it looks like Leslie Silko and Toni Morrison are doing what I'm doing too. When we've talked about our backgrounds in myth and story-telling, it sounds like we grew up in very similar ways. Toni was trying to figure out where we belong, and she kept using that term "magical realism"; she thought we were in that tradition.

Jody: For whom do you write and to what part of them: the mind, the heart, the spirit?

Maxine: I write for everyone, and I mean even people in the future. When I thought I couldn't get the books published I was going to leave xeroxes all over the place and then people in the future would read them. So I was writing for all the people now and all the people in the future. And I was writing for Western people and Asian people, I had that sense of a world-wide and present and future timeless audience. I wanted to be able to take people's preconceptions and break them apart. This means going so deep inside people that I would just shatter them, then take them higher.

In the mythical sense I wanted to take to a point where they would experience enlightenment and they could do it by reading my words. That was why I wrote the visions of light, and what the grandfather saw on opium. I wanted people not to take drugs, but to take what I wrote and be able to see the Tao. Emotionally, I wanted to give the reader the anger that I had been feeling for a long time, and also disgust—physical gross-out—and up to higher emotions. I wanted the reader to feel being separated from people they loved; one would be in China and one would be in America. I wanted them to feel the physical loneliness of that, and then the joy of coming together. So, I would give these emotions and also that other thing which I don't think is an emotion but a spiritual high. I don't know what you call that.

Jody: What do you think about revenge?

Maxine: I come from a culture where revenge is important. So many of the stories and operas I grew up on have that theme of revenge. I think revenge has something to do with justice in our lifetime rather than justice in another reincarnation. But in American culture revenge is really questioned. Christianity says no revenge. The vengeance I will permit myself has to come in a new form. I wrote in *The Woman Warrior* that the Chinese idiom for "revenge" can also mean "reporting to five families." If you can find the words for an injustice and put it in some artistic shape, and let everyone know, then revenge has taken place. It has something to do with broadcasting the reputation of one that you want revenge against. Revenge cannot take the form of an eye for an eye, not like that.

Jody: Is Chinese morality different from white Western morality? And if so, in what ways?

Maxine: Morality is morality: whether we practice it or not, that's something else. But human beings have basically the same morality everywhere, through all time.

Jody: In your books white people are confronted with the way Chinese see themselves and also see whites. In *China Men* readers feel the experience of discrimination and exclusion. Has your writing perhaps made a change in the way people see one another?

Maxine: There is a change that has been happening in the last ten or twelve years. I don't know how much credit to take, but it's the same credit that writers take for changing atmospheres, which is very little, and very humbly. Everything has been happening at once: there have been women's studies and ethnic studies and my books have been coming out, and also lots of new people are coming to this country from all over. The reviews for *China Men* were much more understanding, much less racially stereotypical than for *The Woman Warrior.* Not so many reviewers saying, "sweet and sour" and "inscrutable."

Jody: There are constant references to white experiences, familiar parts of white culture, which you dress up in Chinese clothing, like the story of Robinson Crusoe. Do readers recognize what you are doing?

Maxine: Yes, they sometime recognize it. But I get the same flak about the Robinson Crusoe story from critics that I get about Chinese mythic stories. The editors wanted to shorten it because they said everybody knows what's going to happen. I don't think everybody knows, because what I'm saying is, "Now look, I've done the same thing to Chinese traditional stories as I'm doing to this one. This is one we're all familiar with, so let me tell it in my own voice and see what's going on." I'd heard the Robinson Crusoe story first as a Chinese talk-story. The Defoe novel had become Lo Bun Sun. When I retold it, for some reason, Friday's father became a major figure. *China Men* is a story about a search for my father, or all of us searching for our fathers—and Friday found his father. There's wonderful, loving, physical touching between the two of them. To show these two black men having been apart and coming together is a healing thing for all of us, to look at the Defoe story not as man on an isolated island but man finding man, hugging him and touching him.

Jody: What about craziness, wackiness, female behavior outside the parameters of what is considered normal and appropriate? I'm thinking about the boy who keeps coming to the laundry and the things you did, like effecting a limp and picking your nose. What about craziness as a response to sexual or cultural oppression?

Maxine: I don't think I ever use the word "crazy" about my mother. I tell enough of her story from her own point of view and with enough understanding so I think we all see her as a powerful, positive woman. But if you just look at her from a kind of side view, she is very eccentric. But Moon Orchid is crazy, the lady in the swamp is crazy, Crazy Mary is crazy. The narrator's struggle was to follow the way of the powerful, wild, strong, eccentric women and not go crazy.

Jody: Does that quality in your mother give you permission to have it too? Aren't we talking about the issue of competence and power, i.e., how can one be a beautiful, intelligent woman and also a creative artist?

Maxine: The price for not knowing how to be a beautiful woman is enormous; it's a terrible price: no husband, no children, not being able to play in sexual games that are fun. Have you read Susan Brownmiller's *Femininity?* How do you choose your dresses and eye makeup? What happens to a woman who wears fuck-me shoes and skirts? I've fought hard not to be eccentric like my mother. I am nevertheless most eccentric.

Jody: In her article on you, Rabinowitz made a comment I found particularly interesting. She said, "Women are traditionally bearers of meaning." For me that is a good way to distinguish among the various women in *The Woman Warrior*. Some are bearers of meaning . . .

Maxine: Very nice: and some are creators of the world.

Jody: In *China Men* men are viewed through the eyes of a female narrator. Were you conscious of that at the time as a major reversal?

Maxine: I thought that was such a coup. I had always been much more interested in writing about women. When I started *China Men*, I had doubts about whether I had enough sympathy for men, whether I had enough sense of masculine adventurousness, whether I had enough appreciation of physical labor. I saw men as people who were adventurous and worked with their bodies. So while I was writing I did things like use a ballpeen hammer and an axe, because I wanted to feel those body muscles. As she enters the Land of Men my feminine narrator becomes less obtrusive, but at the same time, she's not killed or anything. She becomes a most understanding person, a very large person, she can understand men and encompass them and create their lives. I'm glad Garrett Hongo said, "This is a man's book." I'm very proud of being able to write the men's story, and I feel very happy when men come up to me and say they want that book autographed. It's surprising, but when I'm autographing books men buy *China Men* and women buy *The Woman Warrior*. And I think, "Why don't they buy the other book?"

Jody: Women respond very personally to *The Woman Warrior*, they feel an intimate connection with it, don't they?

Maxine: Oh yes, they tell me it's their diary. But when I love a writer, I want to read everything else she wrote. I want my readers to feel that way too, because I want them to watch that woman grow up in *China Men*. I believe that in order to truly grow up, women must love men. That has to be the next stage of feminism: I can't think that feminism just breaks off at the point where we get to join the Marines.

Jody: What is the relationship of your life to your art?

Maxine: I think I can't set boundaries. I am very much the same person as the person who is in my books, that same sensibility, but I become older and new stuff happens to me. The books are a way to tell exactly who I am, that I am some being that is in this universe and my life and seeing are immense. There is also that part of me which is living a daily life: I have to eat and clean and in most of my life apparently nothing happens. That part is not in the books because it would be boring. How do you do that? To be very truthful to what a human being is I would have to talk about getting up and combing my hair and brushing my teeth and then repeat that 365 times and that would be truly life. I'm on the last two pages of reading *Moments of Being*. This book is made up of pieces just found in the British Museum. It's incoherent, because Virginia Woolf would start off telling the story of her life and then get sidetracked and put the manuscript away. Then she would start again the story of her life, but different in style and tone. She really teaches me a lot: you have to write about what's happening to you today as you write about what's happened in the past. And what's happening right now affects what happens in the past; the whole thing keeps changing all the time. I used to be less disciplined, so that everything I wrote kept swimming in what was happening right now, I could not stick with one idea. That's my first book, which isn't published. Everything flowed from my today diary— life into the novel, and I could never separate them.

Jody: You kept a diary?

Maxine: It wasn't exactly a diary. I was trying to write a novel, but my life, like going to Safeway, would get mixed up in my book. Those boundaries between life and my work were not sharp. As I've gotten older they've gotten sharper and sharper, and that's these other two books, where I could keep myself as a narrator separated from myself as a writer. Chronological order is very new and difficult. I don't think I answered your question at all.

Jody: Yes you did. Actually, it's the same problem Anaïs talked about with the diary.

Maxine: God, is she an inspiration for me. I really found those books a guide to life, and life as a writer. It was wonderful what she said about creating your life, that your life has to be creative, and your writing has to be creative. Will there be a book some day with the sections of the diary that have not been published?

Jody: Yes. Rupert Pole, her widower, is editing them now.
Maxine: Well, he had taken out all that stuff about himself.

Jody: No, that wasn't Rupert. Anaïs had two husbands: the first was an American banker, Ian Hugo, who was considerably older than herself and whom she married when she was quite young. They lived in Europe but returned to America when World War II broke out. In New York she contin-

ued the psychoanalytic training she had begun in Europe with Otto Rank.
Somewhere along the line, she met Rupert.

Maxine: How long was she married to Hugo?

Jody: Hugo died only recently: ironically, he outlived her. Initially, he had
refused permission to be included in the diaries, which is why at the end of
volume one there is that unexplained stillbirth. Eventually she met Rupert
and came to California with him, but she never divorced Hugo. She made
extended trips to New York to be with Hugo, so she led a double life. Hugo
knew about Rupert, and Rupert knew about Hugo, and each knew the other
knew, but they conspired not to let Anaïs know they knew because they both
loved her. Isn't that the ultimate form of love? Shortly before she died she
married Rupert—which technically made her a bigamist.

Maxine: It's wonderful she was able to live like that. Most people would
break one of their hearts.

Jody: What if she had told the truth?

Maxine: That would be asking too much. She paid a price as a writer,
having to hide part of the diary during her lifetime.

Jody: Have you read Joseph Campbell's *The Hero's Journey*? Were you
aware of Campbell's theories when you wrote *The Woman Warrior*?

Maxine: I haven't read it, but I know his idea of the journey and the quest.

Jody: The journey or the quest is often to exotic lands. From the white
American perspective, it is reversed in *China Men*: America is the gold
mountain, the faraway place, the exotic land: very much what we were just
talking about.

Maxine: No, but I do feel we are on that quest, and he talks about the path,
how the hero dares, and the hero may also get lost en route. I pictured the
hero as the artist, the artist going on explorations, and how it is very possible
to lose your way and not make it to the end of the book.

Jody: "no name aunt" and Moon Orchid . . .
Maxine: Very similar.

Jody: What of women making the journey alone? Historically, women
have not been allowed to go on the journey alone—or not at all. It's a recur-
rent theme in Esther Broner's work, and Margaret Atwood's work, and Alice
Walker's work.

Maxine: Now women are forced into the journey alone. I've often felt that men seem to be playful and adventurous and loose; they tell jokes really well, they're fun. Women are not fun, women are not loose and playful. Why is that? Is it because women are oppressed and not allowed to play? Part of men's going out on the journey seems to be in their sense of curiosity. Women always seem so worried, as though if you let a woman free she wouldn't like going on the journey. But they have to go on arduous journeys because they have to make a living, families break down. The women in my books do not readily set off on journeys: the men left them, so they have to carry on by themselves. But they are not going anywhere; their adventures are within the village. They stay at home and something happens to them anyway, and they are forced to make the journey.

Jody: Well, it's a gift isn't it, in a strange way?

Maxine: Yes, and then it becomes—you're given—a quest. So these women's quests aren't like the men's.

Jody: How large a role did your mother and father play in your choice of a career as a writer? You became a writer and a teacher like your father, who was a teacher and a scholar. Your mother was a teller of tales and you became a literary teller of tales. She was a healer, and a writer is a kind of healer. What are your thoughts about that?

Maxine: Well, I can see those coincidences. I don't know how direct their influence is on my writing. I have a lot of brothers and sisters, and we compare how we see life. "Is that the way it went?" We compare our strange childhoods. Certainly they have the same mother and father, and yet none of them has that mania to put it all down into words. They inherited the same stories, and yet some of them will say they never heard those stories before. Sometimes I think writing has nothing to do with the way one was raised, or genes. Characters come and say, "Tell my story." They only come to some people. Certainly, having parents that found books and writing and storytelling important—whatever I had I guess they nurtured by example. My mother couldn't help it, stories just kept coming out of her—not to give something to me, but because it was something in her.

Jody: Your son has chosen to be a musician. He is the son of a writer and an actor—doesn't that imply certain shared values?

Maxine: It was amazing, when we went to my mother's village in China there was one good building—it's a village with a lot of huts, but there was one building which stood out. It had tiles, it was special, it was large, and it had a sign on it. I took a picture and brought it back and my mother said it was the music building. That was where they went to play their music and put on shows and concerts for each other. For the first time I realized that she came from people that were musical. Music was the whole focus of that village. So now I realize where my son may have inherited his music.

Jody: What "size" is your mother these days?

Maxine: You know, just when I think things are normal, that we're just like everybody else, then she will do something immense and enormous. Recently I said, "Remember you told me the story of the ghost sitting on your chest?"—I was showing her pictures I had taken of her school in China—and I said, "So that really happened?" And she said, "Of course, and not only that, but the ghost had a foot sticking out." And I thought, "My God, she's still adding." I had just written it all down that there was this hairy thing, but I didn't write down that it had a foot. She's the size that she can say, "There's more, you haven't written it all down yet."

Jody: When you tell a story like the one about the newsboy ghost, where the kids follow him in the street and he goes to a house for directions and they're eaten by gypsy ghosts, what is your intention in blurring the line between reality and fantasy?

Maxine: Well, I think all children think like that. And in our culture the mythic is real. There are people who are people, and there are people that are ghosts doing real things, like selling newspapers and bringing milk and driving taxicabs. So I am describing an actual cultural phenomenon. These books have the artistic problem of how to write the true biographies of real people who have very imaginative minds. And there is always the exciting possibility that I will break through into another world that's about to happen.

Jody: Where did the idea of calling white people demons and ghosts come from? Is it personal or cultural?

Maxine: Oh, it's cultural.

Jody: How did you find your voice?

Maxine: I told myself, "Even if it's stupid, write it down." There was a point when I thought that what I wrote was incoherent, that other people would not be able to read what I wrote. The writers who do experimental poetry and those strange books where the language goes far out like *Finnegan's Wake*—that helped a lot, because I thought that if there are readers who are going to try to decipher them, then I could write in my way and maybe it would be all right. Just before *The Woman Warrior* I published a scholarly piece in the *English Journal*. It was a strict essay, with footnotes and everything. That was to reassure myself that I could write in sentence form, that I had the ability to communicate intellectually. That kept me going.

Jody: How long did it take you to find that voice? How long did it take you to get from that first, unpublished book to *The Woman Warrior* and *China Men*, where the voice is consistent?

Maxine: I think I was always searching for that voice: I guess I started when I was about eight and I published *The Woman Warrior* when I was about thirty-five or thirty-six, so I was trying for twenty-five years.

Jody: You talk about knowing you were a writer as a child. Did you also read a lot as a child, and what kind of books did you read?

Maxine: I read all the things that children read, but Jade Snow Wong's *Fifth Chinese Daughter* was important to me. It was published during World War II and for the first time I saw a Chinese American character, and it was told from the point of view of a young girl. For the first time I could see a person somewhat like myself in literature. I had been trying to write about people who were blond, or a beautiful redhead on her horse, because those were the people who were in the books. So I was lucky that at a young age I could see a Chinese American. In Louisa May Alcott one of her characters marries a . . . I guess she calls him a Chinaman, with a long pigtail. He was so funny, he was so weird and different. I was reading along, identifying with the March sisters, when I came across this funny-looking little Chinaman. It popped out of the book. I'd been pushed into my place. I was him, I wasn't those March girls. That kind of reading made me create my new place in literature.

Jody: Was it the foreignness and failure in the muteness of the mute girl which made you attack her? Did you blame your own foreignness and muteness on your cut tongue?

Maxine: I was fighting her for her muteness, yes, but not her foreignness. I now realize she was much like me, although she had pink cheeks and pretty pastel clothes. I think I didn't like her because she was too much like what I could turn into. I wanted to be a tomboy and bad, and I wanted to be a person who could talk and fight. I wanted to change. It surprises me that I never saw that until I wrote it down. Supposedly my mother cut my tongue to make me a better talker and linguist. I guess it worked.

Jody: You spoke of being mute, of your black paintings, of the duck voice: and yet in your books, there is this huge voice, writing to be heard. How did you get from one to the other?

Maxine: I was a teacher for ten or twelve years, I taught high school, mostly. That is the hardest job on earth. If you can be a teacher and last for a few years, you can do anything. That's what did it. When I began teaching I still had my duck voice, and by the time I was through I could do anything. There's nothing I couldn't do. Sometimes I wondered, "God, why did I spend so many years teaching?" But perhaps that was my working out of the voice. A teacher can speak to everyone, a teacher can control mobs. You can break up fights, you can teach a rock to read. Anything you say has to reach an idiot child and a genius at the same time, it has to mean something to both those people plus the other thirty in the class. Maybe that carries over into the writing, where I feel that I'm writing for everyone.

Jody: In an essay on *The Color Purple*, Alice Walker said that her characters came through her, they literally spoke through her. When she was writing the book they pushed her around, told her what to do—they even told her to sell her house and move across the country. You said recently that you have no control over the first draft and you added, "I feel I am chosen by the stories. They come to me without my trying for them. There are things that haunt me, that I keep seeing and won't go away." Then you gave the example of the white triangle and how the story of your father's coming to America came from that image. Do you always think in images? And is it the image which brings forth the story, or does the story come first?

Maxine: No, the images come first. It's almost as if the images are mute: they're visual and the people are visual, rooms are visual. I do hear people say things, and I hear music, but the visions aren't in words. The words I have to strive for and find and somehow connect with the image so that the reader can have the image. There was a time when I was a painter and I thought that was what I was meant to do. That, of course, comes from the fact that I see the images first, so why not directly paint them and then have people go look directly at the paintings? Why go through all of this with the words? I even took art classes in college and I painted a lot for about a year and a half. Then I realized I had already put in fifteen years of apprenticeship as a writer, and if I put in another fifteen years as a painter I might be in the same place, so I gave up the painting.

Jody: Do you still paint?

Maxine: No. I'm writing the big books and I don't have time; but I really like to draw, it's so direct, because I see the picture. So why not be more direct?

Jody: Do you see any relationship between the people in your head whom you talked to as a child and the fact of becoming a writer?

Maxine: Yes, I think it must be the same gift, it's the same state of mind but the people are different. I think it's so weird that they should be different people. I don't know where those other people went. I don't feel like writing about the childhood people, but there were a whole lot of them and they were just as real as the ones I write about, or you or me. I do remember times when those people began to disappear, and how alarmed I was.

Jody: And they never reappeared?

Maxine: No. If I could understand that . . . It would be nice to talk to a psychiatrist to see what happened.

Jody: They did introduce you to a process, again, they gave you a gift: maybe that's why they were there.

Maxine: I learned how I could manipulate them and how I could not manipulate them. I think they were there because they were my friends. And I had my own world.

Jody: How much of *The Woman Warrior* is also a fascination with fore-mothers?

Maxine: Oh yes, but it comes from them, not only from me. Those women who are so marvelous, so magic, so overwhelming took my life and my abilities and said, "Write about us." It's not as if I had any choice: I didn't go looking for them.

Jody: How about the men in *China Men*?

Maxine: They were people I could appreciate when I became a more subtle seer. They are people I searched for and found.

Jody: Did you make up details like the aunt's marriage with the rooster?

Maxine: No, no. I never make up anything: they're all gifts.

Jody: What is the lesson you would like people to learn from your books?

Maxine: I want people to realize how large and marvelous the universe is and what a shame to blow it up.

Jody: You repeated just the other day that to tell lives truly one must tell people's imaginative lives.

Maxine: Yes.

Jody: Is this one of the major sources of your unique vision and of the energy behind your work?

Maxine: There's more to people than their going to Safeway. Although it looks like they go to Safeway and they bring food home and cook it and eat it, there is a universe of adventure going on in each one.

Jody: You said that our society doesn't feed artists, that each artist must find his or her own path. Can you look back at your life and identify any of the significant markers or events along your own path to becoming a writer?

Maxine: Yes, there are many events. I told you about painting. There was a man who came to the laundry when I was a little kid—this was about the time I was reading Jade Snow Wong—and he could draw anything. He said, "You don't have to have money to be an artist. All you need is pencil and paper, that's all you need." Then he proved it by being able to draw anything. Then, I told you about being able to write a scholarly piece so I knew I could think. At UC Irvine I talked about being able to make a living while writing constantly and flowingly. Reading Virginia Woolf's *Orlando* was an event . . . it's all right to make your man turn into a woman, it's all right to have a century of time flow by here and a moment of time flow by there. She showed me various freedoms I could take in writing.

Jody: The *L.A. Times* did an article on the occasion of your return to Stockton, California, to be honored by the Stockton Arts Commission. How did you feel?

Maxine: Actually, I felt lots of dread because I was going to run into all those people I wrote about, I was going to have to face them. And my grammar school and high school teachers and Chinese school teachers were going to be there; it was going to be like a high school reunion, all these people. I dreaded it a lot, but it turned out OK. It was also a power thing to give me an event like that; there were various political enemies who wanted to confront one another. People with their own feuds showed up. It was the wild west, it was a Stockton event, and Stockton is where stories come from. So the people from my books were there, plus people I didn't have time to write about. They were all there.

Jody: What are you working on now?

Maxine: I'm working on a novel, and this one is very different. I'm making up everything now. With the other books you could pick out almost any image and it's either cultural or it actually happened. But in the new book I'm inventing everything, so it feels very free in a way, and in another way very difficult, because I don't have boundaries, I could just keep inventing this world forever. At one point it was a thousand pages and I was very alarmed that I would never finish. But I have found its boundaries, so I'm almost finished now. It's set in 1963 and it's about a young, hip, Chinese American man who has the spirit of the trickster monkey. He has to solve all kinds of problems about who he is, and how he will make a living, and how he will be an artist, and how he will be a Chinese American, and what's he going to do about domesticity (that was a big issue at the time). And it's about theater, and actors, and it's dedicated to Earll, who is an actor.

Jody: When will it be finished?
Maxine: I think it will be finished this year.

Jody: Your books are a lot about people's inhumanity to one another, so I wondered where you find comfort and balance?
Maxine: I ask that of myself a lot: where are the sources of life so that you can renew yourself! I find help in nature. We should always remember to plop ourselves under the trees because every time I've ever done that I feel the earth giving me energy and the sky giving me perspective, and I come as close as I ever do to satori. Then I realize that life in the city cuts me up into pieces. I know that, and yet I don't leave it. All I have to do is go out into nature and it gives me strength to come back and work on. And I read—there are writers who give you life whether or not they write well, it's very odd. I feel that way about Anaïs Nin, who sometimes I don't think writes well. I re-read *Orlando* whenever I feel stuck, and I read poetry.

Jody: Is there beauty as well as sorrow in the human experience?
Maxine: Oh yes, it's all connected, sorrow and beauty. I think somewhere in my book I described the bombs that fell on Hiroshima and Nagasaki and how beautiful they were. After the little girl draws in black she starts drawing the bombs (because the bombs fell when I was about five). She can't help but draw the explosion—beautiful, boiling, red and orange clouds, yellow and white. The light of the bomb is like the light of enlightenment, it would annihilate your problems, it would be reaching a purity. We want to bomb each other because we don't know that it's actually not the same as the beauty of enlightenment.

Eccentric Memories: A Conversation with Maxine Hong Kingston

Paula Rabinowitz / 1986

From the *Michigan Quarterly Review* 26 (1987), pp. 177–87. Reprinted by permission of the interviewer.

Kingston is the 1986 Thelma McAndless Distinguished Professor in the Humanities at Eastern Michigan University. This interview took place in September 1986.

PR: The special issue of *Michigan Quarterly Review* in which this interview will appear is devoted to the theme of "Women and Memory." My questions to you range from broad philosophical matters to more narrow concerns focused on your work, but all address the significance and politics of memory for women writers in the United States today.

In your 1983 lecture at the University of Michigan Hopwood awards, you said that you had not wanted to go to China before you had finished working on your two books. In an earlier interview you said you had not wanted to ask people to repeat their stories to you while you were working on the books, either. I saw some connection between the use of memory and the function of imagination—the image of China, in particular for you as a writer, and in general for Chinese Americans.

MHK: The artist's memory winnows out; it edits for what is important and significant. Memory, my own memory, shows me what is unforgettable, and helps me get to an essence that will not die and that haunts me until I can put it into a form, which is the writing. I don't want to get confused by making new memories on top of the old ones which were already such a large vision—the mythic China. Going to China would have meant the creation of, and the beginning of, another memory.

PR: So, when you subtitle *The Woman Warrior*, "A Memoir of a Girlhood Among Ghosts," "memoir" and "ghost" represent the same thing. And they both needed to be exorcised.

MHK: Yes, but not *exorcised.* I have learned that writing does not make ghosts go away. I wanted to record, to find the words for, the "ghosts," which are only visions. They are not concrete; they are beautiful, and powerful. But they don't have a solidity that we can pass around from one to another. I wanted to give them a substance that goes beyond me.

PR: Then memory is essentially a visual quality?

MHK: Visual, and emotional. Sometimes, there are words, too, like when someone says something that's violent and it echoes through time.

PR: Like the father's insults in *China Men*?

MHK: Yes.

PR: Well, in that context, memories have meaning for you in a sense very different from the Freudian notion that what we remember is insignificant, since what's significant is repressed and we never entirely get it back.

MHK: Yes, that makes sense, in a way, in that memory is really nothing. It's not substantial, and it's not present. It has to do with past times, and in that sense, it's insignificant, except when it haunts you and when it is a foundation for the rest of the personality. Somehow, though, words are a medium to get to the seemingly subconscious.

I think that these visions don't just come full-blown and with details such as chairs and clothes, and where everything is placed—the relationships between bodies in a room. All that becomes more and more accessible as I approach them with words. Words clarify the vision and memory.

When you think about it, words are also insignificant, insubstantial, not things. So we can use them to arrive at insignificant, insubstantial memories. As I paint part of a vision, the next part of it becomes clear. It's as if I am building the underpinnings of a bridge, and then I can cross it, and see more and more clearly.

PR: So, memory is the starting point for your work, but once the writing begins, it's actually language that takes over the next level of memory, and words become traces themselves.

MHK: Because then you find the next memory, all of the time keeping an eye on what's happening in real life, right now. I think that my stories have a constant breaking in and out of the present and past. So the reader might be walking along very well in the present, but the past breaks through and changes and enlightens the present, and vice versa. The reason that we remember a past moment at all is that our present-day life is still a working-out of a similar situation.

PR: Because the present reenacts the past. Memory becomes a structuring device to mediate past and present.

MHK: Understanding the past changes the present. And the ever-evolving present changes the significance of the past.

PR: I was wondering about your decision to divide off your narratives in terms of a male and a female ancestry—dividing them off by gender. Did you feel that one narrative could not fully contain both kinds of memories?

MHK: At one time, *The Woman Warrior* and *China Men* were supposed to be one book. I had conceived of one huge book. However, part of the reason for two books is history. The women had their own time and place and their lives were coherent; there was a woman's way of thinking. My men's stories seemed to interfere. They were weakening the feminist point of view. So I took all the men's stories out, and then I had *The Woman Warrior*.

Historically, of course, the men went to a different country without their families, and so they had their adventures by themselves. It was as if they went to a men's country and they had men's stories. This is hindsight now; but it does seem as if the women's stories have a convolution and the men's stories have more of a linear passage through time. The men's myths and memories are not as integrated into their present-day lives, and that influences the structure of both those books. In *The Woman Warrior*, when the girls and women draw on mythology for their strengths, the myth becomes part of the women's lives and the structure of the stories. In the men's stories, I tell a myth and then I tell a present-day story, a myth, and then another present-day adventure story; they are separate narratives. The reason I think that happened was that those men went to a place where they didn't know whether their mythology was giving them any strength or not. They were getting very broken off from their background. They might not have even been drawing any strength, or they may have gone against the teachings of the myth. They were so caught up in the adventure of the new land that they thought, "What good are memories and the past?" Memory just hurts them, because they can't go home. So, the myth story and the present story become separated.

PR: What you are saying, in a way, is that there is geographic difference in terms of genders. One might roughly say that China is a landscape inhabited, at least in the narratives, by the women and their myths, and the Gold Mountain, America, is really where the men are and that's where history is.

MHK: Yes, those men were making history. They were making a new myth, too. They were not so caught up in the old myths as the women were.

PR: Yet, even in the narratives of the men, the sense is that these are narratives that have been retold through women. Perhaps, then, the women's voices and women's memories become a cultural connection between those China myths and that American history?

MHK: Yes. In fact, I wrote the characters so that the women have memories and the men don't have memories. They don't remember anything. The character of my father, for example, has no memory. He has no stories of the past. He is an American and even his memories are provided by the mother. She says that he went dancing, or whatever; he is so busy making up the present, which he has to build, that he has no time for continuity from the past. It did seem as if the men were people of action.

But I am trying to think whether we can make any generalizations about men and women. I have thought about the animus and the anima, Jung's terms, as I work. I have had dreams about two women, and they both have a left toe on all four feet. Somehow, if I could get to the point where one is a man and one is a woman, I'd be a more balanced person. Somewhere, in the writing of the two books, things did sort out: there was a man and a woman.

PR: Since I just reread them, I was struck by the way you played with intertextuality in the two books, where an insignificant reference in one of the books will be elaborated to a great extent in the other one. Some little statement that Brave Orchid makes in *China Men* had been a whole section in *The Woman Warrior* or vice versa.

It struck me that the way the two books work is the way that memory works, where some large memory often just comes out of the most ephemeral beginnings and then gets blown up from there. So that you don't ever really remember the whole picture. What you remember is a smell or a "sharp white triangle."

MHK: Yes. Yes, and then, that triangle turned out to be the trouser leg glimpsed on a ship while my father was stowing away. I think life works like that. There are various themes and people, and obsessions, that come and go and sometimes they take a major role in life. And then, on another day, you have to devote your whole day to going to the grocery store. . . .

PR: Yes. I wanted to ask, now that you have been to China, what happened?

MHK: I was very afraid to go because it's really there. What if China invalidated everything that I was thinking and writing? So, one of the great thrills was to see how well I had imagined it. Many of the colors, and the smells, the people, the faces, the incidents, were much as I imagined. Many people said to me, "Welcome home." I did feel that I was going back to a place that I had never been.

Actually, it was a new adventure, too, but there were just small things that I wish hadn't happened, in a way. There were some things that I wish I had seen before I had written my books. The tight quarters of the rooms and of the villages. If I had been in those rooms earlier, I would have understood even better the sense of a village and how each person's drama reverberates throughout the village. I would have seen that people did not have to walk as far as I said to go from one place to another. At my father's village, the well where the aunt drowned herself was right next to the Hong family temple. My mother said that the guys used to hang around on the steps of the temple and make remarks at the girls to try to get them to drop and break their water jars. That is so real to everyone, of all cultures. You know, guys whistling at girls, and, also, it's so sexy. I wish I had had it in the book. I saw small things like that that I wished I had had earlier, but nothing large that invalidated the whole work.

The trip made me see another use of memory or imagination or talk-story. Toward the end of *The Woman Warrior*, I wrote about the savage barbarians shooting off arrows with whistles on them. I wrote that, and then, not very much later, I saw one of those whistling arrows in a museum. I felt that I created it. I wrote it; and therefore, it appeared.

I think that I found that China over there because I wrote it. It was accessible to me before I saw it, because I wrote it. The power of imagination leads us to what's real. We don't imagine fairylands. I've begun lately to realize that if I were to know you, as my friend, the best way is for me to imagine you at life so well that I sympathize with you. Well, that means that imagination is reaching toward a real person. Now, if I imagine something about you that is totally off the wall, that's not you, then my imagination is off. To have a right imagination is very powerful, because it's a bridge toward reality.

PR: Your books also seem very American, even though they are about "China Men" or "Warrior Women" in China. I was wondering if you were also imagining America?

MHK: Oh yes. Actually, I think that my books are much more American than they are Chinese. I felt that I was building, creating, myself and these people as American people, to make everyone realize that these are American people. Even though they have strange Chinese memories, they are American people. Also, I am creating part of American literature, and I was very aware of doing that, of adding to American literature. The critics haven't recognized my work enough as another tradition of American literature.

PR: What tradition?

MHK: I directly continue William Carlos Williams' *In the American Grain*. He stopped in 1860 and I pick it up in 1860 and carry it forward. When I was writing "No Name Woman," I was thinking about Nathaniel Hawthorne and *The Scarlet Letter* as a discussion of the Puritan part of America, and of China, and a woman's place. I use the title, "The Making of More Americans," from Gertrude Stein, because when I read *The Making of Americans*, I thought, "Yes, she is creating a language that is the American language; and she is doing it sentence by sentence. I am trying to write an American language that has Chinese accents; I will write the American language as I speak it." So, in a way, I was creating something new, but at the same time, it's still the American language, pushed further.

PR: In that sense, then, there is a kind of political agenda to your writing.

MHK: Yes, there is. There has been exclusion socially and politically, and also we have been left out of literature.

PR: I was thinking about the way, in your two books, the characters become Americans by appropriating bits of American popular culture.

MHK: Fred Astaire—yeah.

PR: Or the comic books that the little girl reads, and I was wondering whether that appropriation is an example of a kind of subversion of the erasure of Third World cultures. In other words, instead of seeing it as, "Everyone comes to America and—

MHK: And we disappear"—

PR: —rather it's a way of turning America into yet another aspect of one's own culture?

MHK: Yes, and I think that the highest form of that appropriation is art. In a sense, when I wrote these books, I was claiming the English language and the literature to tell our story as Americans. That is why the forms of the two books are not exactly like other books, and the language and the rhythms are not like other writers, and yet, it's American English. I guess my thought is, "If I can use this language and literature in a really beautiful, strong way, then I have claimed all of it for us."

PR: I don't know if you saw Mel Watkins' article in the *New York Times Book Review* berating Afro-American women writers for not presenting positive images of black men ("Sexism, Racism, and Black Women Writers," June 15, 1986).

MHK: Yes, the men are doing that now.

PR: Well, I recently read in Elaine Kim's book that you had gotten some of the same kind of criticisms (*Asian American Literature: An Introduction to the Writings and Their Social Context*).

MHK: All the minority women get exactly the same thing from the minority men.

PR: What do you think is going on?

MHK: Oh, I think what's going on is that the men have had a very bad time, and the men writers are equating the novel with their manhood. They are not publishing as many novels as the women are, but their anger is toward the wrong people—us. I mean, they are angry at what they think is the white publishing establishment. But they also think that the women are in conspiracy with the white male publishing establishment to get our work published. We are getting to be anchors on television news programs—and the men, where are they? But their anger is misplaced. They aren't reading us right. Instead of being angry with us—I mean, it takes a lot of words to write articles against us—they ought to be home working on those novels. The other possibility is that they feel that they have been castrated by American society. Maybe what they say is exactly what's going on: the novel is castrated out of them and all that's left is tremendous anger at women.

PR: Well, I was thinking about this in another context, which is the white, male, postmodernist establishment of writers, who have outlined the boundaries of what is considered contemporary writing. Certainly the critics who write about them would never consider putting your work in that category. Your work seems as insistently reflexive about questions of narrative, form, representation, and language as theirs, and yet, because your work is about culture, and comes out of a history that has been kept silent but now has a voice, it lacks that whole sense of ennui. So, it seems that you and other minority writers have been put in a peculiar spot, an "eccentric" position. You are being deleted from the mainstream of contemporary American literature, while being denied a position as writers within a Chinese American or Afro-American tradition.

I was wondering if you feel, therefore, an affinity with other minority women writers? Do you see a connection between your work, and say, that of Toni Morrison or Leslie Silko?

MHK: Yes. Yes. It's funny you mention the two of them, because we went to China together. I do feel an affinity not only because I love them as people but because we seem to write alike. There is so much human emotion and richness and story and imagery and colors and things to eat. Nobody is alienated from life; everybody is warm. I feel that we write like that because we are warm, and even though we all—I hate to say master—we are all very good with words, words aren't the only thing that's important. We care about stories about people, and also that magical real place that we are all visiting. When I compare our work to some of the mainstream work, it seems as if many of them are *only* playing with words. The "language" people's world seems gray and black and white. Toni's and Leslie's and my aliveness must come from our senses of a connection with people who have a community and a tribe. We are living life in a more dangerous place. We do not live in new subdivisions without ceremony and memory; and if those other writers have to draw from that non-magical imagination, then of course, their writing will be gray and black and white.

PR: So then the idea that you are speaking out of a cultural community is crucial?

MHK: I don't see how I would live without a community, family, friends. But I am always very interested in how one can be an individual and be part of a collective people and a collective memory. Of course, that's very American too, because Americans strive to stand alone. I am always figuring out how the lone person forms a community.

PR: Well, it seems that memory does that for you in a way. It becomes the translation between an individual narrator and the family, whose stories have been narrated, and the history in which that family has lived its stories.

MHK: Yes, and then that brings us to the tribal memory, the family memory, the cultural memory. Well, I guess I contain them all in my own individual memory, but some of the stories that I write began with memories that we all have. Those collective memories are the myths. For example, immigration stories about how you got through Angel Island—having four or five versions of your immigration—that's not just the way my head works, that's the way narration and memory and stories work in our culture. So, that's a gift given to me by our culture, and not something that I imagined on my own. I invented new literary structures to contain multiversions and to tell the true lives of non-fiction people who are storytellers.

PR: Your books are categorized as autobiography or cultural history and as fiction and I am wondering what you see as the relationship between fact and fiction?

MHK: It doesn't bother me very much; it bothers other people more than me. It has caused problems. When the British reviewed my work, they could not get past the question, "Is this fiction or nonfiction?" There have been articles that just addressed that, and never got to what I am talking about.

The question of fiction or nonfiction has become a very political debate. Some minority critics have really elevated the novel as the highest form. They say that autobiography is a lesser form because you are not using imagination, and you present yourself as an oddity, an anthropological specimen, not as a literary creator. Since both *The Woman Warrior* and *China Men* were called nonfiction, I have had attacks from that point of view. When people pointed that out to me, I said, "Sure. I could have classified them as fiction." Our usual idea of biography is of time-lines, of dates and chronological events; I am certainly more imaginative than that; I play with words and form.

After going back and forth on my classification for a couple of years, I've decided that I am writing biography and autobiography of imaginative people. I am writing about real people, all of whom have minds that love to invent fictions. I am writing the biography of their imaginations.

PR: What are you working on now?

MHK: I am working on a novel that I should finish soon. It is definitely fiction. I mean, I made up everything; I invented the characters and the situations. I can tell the difference between fiction and nonfiction. In a sense, fiction is so much easier, because if the narration needs an exciting moment, I can invent the exciting moment. Whereas, in the other two books, structurally it may be time for an exciting moment, but if the characters decide to go do their laundry or something, then somehow I have to make that a compelling part of the whole narrative.

PR: So you are saying that you felt constrained by the real people who were inhabiting those memories.

MHK: Yes, but they were an inspiration and a guide, too. They were always helping me shape the books; whereas in this fiction that I am writing, there is another kind of shaping, where I, as the writer, have a lot more power. In writing the other two books—finding the form, finding the language—I didn't always feel that it was me who was the most powerful. Some of the characters helped shape it, the way they spoke—

PR: Certainly Brave Orchid looms—
MHK: Yes, she dictated it, dictated it.

PR: So for the writer, fiction gives more power than writing autobiography. That's interesting, because one would think that if you are constructing the story of your life, you have a power; but you are suggesting the opposite.
MHK: Different kinds of power. Now that I have written fiction and two non-fictions, I just don't see why everybody doesn't do both. Each kind of writing draws on other kinds of strengths needed to find new ways to create a literary reality, to get at life. Just playing with another form, I feel that I am in another world.

PR: Do you think that fiction comes out of the same locus of memory and imagination that generated the other two books?
MHK: There seems to be a fantasy at work that's different from memory and imagination. For fiction, we fantasize about what we would like to happen: I am making what I would like to happen happen. And so, this writing always feels new and going forward. If there is such a thing as reverse memory, maybe that's what I am getting into; because it seems to me, I'm writing the memory of the future rather than a memory of the past.

Talking with the Woman Warrior

William Satake Blauvelt / 1989

From *Pacific Reader: A Review of Books on Asian Pacific Americans*, 19 July 1989, pp. 1, 8. Reprinted by permission of the *International Examiner*.

The following interview with Maxine Hong Kingston was conducted on May 12, 1989 while she was in Seattle for a reading of *Tripmaster Monkey: His Fake Book*.

IE: How did *Tripmaster Monkey: His Fake Book* come about?

MHK: The 1960s were some of the most important years of my life and they go into forming me and the country the way it is now. I wanted to write a story about that period that came after the beatniks and before the hippies. I think of it as a dark time because Asian American theater was really dark then—there wasn't any. All those nightclub shows—they were closing. There wasn't a modern Chinese American theater. That was a dark time full of possibilities and I don't think anybody else has written about that period.

IE: When you say Chinese American theater, how inclusive are you being? You mentioned nightclubs—I assume you mean places like the old Forbidden City in San Francisco. Are you also referring to Chinese opera?

MHK: No, I'm talking about the kind of shows we have now like David Hwang, Frank Chin. Nobody was doing anything—it was only for a few short years. I know there were a lot of shows in theaters during World War II because there's always a lot of energy during a war. [There were] a lot of Chinese shows to raise money for the war. Then the war's over and the shows go. People are kind of fallow, waiting to see what happens next.

IE: Tell me about the book's subtitle, "His Fake Book."

MHK: That is a jazz term. Jazz musicians used to compile a book of basic tunes, songs, chords. Sometimes it would be just the beginning of a tune, then they would improvise. So I was trying to write a prose book with basic plots, suggestions for social action, for trips. I hope to trip the reader out and have them improvise further.

IE: The language of the book reveals quite a bit of different influences including Chinese, Chinese American, Japanese, and Hawaiian pidgin. What were you trying to do with the language?

MHK: When I started to write the book, I wanted to do '60s slang because I thought that period had such wonderful words. People were inventing new words to describe psychedelic states, new visions. There were even new words for new ways of social protest such as the sit-in, the love-in, the be-in, the teach-in. There were all these words such as "tripmaster," and I wanted to use that language.

Another reason is that, in my first two books, the English that I was inventing was a way to translate the dialogue of the characters who spoke Chinese. When I finished those two books, I really had more language in me, and that's this modern language I speak that I wanted to play with. So, I wrote this really new American language, and it really surprised me how free it is—how much room there is for other languages.

IE: *Tripmaster Monkey* is quite different from *Woman Warrior* and *China Men*. What were you trying to accomplish this time?

MHK: One big thing I'm trying to show is how there is a force of history. I take history clear back to monkey times, and show how it is acted out in myth and personal lives right up to the present. I show the history of human migration, which I think is going faster and faster, so that, here in the U.S., now everybody from all over the world is here. We are going to form some kind of new human being out of all this.

I'm also showing the history of theater from monkey theater and talk-story theater, story boats, song boats, Ramayana, minstrel shows—right up to the time of the book which is the one man show which was Lenny Bruce, Leroi Jones—one actor getting up there and engaging a whole audience.

IE: Could you talk a little about the monkey—when you first heard of him and how you decided to incorporate him in your work?

MHK: It seems like I've always known about him. It must be one of those stories my parents told as bedtime stories. I've encountered the monkey in all its forms—in cartoon form, acrobatic shows and operas, as toys.

As I wrote about the '60s, I began to understand that the spirit of the monkey has come to America. You see in the Buddhist story he goes to India, but I have him continuing on and he arrives in America in the '60s. You can see his spirit in the Chicago Seven, who were like seven monkeys bringing chaos to the establishment. All those love-ins and Woodstock—all that is the monkey. The monkey loves to go to parties, and if you have a wonderful enough party, you can change life.

I think of the monkey as an underdog—he doesn't have a lot of power, so he uses trickery. He has to think of new ways to change things. I even think of Martin Luther King, when he thought of those demonstrations, nonviolent acts, new acts in order to change the world. To me, that is evidence that the monkey was here. I now think he continued around and did the Cultural Revolution. Sometimes he's not so nonviolent; he causes a lot of trouble.

IE: Where does your book's incarnation of the monkey, Wittman Ah Sing, come from?

MHK: At the end of the book, I wrote down names of a lot of my friends and thanked them for various ideas, things they did, parties they gave. In a sense, Wittman is like all those people. He's like me. I think what I am is a person who has built my mind on what I read. Readers do that—your mind is made up of what you read.

Wittman is a reader and an English major. I was an English major. When somebody graduates from college as a business or engineering major, right away they apply their knowledge in the real world. What happens if you're a reader and an English major? How do you apply your knowledge? I think that's very important because, when you read, the jewels you find are values and ideas for a better world.

There's other characters like that—Emma Bovary and Don Quixote—they were readers. They went out into the real world to try to apply their knowledge, and both of them just mess up their lives completely. I didn't want Wittman to be like that. I want him to win. I think he comes up with a great solution: he puts on a show and puts in everybody he knows.

IE: Wittman Ah Sing obviously has a connection to Walt Whitman. Why did you choose that particular bit of symbolism, and could you explain a bit about his name?

MHK: His father named him after the most American of the American poets, but he spells it kind of funny. I think it's more typically Chinese American to spell it kind of funny—those two syllables. I mean to carry on in the tradition of Walt Whitman. Whitman says, "I sing the body electric" and "I sing the body from top to toe." He writes about his goal of celebrating the modern man as he calls it, and he sings the American self.

I wanted to sing the Chinese American self. This book actually does literally celebrate a Chinese American man from top to toe. I write his skin, his eyes, the teeth, ears, penis, the chest, hair, toes. I try to find new words to describe the kind of skin that we have, the kind of hair. I sing the Chinese American from top to toe.

IE: Why did you choose to have a male main character or hero as opposed to a female one?

MHK: Well, I said I wanted to write this story of the '60s. I think guys had more interesting, adventurous, dramatic lives in the '60s than the girls did—at the same time they called them girls.

I think that, if I wrote about a girl of the '60s, it just would not be so interesting because, for one thing, the young men were in danger of the draft, and I think that is a very dramatic story right there. During those years I worried about my brothers—both of them went to Vietnam. I just thought girls and women had it easy compared to that.

I have a son, he's Wittman's age. I have this attitude about him, wondering whether I gave him the right strengths, upbringing, education, values. What's his identity going to be? So, those concerns I have about my son are also concerns a novelist has about characters. The narrator [in the book] in a sense is so omniscient to a certain extent, and gives him various girlfriends and tries to match him up. I don't know—maybe if I had a daughter, I would have written about a girl.

IE: Wittman seems to bear a striking resemblance to Frank Chin. A lot of people think it is him. There's some references I can see. How much of that is true?

MHK: I suppose he resembles Frank—and a lot of people. You know, when I try to write about myself, I think I may end up writing about Frank because his background and mine are very similar.

We were born exactly the same year, we identify with being dragons and come from northern California. I guess he comes from Oakland, and I live in Oakland. We went to school [at U.C. Berkeley] exactly the same time, too, and had the same teachers.

I think he may have been the only Chinese American male English major of that period. I may have been the only Chinese American girl English major. I know the same teacher appreciated both our work and encouraged us. I think we come from such similar backgrounds with so many similar concerns and values. If I write about myself I probably end up resembling him because I do resemble him in real life, although he's tall and I'm short [she laughs].

IE: So, you were in the same class. Did you sit together?

MHK: Yeah, we were in the same class, although I don't think we were in the same classroom because we never met each other. But I heard about him because he already had a reputation as a writer. He was publishing in the college literary magazine. I was working on the *Daily Cal* because I thought I was going to be a journalist.

IE: Everyone knows that Frank Chin is your most vocal critic and sort of bothers you. . . .

MHK: Oh yeah. He threatens me, it's not just bother—he threatens me.

IE: Is *Tripmaster Monkey* or Wittman a way of getting even, so to speak, or a way of answering Frank Chin?

MHK: Oh I don't know, I actually don't believe in revenge. I see this book as a kind of big love letter. If it is answering—if it is—then it's like him sending me hate mail, and I send him love letters, it's like that. I sure hope his soul is big enough to understand that.

Oh, that reminds me: I just saw the Seattle *Weekly*, and Sam Solberg wrote a review in which he says my book is a *roman à clef,* saying it's really all about Frank and other people, and you just have to match up things. He says it's a very bad portrait of Frank. He's saying I'm trying to imitate Frank's language and doing it badly. I think it's just a mistake, because it is not a *roman à clef* and I'm not trying to capture Frank or his language. I just think Solberg never read my book for itself.

IE: Speaking of language, how has your writing changed from your first book to this new one?

MHK: A lot. Even from the first work to the second. For 30 years, I wrote from the "I" point of view and that's all I knew. At a certain point in my 30s, I began to see this as a personal and artistic shortcoming. I thought there was something really wrong if I can't even use other pronouns, especially the omniscient narrator, and get myself into the point of view of other people.

I struggled with that toward the end of *Woman Warrior.* I did successfully write one chapter from the omniscient viewpoint, but by the last chapter, it reverted back to "I" again. *China Men* was really supposed to be about those men, but I could only approach it from "I" again. But as the years went by writing *China Men,* I see that the "I" began to fade away and in the end she [the narrator] becomes a listener. Those men are very much presented as themselves.

By this book, I find that I'm very different—I've achieved that omniscient narrator. Quite often I say "you." I'm talking directly to the reader. I also feel tremendous because I can say "we," because I finally understand community and I know who "we" are. I feel very confident speaking with the voice of a communal people.

I think that, in most of the literature we read, the omniscient narrator is a white man. This is because the nineteenth-century novel was written at a time when we believed in a white, male God. I think of my narrator now as Kuan Yin. This is a big change—a narrator who people can see right away is a woman. She is always helping the woman characters out in there, giving Wittman a bad time.

IE: I understand that you were writing well before *Woman Warrior*. What kind of writing were you doing?

MHK: I started when I was eight years old . . . with poetry. I first published when I was 15. It was an essay in *American Girl* magazine, and as I look back, I see my concerns are very similar. My essay was titled, "I Am An American."

In a way, that's like the speech Wittman gives at the end. Then I didn't publish again until *The Woman Warrior*, but I wrote many things, including a novel which I keep in the closet because it's my experimental laboratory work. So, in a way when people call this my first novel, it's not really.

IE: There's been debate over whether your first two books should be considered fiction or nonfiction. Do you consider, say, *China Men*, a novel?

MHK: I would consider it nonfiction because it is about real people and all those things they did—they really did them. I try to guess why people think it's fiction. One, it's beautifully written. I think there's an idea that only fiction takes art and craft—nonfiction does too. Also, I do tell about people's dreams and visions. This isn't the way most biographies work. How do I know what their dreams and visions are? I know because I come from this talk-story tradition.

I'm so lucky it didn't die out with my parents. We would wake up in the morning for breakfast, and everybody tells what each other's dreams are. This was confirmed for me when I go to Asia—I look up my relatives. One of my aunts in Hong Kong came to pick me up. The first thing she asks is "How is your mother and what is she dreaming?" I thought "Wow! What a question," and I felt really happy because I could tell her because I knew—my mother told me.

So, yeah, we can call those nonfiction because it's the truth, the dreams and people are real. I had to find a form so I could tell where the lineage of the stories themselves come from. What I think I'm doing is a whole new form and probably somebody should think of a name for it.

IE: For a long time Asian American literature was dominated by autobiographies that were manipulated by outside forces for various reasons. They were used to, say, promote circumscribed assimilation or to identify "good" and "bad" Asians, depending on the climate of the times. You've mentioned that *Fifth Chinese Daughter* was the only Chinese American book you knew of for a long time. How much did that influence you?

MHK: I must have read *Fifth Chinese Daughter* when I was in 6th or 7th grade, and it was really, really important because, up to that moment, I had not encountered a Chinese character in a book, let alone a writer. It made me realize we were left out.

I was reading all of Louisa May Alcott. In her book, there is a white girl, and I suppose it's sort of daring, but she marries a Chinese guy. He has a long pigtail. He's fat, short, weird. He was mainly a character of fun and so stereotyped, although I suppose it was accurate—by that time they hadn't cut off their pigtails yet. Up to that time, I had identified with all those little women, then I saw this guy and I thought, "My God, that's who I'm supposed to be—this little 'chinaman' guy." It ejected me out of literature.

A few years later, I read Jade Snow Wong and she brought me back in. There were such wonderful illustrations of little kids that looked like me, and most importantly, written by a Chinese American woman. So, she gave me this great welcome and send-off, so I continued writing.

IE: Many Asian American authors, and other writers of color, have dealt with the theme of self-contempt. In the new book, Wittman goes up and down with it. How do you feel about that theme, and how do you deal with it in your work?

MHK: Yeah, he fights it, and sometimes he wins and sometimes he loses. I suppose, in my work and my life, it's about the same. I think it's very hard for us to see our own beauty and one another's beauty, because everybody in this society is so brainwashed by television—the movies who make blond people the ideal of beauty and attractiveness.

We are not taught to find one another beautiful. In Hawaii, I taught writing at a private school that had mostly Japanese Americans. I teach them how to write short stories. Of course, teenage kids want to write love stories with a beautiful blond in it, because we are taught in this society that that is the kind of woman that is worthy of love, and those kids buy it. It's my task to show them—you know, what if you made this person look like yourself? That teaches them a lot, because, pretty soon, the stories are no longer about stereotypes.

IE: For a long time, there's been debate over your work, with critics charging that you're being manipulated by white editors and feminists. How do you feel about that?

MHK: That's what Solberg said in his article! Do they have any facts to back that up? What do they mean, "manipulated"? I don't even sign a contract until my work is what I feel is perfected. I send it out, and I have no trouble publishing. I hardly have any rejection slips. Even *Woman Warrior* got published right away.

There isn't anybody saying do it this way or that way. Once the book is done, the editor has very few changes that he discusses with me, hardly anything. In fact, sometimes I want heavier editing because I don't want people to let me off too easily. I want it as good as I can get it.

Solberg wrote all that and I thought, "Why does he say that when he has no evidence for it?" It just makes me so mad. It's his stereotype of women being manipulated by white men. He actually says stuff like "selling out." I mean, it just doesn't make sense.

Continuing on about publishers—I learned something new. When I was at UCLA, some young girls came up, young writers. They asked me, "Do you know there is a generic Maxine Hong Kingston rejection slip?" They said that they sent in some writing and the publishers reject them, but on top of that, they advise them to read my work.

I'm sure it made them feel that publishers have in mind that Asians ought to write like me, and then they might get published. This one girl said, "I don't know anybody who plays mah jong, and I would have to inject that into my work?" I guess that their idea of the publishing industry is that, once there are some successful Chinese American works out there, then they think other Chinese Americans ought to write the same way.

I just had to remind them that they have to write like themselves. They have the task of figuring out—if they don't play mah jong, then what do they do? What is 1989 Asian American life, or what is life? What is that like and write about it, and send their own work out there and not be so affected by the market place. They have to change the marketplace.

IE: What are you going to be writing about next? Are you working on something now?

MHK: No, I'm not, but quite a few people have been asking me, "What does Wittman do next?" So, I've been thinking, what if he grows up, after all he's only twenty-something. What if I show what happens when he becomes 40, or even 50?

If I could manage to make him grow up a whole, good, effective, socially responsible man, then maybe I will show the whole American society how to grow up. I mean, I will make Huck Finn, Tom Sawyer and Holden Caulfield—all those American adolescent heroes [grow up]—because Americans are so adolescent.

If I can do this, I'll give a role model to America, but it will be very hard because I have to grow up and be wise. I don't know whether I can pull it off at all. I find this really challenging. I might not even be able to do it [she laughs]. I don't want him to be tragic. I don't want Wittman to be a martyr, either. It can't end in a shoot-out or that kind of despair. So, those are the ideas I have. I hope I can do it.

Writing the Other: A Conversation with Maxine Hong Kingston

Marilyn Chin / 1989

From *Poetry Flash* 198 (September 1989), pp. 1, 4–6, 17–18. Reprinted by permission of the interviewer and *Poetry Flash*.

The following conversation between the prose writer and the poet, Maxine Hong Kingston and Marilyn Chin, was taped before Maxine Hong Kingston's reading for the Living Writers Series which Chin coordinates at San Diego State University, after they had spent a rich day together. Marilyn Chin, a generation younger than Maxine Hong Kingston, is also Chinese American. The fact that Hong Kingston has been an inspirational role model for Chin has acted as a generative spark to bring their talk to the pages of *Poetry Flash*.

MC: The opening chapter of *Tripmaster Monkey* made me cry.
MHK: Really? I'm so glad.

MC: You're glad you made me cry?
MHK: Because everybody is saying it's *tough,* or they're saying, "That Wittman has such an obnoxious personality." I am so glad that it brings out a softer emotion.

MC: Well, I recognize that squalor, that desperation. Being an unemployed poet, going through life in San Francisco where the immigrants are making their dream. I remember sitting in coffee shops, writing up my resumé while the immigrants were out there working hard and buying their houses, working toward this 'dream.' I said, how have I lost that dream? I recognize that desperation in Wittman. And those piles and piles of unfinished poems in the false bottom of his Gold Mountain Theater truck. . . .
MHK: That dream that he's gonna be a poet. You know, lately I've met new immigrants that have been coming in and they are so different from my parents. I've met a whole bunch of brand-new people who are musicians, and their strength and their music is so strong. They come here looking for part-time jobs. They don't want to open a restaurant or a laundry, but they will take a menial job in a restaurant in order to practice their music. And their dream . . . they've come here with the ancient instruments—their *erh hus* and

86

yuehs [2 string fiddles and moon guitars], and they want to introduce American people to this music. And they think they can introduce those ancient instruments and make music and compose and make a career.

MC: Let's talk about the opening chapter. Why Wittman Ah Sing . . . and not 'Wilma Ah Lan'? Why a male protagonist this time? That surprised me when I opened the book. I wasn't expecting a male protagonist.

MHK: Oh, many reasons. One of them is that my life as writer had been a long struggle with pronouns. For 30 years I wrote in the first person singular. At a certain point I was thinking that I was self-centered and egotistical, solipsistic, and not very developed as a human being, nor as an artist, because I could only see from this one point of view. I was only interested in myself. So for 30 years I did that—all my poems, my prose, everything that I wrote. And then in about the fourth chapter of *The Woman Warrior* I felt the claustrophobia of that very strongly. I thought that I had to overcome this self-centeredness. I guess what I'm saying is that I think you can't write well unless you're a good human being. That you cannot fake wisdom, or good values, in a book. You have to be a good person in order to write that way. So about three-quarters of the way through *The Woman Warrior* I was thinking, I have to care about other people more than I do. And so, very artificially, I wrote a chapter that's done with an omniscient narrator. So I could use a third person. That's the chapter about my mother and her sister going to Los Angeles to reclaim that bigamist husband.

MC: That was a wonderful vignette.

MHK: I liked it, because it really fell into place as a classical short story shape. And actually what gave me a lot of help was thinking of "I Love Lucy." I thought, what an easy form; I could work in that form. The first half of the show is Lucy and Ethel. That's my mother and my aunt, and they are stirring up everything. They are plotting to do something that will get their husbands into a lot of trouble. And then, by the second half, there's the confrontation, where all of them, Ricky and Fred, and everybody, they all clash, and they're chasing all over the place, and there's all this excitement, and then the resolution. I use that form, to help me be able to manipulate four characters, to be able to look at people from the outside and not as before, always interior. Even when I wrote about other people, I would do it first person.

What was happening next, though, is that I continue that struggle in *China Men*. So it does begin with a strong narrator, myself. Then, as I go along, I disappear. And I become a listener at the end. I can tell their stories from their own point of view. And then, what's happened in *Tripmaster Monkey* is that I have, as the narrator has, totally disappeared. I feel that this is an artistic as well as a psychological improvement on my part. Because I am now a much less selfish person. And I can write the Other. . . .

MC: There was a letter that Ezra Pound wrote to James Joyce after he finished *Ulysses*. He said something like, at last you have been able to write the Other. So The Other for women is a man. At last you have found your 'other' characters. It's also the maturation of craft. To be able to work with another point of view. The first person is something we do in our youth, perhaps.

MHK: Another thing about the first person was that, in that first book, the reader is reading the first person. So I was thinking that I was creating this world, that the 'I' is so strong that the reader is caught in it; the reader believes it. But then I wanted to show them, who is this 'I' after all, in the context of the rest of the world? It's just some dumb kid who sits in a corner. I want to show her place, socially. How other people see her. She is just some kid who doesn't know anything about anything. She has no business in the drama of the adults. I just want to give the different perspectives. But, anyway, this new book, I think that it's a real triumph to do an omniscient narrator. And she is actually pushing Wittman Ah Sing around, telling him to shut up. She gives him various girlfriends; she gives him different difficult human situations to contend with. And, as I was writing along, I saw that she has a personality. First of all, the omniscient narrator is a woman. And, second, she has a memory that goes way back to China. She has a memory that sees a little bit into the future, toward the end of the Vietnam War, in the movies that were being produced. And she is also sometimes very tough on Wittman, and she captures him. Remember, in the *Monkey* story, as Kuan Yin takes a rock and throws it on top of the monkey for 500 years? I felt that as narrator I took a rock and threw it on top of the protagonist and captured him. And kept him in place. So I was beginning to see that my narrator is Kuan Yin, and she is very merciful. I mean, nobody is going to get killed or hurt. She keeps giving people wonderful opportunities.

MC: At the same time, life is not a bowl of cherries for Wittman.

MHK: She gives him a lot of hardships and problems he has to deal with, such as, what are you going to do with your life after you have your degree in English? How are you going to apply what you have learned? How are you going to bring what you have learned back to your people? There are no ready-made answers, as there are for your engineers and the business majors. So this is Wittman's task. And I wanted him not to end up like Madame Bovary, who's a reader, or Don Quixote, who's a reader. Literature took them to all the wrong places. I wanted to see whether Wittman can take all this wonderful literature and make the world a better place, given what he knows. As craft, though, I felt so good, so revolutionary, in that I have a woman, goddess narrator, as opposed to those nineteenth century omniscient narrators, who were really men—they were white men because God in the nineteenth century was a white man. I'm saying that's not so, anymore.

MC: That's great, the Goddess of Mercy is the omniscient narrator. I had a feeling Kuan Yin was in there.

MHK: Oh, I'm so glad you got that! Nobody's gotten it.

MC: Ah Sing's long-winded style is mimetic of the bombardment of the multi-cultural society of San Francisco and the Bay Area. And he's a precocious and unhappy and alienated anti-hero, wading through the shit of American life. And a lot of the shit is his own making. I can see Kuan Yin up there, often judging him.

MHK: Yes, often.

MC: And he not liking it. They struggle. There's a struggle going on between the narrator and the protagonist.

MHK: Yes. And his struggle is also with the society around him. It's also with women. He's a very macho spirit. The narrator is the great female, so he struggles with her and fights with her and refuses to accept reality. He has to learn to be one with the feminine principles of the world. But he starts out alienated. It's a struggle against alienation. And he tries for integration so much. He sees it on some simple levels, such as integrating the buses and the bathrooms and the johns and all that. But he also has to work on integrating himself. And then there's that large integration between him and the rest of the universe. And America.

MC: And you go toward that, by putting out his vision of the theater—an integrated theater. And that vision is complete. What he has is a spirit of play, which the Monkey King had.

MHK: The Monkey King was always mischievous, and he was always looking for the Elixir of Life. And the gods in heaven put him through so many trials. But he always bounced back; no matter how the evil prince and his army chased after him and so forth, he always bounced back. He ended up a very important figure in Chinese literature, and unforgettable.

His bouncing back has to do with irrepressible joy and his spirit of fun. Somehow we are going to solve the world's problems with fun and theater. And with laughter. The reason this is all set in the Sixties, too, is that the monkey was here, in the Sixties. Abby Hoffman, Allen Ginsberg, you know? They were monkey spirits, trying to change the world with costumes and street theater.

MC: And thumbing their noses at the establishment.

MHK: That's it. The monkey's task was to bring chaos to established order. So Wittman has that also.

MC: In the Sixties there was a self-empowerment movement.

MHK: Self-defining. Life is beautiful.

MC: So Wittman Ah Sing could be an Asian American emblem of that era. Some of the Asian Americans then considered themselves separatists, with the blacks, with the Sixties self-empowerment movement.

MHK: But then there were lots of Asians in the Rainbow Coalition. I thought that was great. I thought they were so big to have done that, because Jesse Jackson didn't remember yellow until quite late in the campaign.

MC: Your *Tripmaster* is really a poet's novel. The play in the language, the puns, the cacophony, the history, the invective, the pieces of Americana, filled with the stuff of life.

MHK: Thank you. I love that.

MC: Poets should read this novel.

MHK: He starts out in the book as a poet, as I started out a poet. And then, he wants to make a difference, socially. And he wants to form community. His being a playwright would do that better than being a poet. So he picks a more social art.

MC: I remember on page 33, Nanci, his girlfriend, says, "An actress says other people's words. I'm an actress. I know about saying other people's words. You scare me, a poet saying his own words. I don't like watching." Something interests me about this. That's saying that the act of poetry writing is akin to masturbating; that the reader watches while the poet goes on. . . .

MHK: No, that's Nanci . . . But what I feel is that a poet speaks directly. When you get up there on a platform and read your poetry, you are saying your own words. It comes directly out of your body, your voice, your mind. And Nanci is an actress. She uses other people's words. But she's scared of him because he has just put on a one-man show for her. And she's all by herself. She's this one person audience. And he blasts her, with his language. It comes straight from him, blasting at her. She gets no help from other members of the audience. And she is sort of like an unworthy audience. She doesn't understand it, and she's scared.

MC: She's one of those Philistines.

MHK: Well, she's not the girl for him. She's not the perfect listener or the perfect reader, which I try to be for those China men.

MC: I want to tell you that *The Woman Warrior* was a very important book in my life. I discovered it in 1977 in the Jeffrey Amherst Book Store in Amherst, Massachusetts. I was an undergraduate there.

MHK: I was just at Amherst. So many Asian American kids there. They gave me a standing ovation. I was reading, and they were standing in the balcony, clapping. I felt like I was at a revival meeting.

MC: The Asian Americans there, they hunger for this. I think we're very spoiled on the West Coast. We get more of this Asian American culture. The streets of California are littered with budding writers. And we get more of the cross-cultural stuff. And they don't, back there. When I discovered *The Woman Warrior* I recognized Brave Orchid as my grandmother and Moon Orchid as my sad, sad mother. And my father was Moon Orchid's doctor-bigamist husband. My whole family was in that book. All those faces, with the composite physiognomy of that first generation of Chinese American chaotic families. But it was wonderful. I think it gave us permission to go on. That book set precedent. That summer I was wallowing between law school, and becoming a poor, starving poet. So that book really made a difference in my life. And I'm certain that it made a difference in many, many lives.

MHK: You mean it helped you think that you should continue as a poet?

MC: Yes.

MHK: How did it do that? I don't know how it would do that.

MC: Well, for a long time I was in despair. I thought, there was really no audience for my voice. And the narrator, the protagonist in *The Woman Warrior*, she was working hard to let her voice out. She had to wade through the contradictions of this dual culture, this heavy-duty heritage. If she had the power and the fortitude to continue her 'pressed duck' voice, to eke out that voice, I said, perhaps so must I continue my struggle. Poetry was my passion. This was what I wanted to do. That summer I decided to not go to law school and to become a poet. And here I am, a starving poet.

MHK: So that's what I've done for you.

MC: Oh, I'm sure you've done that for many, many Asian American women.

MHK: I've done it for a lot of women. I was so amazed when I was up in Seattle. A young black said that I started her writing again and that she wanted to thank me. So she gave me a rap. She did it, and the audience snapped their fingers along. It was a poem in praise of me, with my Chinese name—Ting Ting—she played on the rap rhythms, and it was just lovely. And then the audience cheered. I thought, my gosh, what a wonderful response to my writing! And I've heard that before, from writers who say that I get them going again. It makes me feel that in my life I am at the source of life and words. I feel that I'm sort of standing over this hole in the universe, and it's all pouring in. I can be a conduit. The people who read my work feel more alive, and they can work. I feel like that about other writers that make me keep going. When I read Virginia Woolf's *Orlando* or William Carlos Williams's *In the American Grain*, I can feel like I'm dying, or I'm stuck, both in life and in work. I read those books, and then I start flowing again. I'm happy that I can do that for other people.

MC: You are a positive force. It's wonderful to have you in California again. You can't imagine how important your work is. Do you as an Asian American writer, now in the prime of your literary life, still feel the same contradictions that Ting Ting, the protagonist, felt in *The Woman Warrior*? That struggle to get out, the struggle to have a voice?

MHK: No, no. I feel much more integrated. I think that it takes this long, to be middle-aged—it takes decades of struggle. When you are a person who comes from a multicultural background it just means that you have more information coming in from the universe. And it's your task to figure out how it all integrates, figure out its order and its beauty. It's a harder, longer struggle. I feel that I am now a pretty integrated person. I still have a way to go, but when I compare myself to other women . . .

History is all these migrations, from the very beginning. People are probably a migratory species. And they go faster and faster and faster. We're all here in America now. Lately I met an Indonesian-Chinese woman immigrating to Japan. She learned Japanese language, then came to America in the middle of the civil rights movement, joined the civil rights movement and identified with all these black people. Then there came a time when the black people decided they had to consolidate their own forces. So they threw everybody else out of the movement. So she was thrown out. And I was thinking, my god, what a beautiful, strong woman. How is she going to integrate Indonesia, Chinese-ness, Japanese-ness, her blackness? She had to do all that, and she has. So I look at myself. I just have two. It's not that bad.

MC: It's a hard life. To be a writer is marginal. There's no place for a writer in this country. Even being a reader is weird. It's like being Kafka's character who wakes up one morning and turns into a cockroach, and the family ends up crushing him to death. There are times in which I feel, as a poet, that it's almost hopeless, but then, of course, when we're reading people that we love and when we're writing well and the spirit, the muse is with us . . . it makes it all worth it.

MHK: That's true about writers being marginal. It comes to me when I'm on an airplane. I guess because I've been on a lot of airplanes lately, but, you know, your seatmate might ask, well, what do you do? I always struggle. I cannot just say, I'm a writer. It's just awful. I hate it. I've resorted to lying. If you say you're a writer, they say, well what do you write? Then they feel defensive, because they don't read.

Since you're an Asian Lit specialist, I want to tell you that when I went to China—I was there last year—it was a trip sponsored by UCLA and the Chinese Writers Association—there was this whole group of writers. We were guests of Chinese writers, poets, scholars. One told me that I was writing in the water and grass style. And then I read an early draft of *Tripmaster Monkey* aloud to them, and they had it translated, and they read it. A poet told me that I was the only Chinese that was writing in the tradition of the *Dream of the Red Chamber* because here is Wittman as the effete, young man battling to keep his manhood among the matriarchy, the twelve women of that book. He said that I was writing in the tradition of the past. And, in part of the conference, they were telling us that there was a "roots literature" movement in China—because in the Cultural Revolution they cut off the roots.

So they had cut off their ties to the West, and cut off the bindings of feudalism, the imperial arts and all that. But then they weren't left with anything. So, as I came to the end of the trip, when we got to Shanghai, they

were crying and talking about all this Cultural Revolution stuff. Then I
thought, I know why they invited us American writers there, especially me,
because they felt that I was working in free conditions. Here I was in
America, where I had free speech and free press. And I spent this lifetime
working on roots. So what they were saying was that I was their continuity.
And they wanted help in figuring out where to go.

They thought Gabriel García Márquez's would be the way, because of his
richness, because his work can be multilayer. He can use the Indian past and
the Catholic-Spanish heritage. Keep it all. You don't have to cut that out, cut
this out.

MC: And also, keep in the political realism, which is very important.

MHK: Yeah. But, God, I felt so terrific. Because they were telling me I
was part of a Chinese canon. And here I was writing in English!

MC: But that's important, to think that there is continuity. I always think
back to the T'ang Dynasty when I write poetry. I feel that I am very much a
part of that Chinese tradition. I don't want to be cut off from it. That's why
I studied classical Chinese. I feel it's very, very important. I don't know if
other Asian Americans feel that way, but I know you feel that way. Our roots
go way back. We're old souls. We need to speak for all these people who
didn't have a chance to speak, all these women who were illiterate, all those
court women who were embodied in architecture and couldn't get out—their
feet bound, so they would not wander away from the courtyard. We're almost
like mediums for these ancient voices. I feel close ties to my Chinese roots.

MHK: I do, too. I think it's partly because my mother came from China,
so I live with a person who remembers that history. I feel directly concerned.
On the other hand, I've also realized that I'm an American. There's such a
struggle to establish one's claim to America. And I keep thinking, maybe I
shouldn't be interested in T'ang Dynasty poetry because that's going backwards. Because I am writing in English, after all. And I have to show that the
connection is here. Because the moment I let go of my hold to this country,
there are people out there who will say, well, go home then. Why don't you
go back where you came from? Which is not where I came from. I come to
my Chinese roots very tentatively. This is why Wittman can't help it—it's in
your genes or something, this concern for China. But, see, we get scared
about that, because it's like the Japanese Americans, when they burned their
diaries, when they burned their art work. Because they didn't want people to
think that they should be put in camps. There is this wanting to be American

and to write American. But, when I was writing *The Woman Warrior* and so concerned to just throw out any exotic imagery, because I didn't want people to think I was exotic, I only kept the ones that I thought were absolutely necessary. They were so much a part of my life here that they are American imagery. And yet, when I look at it now, it still looks really Chinese. You know, in *Tripmaster Monkey*, at the beginning, it comes pouring out of Wittman, all this Chinese history and poems of Chinese theater. And then, all of a sudden, he looks at it and says, oh my gosh, what am I doing? All this Chinese stuff. I'm an American. I gotta write American stories. So he takes it, and he burns it.

MC: He keeps going back and forth, doesn't he? I mean, he looks at FOB's ['fresh off the boat'] on the street, and is ashamed of them.

MHK: There's that part of him that's like a mainstream, racist American because he's got a Mayflower complex, himself. He's been taught by America that, if you were born here, then you're a real American. If your people go way back, then you're a real American. His people do go way back, except that there are a lot of white Americans who will come up to you and say, where do you come from? There is a refusal to understand that an American can look like one of us and doesn't have to be white. He just doesn't want to be taken for an FOB.

So he takes it out on them by being nasty to them and not liking them and saying I'm not one of you. Like minority guys who beat up minority women.

MC: Yes, let's talk about that.

MHK: As we were saying, among the minority writers, it looks like there is the same argument going on, between black men and black women writers, between the Chicano men and the Chicanas, between the Asian American writers, the men and women, the same argument is being carried out. And it's not even an argument; it's so one-sided. Attacks by the men on the women. Saying that somehow we have achieved our success by collaborating with the white racist establishment. We are in bed with the white literary establishment; that's how we get published. Or they say, we pander to the white taste for feminist writing. We're just panderers if we write this kind of stuff. We write, we put exotic visions, images, because whites find it romantic. All these issues that David Hwang did in *M. Butterfly* are very feminist. It's just a one-sided argument because women don't answer. We let them say those things because we don't want to be divisive.

MC: And the analogy . . .

MHK: Yes. What is so sad is that here we are, the literate people, the artistic people, and we're replicating a battle that's going on among more primitive, unenlightened people. The minority women go out there, and we can get the jobs, no matter how menial. And we come home to the unemployed husband, and he, because racism has messed with his manhood really badly, instead of understanding he's got to go out there and change the world, he has it all wrong, who the enemy is—so he hits his wife. It's appalling, that it takes place on that level of people who solve problems with their fists. We're doing the same thing. It's so sick. And it's all because we're buckling under the racism.

MC: How do you think that we can overcome this? I think you're right. It's happening not only in the Asian American world; it's happening to really very good ethnic women writers. Powerful writers. They deserve their success. They're talented.

MHK: I was really shocked when I came out with my first book. At that time there were some Asian American men who were all we had of our literary community. And I expected, when my book came out, for them to say, welcome. Welcome to the community of artists. Because there are so few of us. So here's another one to add strength to our numbers. And, instead, the men just right away went into this big thing. It's a very crazy plot they have in their heads. Their assessment of the publishing industry is so wrong.

MC: Do you think it's mostly professional jealousy?

MHK: You know, it's true that Asian American men are not writing the novels. Where are they? How come they're not writing the novels?

MC: And is that true about Afro-Americans?

MHK: No, they have small presses that bring out the novels. But they're not writing the big books. The other day I was talking to a critic in Seattle. She was saying she didn't think Japanese Americans had big novels because they're so careful about not hurting people's feelings and exploding emotionally. So I don't know. No, that's not true.

There is a new novel coming out by a British man—Kazuo Ishiguro. He is so good. He's about 35 years old; this is his third book. The command of language—his language is so superior. The moment that you start reading his book you enter the land of story, because of the way the words are put together. God, that man is so good! So, they're doing it in Britain.

MC: You know, I wonder if you realize that your work not only crosses cultural boundaries, but, in terms of the university, your work crosses disciplines. I've seen it taught not only in Literature departments, but in American Studies and Anthropology, Ethnic Studies, History, Women's Studies. And your books are being taught in high schools, colleges and universities.

MHK: I was taught once in Black studies. I was so proud.

MC: It must be wonderful! This longevity—*The Woman Warrior* came out, what, in '76? And people are still reading it. It survived the test of time, the test of great literature. It's already in the American canon. You're a celebrated author, and your work will survive. The way the publishing world is now, often the book comes out, and disappears.

MHK: Yes, a shelf life of six weeks. It is amazing. Two teachers back east on my tour told me that I was the living author whose books are most taught in colleges. Somebody just told me they did an informal survey, walking around the UC Berkeley book stores and found it in twelve courses in one university. And the MLA is coming out with a book on how to teach my work.

MC: That's really exciting, to have an Asian American writer be a very popular writer. We should all celebrate this.

MHK: You know what happens, Asian Americans are so cautious about saying that my work speaks for them. They don't want to say that since there are so few works that come out from us. Every one that comes out has to represent everybody. They give it a lot of weight. They make it take on many responsibilities.

MC: That's very unfair.

MHK: I understand what happens. I met some readers who get so offended when a white friend of theirs says, "Oh, I just read *China Men*, and now I understand you!" Nobody wants that. And then a lot of Chinese Americans get mad, because they say my experience is nothing like theirs. Of course, they may come from a different class of people; they come from a different generation of migration; they're a different generation American. There aren't enough books out there. If there were lots of books, then you could see the variety of people in the books, reflecting the variety of people in life. But since there aren't a whole lot of books . . .

MC: They expect everything from you. Can *Moby Dick* speak for every American? It's impossible. But there are more Asian American writers now, are there not?

MHK: Something wonderful is happening right at this moment. Right now, just in the last few months, I mean. Amy Tan published *The Joy Luck Club*, and Hisaye Yamamoto published *Seventeen Syllables*; Frank Chin has a collection of short stories, and I think maybe Ruth-Anne Lumm McKunn just came out with her book on Chinese families. Jessica Hagedorn's in the spring, and Bharati Mukherjee's is in the fall. She won the National Book Critics Circle Award. Something great must be going on.

MC: It's mostly women.

MHK: Yes, I know. And then the poets, too. You can just see the poetry in all the magazines. It's amazing.

MC: Yes. It's clearly a second blooming. Don't you think it's a hundred flowers blooming? I think that my generation is taking literature seriously, especially a lot of us coming out of writing programs, for better or worse. Not going to law school, and not going to engineering school.

MHK: I went to engineering school. I didn't last.

MC: I can hear Brave Orchid saying, "Go to engineering school!"

MHK: Yes, and I did; I did. And I was so miserable. I always thought taking English was just fun. There was no good reason for doing it. When I went from engineering to English, I felt I had abdicated all my responsibilities! I was just living life for the fun of it. I guess it was the way I was raised, but everything had to be hard. Engineering was worth it because it was hard. But English was easy for me, so I shouldn't do anything that was easy. I thought it was like that. There was something wrong with me if I did something that was easy and fun. But there is something about that generation, too, that wanted all their children to be mathematicians, engineers . . .

MC: You know what it was. They wanted us to be safe. They were protecting us. Because they know how hard it is to survive out there.

MHK: Stability.

MC: It's a generation that did everything for their children. They pretty much sacrificed their lives so their children could have an education, so that the children could go on. This has left the burden of guilt on us.

MHK: That's right. But they were also people who . . . well, at least, my parents read Tu Fu and Li Po. My mother will read T'ang Dynasty poetry all night, aloud. And my father listens. They forget that those guys were drones wandering around in the forest. They were ultimate hippies. They were writing on rocks and leaves.

MC: And Li Po was writing poetry in brothels, and he was a swashbuckler, and he might have killed a couple guys, they say.

MHK: I guess they didn't want us to be like that. Because they know that a poet is like that in China. And they're like that here. And so they don't want that for their daughters, especially.

MC: Oh, yes. My grandmother's illiterate, but she memorized Chinese poetry. And she memorized long poems, dating back to the Shih Ching. It's wonderful. But, then, when it comes to their children's future: No! No poets! And don't you dare marry one!

MHK: Before I could even talk, I could hear my parents reciting that poetry.

MC: It's that rhythm. And I recognize that rhythm in your work.

MHK: Oh, good. I'm so glad. I see it in your work too, in the images. They're all there. You know, my mother did the chant of Fa Mu Lan. I learned to talk by repeating those things. I never knew, until I got to college and was taking an Asian Lit class, that that was important poetry. I just thought it was my parents' tales. My brothers thought, oh, those are just village ditties. They sing that on the farm. And then I thought later, oh, Tu Fu and Li Po—this is important stuff.

MC: The greatest poets in China.

MHK: But, you know, that was how I got a lot of my literature. I didn't know until I got to school that *Robinson Crusoe* was an English novel. Because it had gone into Chinese as a spoken story. So my parents spoke the story, *Robinson Crusoe*, and that was the same kind of discovery. I got to school, and I thought, oh, so this is what this stuff is.

MC: It's been written down.

MHK: The culture was handed down orally. It wasn't necessary to be literate. Most people in China were illiterate. That's why telling stories is so important.

MC: And my grandmother's four-character phrases with which she admonished us. She'd dig this stuff out of Confucius . . .

MHK: You know, they used to memorize the whole thing, *The Analects*— they memorized all of it.

MC: We don't have that oral tradition in America. Who are our soothsayers? What happened to that oral tradition?

MHK: I guess what we have is Garrison Keillor. Isn't it amazing that he started off so small, on a small radio station, and now he's an international superstar. And he's carrying on 'told stories' by radio. The good thing is that we have him at all. The bad thing is that most people don't even realize that we ought to do it every night among ourselves.

MC: Anything else you want to say?

MHK: In *Tripmaster Monkey*, I work a lot more with American rhythms, and directly with American language that I usually speak, that my friends speak, and that is around me. And when I wrote *The Woman Warrior* and *China Men*, as I look back on it, I was trying to find an American language that would translate the speech of the people who are living their lives with the Chinese language. They carry on their adventures and their emotional life and everything in Chinese. I had to find a way to translate all that into a graceful American language. Which is my language. But, after I finished, I started thinking, I'm missing a lot . . . I haven't had a chance to play with this language that I speak, this modern American language—which I love. I already finished writing all those Chinese rhythms. So I was trying to write a book with American rhythms. This is what *Tripmaster Monkey* is, too. So I can let Wittman talk. I love that language of the Sixties, the slang of the Sixties. And all those words that were invented to describe psychedelic states, visions, new social . . . Zen gestures, pacifist activities, like sit-ins, and be-ins, and love-ins. All those words that were made up, 'Flower Power,' and all that.

MC: It's interesting that you went back to the Sixties. Not very many authors are doing this.

MHK: No, especially not the age that I talk about.

MC: You're fond of the Sixties. You feel a connection . . .

MHK: Whenever I feel something's missing, that's when I realize: Oh, this is the next book. When I was reading William Carlos Williams's *In the American Grain*, and it ends at the Civil War, where Abraham Lincoln as a woman, with a shawl around her—the mother of our country—is walking on the battlefields, sort of tucking in the soldiers, I thought, wow, this is it. This is the way to write about America. This is right. This is history, the mythic history. So I'm sure there was going to be a volume two. So I ran to the library and turned this one in, looking for volume two. There isn't a volume two; that's it! That was when I thought, oh. I've got to write volume two. If he didn't do it, then I've got to do it. So that's *China Men*. They bind the country together with steel, the bands of steel that are the railroads. That's the same kind of missing feeling; after I finished the first two books, I thought, oh! there's more language in me, this other kind of language, this very slangy, American, present-day language. And the other thing that was missing was that, well, I wanted to read some books about the time that the Beatniks went away—those are our forefathers, our immediate forefathers.

MC: Yes, right! Especially for those of us on the West Coast.

MHK: And so they were going away, but there weren't any Hippies yet. The new artistic wave hadn't come. There's a dark period in theater that coincides with a dark period in Chinese American theater. There's something missing. I could sense it, and so, when I'd get that feeling, I think, oh, I've got to do it, I've got to plug it in. My first thought is—I always do this— who's doing it? Where's that book? As a reader, where's the book on this? Where's volume two? Where's the book about that dark period? What an interesting period! Isn't that funny nobody wrote about it? I wish somebody would write about it so I could read it! And then comes this thing, oh! It's me!

MC: It's your calling.

MHK: It's me; I'm so scared, because there's no other volunteers.

MC: Well, what happens after *Tripmaster*? What are you doing now?

MHK: You know, I've been writing for forty years. I started when I was eight, and now I'm forty-eight, so I've been writing straight for forty years!

MC: Wow!

MHK: After I finished this book, for the first time there wasn't another one just coming along. So I thought I should take a year off and just live and not do this writing stuff and not live with these characters for years—I lived with Wittman Ah Sing for eight years! Many people have said that he's obnoxious, and he is.

MC: He's a difficult birthing. Well, some of our children are obnoxious.

MHK: Yes, and you love 'em anyhow. My niece has been reading this, and she says, "I can't stand him!" She says, "If he sat next to me on the bus, I'd move! Who would want to go out with him? Yuck!" She's a business major in college.

But I was going to say . . . I am beginning to have an idea that Wittman ought to grow up.

MC: Wittman ought to grow up? He should be enlightened.

MHK: Well, he has to get older, has to grow up. This is in response to some people who said, "Well, what happens to him next?" But I was thinking he is only about twenty-three years old, and he has all these ideals. To me, to grow up means to be able to effectively carry out the ideas into the real world. Now, he does begin to do that, because he puts on a show. But that's just one show. Will he be able to grow up and change and be a good man? If I can write a novel in which Wittman grows up to be a socially responsible, an effective, good man—forming a community around him, bringing joy to people—if I can write such a novel, then it means that I will have made Holden Caulfield grow up; I would have made Huck Finn and Tom Sawyer grow up. American Literature is made up of great novels about young men. It has to do with our being a young country.

Now, what if I could write a continuing volume that shows him at forty, at fifty, as an integrated whole, a powerful, good man? Then I would have helped us all grow up. There are books now . . . about grown men and grown women, but quite often they are tragedies. Those people are martyrs. Even the French novels about Communists, socially committed people, quite often they end up to be martyrs. People keep writing these tragedies, the tragedy of when you grow up. I would have to change the whole novel form to write it. And it can't be a utopian novel, in the sense that utopian novels are often so unrealistic.

MC: Absolutely! But, you were willfully keeping Wittman adolescent. I was waiting for an enlightenment. I said, oh, yes, we will have a sequel. We will see Wittman in another light. One cannot grow up at twenty-three.

MHK: It's already phenomenal that he could put on the one-man show and have his people around—for a twenty-three year old that's pretty good.

MC: I thought you were willfully keeping him young.

MHK: You know why? Because that's as wise as I am. This glimmering that I have of the grown-up novel—I don't understand it yet. I'm not sure that I'm wise enough myself to understand how to make him mature like that. I don't know whether I can do it. I don't know what will happen until I actually write it.

MC: Do you feel committed to finish off the Wittman character? Do you feel he's like a bud that needs to be burst-bloomed?

MHK: Well . . . you know, my son is just about that age, and he's an entertainer. At the moment he's a singer and a musician, plays the bass and also the ukulele. He's on those cruise ships that go around the islands in Hawaii. They stop at four islands. He's in a trio with some beautiful sisters. He gives ukulele lessons to the tourists and helps them put on their talent show on the last night on board. He puts on the show; he's just like Wittman.

MC: I bet you got the energy from him.

MHK: It could be. My son is a real James Dean type, sort of non-verbal, and glowers a lot.

MC: That's not Wittman. Wittman is very verbal.

MHK: My son communicates more with his music. But he's coming out of that glowering stage. That death wish stage. He's alive now, with the music. So maybe I need to see what becomes of him further. Maybe it's just that I have to recognize myself as a person who's growing up and see what that's all about.

Coming Home

Paul Skenazy / 1989

This interview with Maxine Hong Kingston occurred in early October, 1989. She had just returned from a publicity tour for *Tripmaster Monkey*. We started by talking about her travels, especially her time in Australia.

MHK: I was very welcomed in Australia. You know there are some writers that seem to have found their readership somewhere? Like Nelson Algren and James Baldwin are appreciated in France, Henry Roth is appreciated in Italy. I felt that way in Australia. Australia is a wonderful place. They are the country which buys the second most books per capita—and the one that buys the most per capita is New Zealand. I felt I was among readers. The people understand my work. The Australians and I were in love at first sight. The reviews and articles in the paper are 100% favorable, and they're well written.

I sense a wonderful connection between me and Australian readers. Part of it I think is that they're consciously building a multicultural society, and some of the things I write about they see and understand. They felt like I belonged there and that I was giving them a lot of their meanings. Like they had a whole series of the Monkey King adventures that was playing on Australian television. It's filmed in China and it's very beautiful. It plays every week, with the most amazing-looking costumes. It shows the Monkey on a quest going through China and you see the wonderful mountains and roads. So people in Australia know this myth. I was flabbergasted when white Australians sang me the Monkey myth theme song in Chinese. So when they started reading *Tripmaster*, they didn't feel that they needed to do research to figure out what the story was all about.

Also, the buscars in the streets are all Chinese. All these recent immigrants, all these people who are in exile from China. I saw one man in front of the *Batman* movie, he was doing birdsongs and bird imitations for money. There are some that have ancient Chinese instruments that are electrically amplified. They play in the streets, passing the hat. It really seemed like half a dozen portrait artists were Chinese. There they are, right in front of people's eyes, and that's the whole point of *Tripmaster Monkey*. What I'm saying is that immigrants don't come just out of dire need and desperation. They also come to sing and play and bring their theater and their music. And there it was in Australia. That historical ideal was right there. It affirmed what I was writing, or my vision of history. And all so immediate. It was obvious to them what I was saying. Not like here where I had to prove this thesis or it seemed like a far-out, far-fetched idea. But in Australia it wasn't a far-fetched idea; they could see it for themselves. So I think there are a lot of strange reasons why I seem to go over very well there. Unlike in England, where they're still trying to figure out my writing style and writing papers on genre.

PS: Is there a tradition of playful, postmodern prose in Australia?

MHK: I don't know much about Australian literature, but the people seem very playful and their language is so slangy. Oh! They have a game there that I've never seen before, that they play in the pubs, that the writers play in the pubs, and that they got from improvisational theater. Before I got there, I got a letter that said, we have a game called Writer Sports; would you like to participate? They have a row of typewriters, and then writers are asked to write three minute poems. And I thought no way. And then they asked, would you be the judge? So I thought, OK. I can do that: you know, just hold up a sign that says "6" or "10," something non-verbal.

Writer Sports has usually been in a pub. Everybody's been drinking. They tell me that three out of four of the invited writers usually turn them down because it's too hard to do. Well-known writers compete alongside locals, from just within town. But this time it's not going to be in a pub, but in a big auditorium. They charged $11.00 each admission and they had an audience of 1,000 people, with all these spotlights like a boxing arena and four type-writers and microphones over each of the typewriters. There was an MC who was like a sports announcer, giving running commentary.

In other words, they set up all the conditions that are against creativity, everything that would intimidate a writer. The crowd is yelling and scream-ing. Then they start. So this is the genre game. You pick from a hat; then they say, this person is going to write magical realism, this person is going to do minimalism, this one is going to do maximalism, this one is going to do romance. And then they get the audience all stirred up and ask them to name some characters. One set of characters was Lefty and Dolores, I thought that was really neat. And then they call out settings and themes and lines, they call out the main danger. Then they ask for last lines; I remember one last line was, "I can do jealousy better than anybody." In another contest, they

had to write a piece of advertising for a commercial, and they had to sell—
this is what the audience yelled out—they had to sell home-grown nuclear
waste. Then they had a three minute poem, and the writers are writing and
editing the whole time. And there's a woman running around with a bullhorn
shouting out the time and looking over the writers' shoulders and calling out
all kinds of things. Then they read what they've written and there are prizes.

PS: And how do the writers respond to all this? Does it open things up
rather than shut the creativity down as you'd expect, realizing they have only
so much time, and writing in public?

MHK: Nobody had a block, except for this one guy who was typing away
like crazy and then all of a sudden yells out, "I forgot to put in the paper!"
He says he's been using a computer and forgot about paper. And then the
audience is on him. When the time is up, they read out what they wrote, and
then the judge does not just hold up a number. The judge does instant literary
criticism. On every piece! I just thought, I can't do this. I've got to sneak out
and get a drink. I actually did sneak out, because I was going to get a drink,
and then they wouldn't let me bring the drink back in, and it was my turn to
judge. I judged the relay, in which there were four writers, so there's sixteen
of them, and one types away until they blow the whistle, and then the next
one comes on and continues the story, and they are all wearing funny hats.

So I had to listen to what they said and instantly do a literary analysis to
justify the 7 or 8 that I was holding up there. And the first thing that upset
me was the Australian accent. I couldn't even hear to judge. But I had to
listen and let the words in so I could have my inside response, and then do
the spoken coherent analysis. I gave a whole bunch of points for one that I
thought said, "The koala bear was eating aphrodisiac gumbies," because I
thought this was such a wonderful creation of words—gumbies. And the
audience yells out, "Gum leaves! Gum leaves!" And I found out that the
person they yell most at is the judge. If you rate somebody down they boo
you and they throw things at you. But I found I could do criticism, I just took
all these phrases like deconstruction and postmodernism and multicultural
aspirations and stuck them onto whatever came up. The Australians were
very proud of this game. They didn't think they could export this to America
or to the U.K., because they said that we are too shy and we don't want to
make fools of ourselves. It was all great fun, but once the writers sat at the
typewriters they took it very seriously. They're very competitive and wanted
to write the best they could.

PS: If the audience is rooting for the writers and against the judges, then it really validates the writer in a way they seldom are in this country.

MHK: Yes. What I was wondering is whether I can adapt it to my classroom, without bringing in liquor. It could be done even more wonderfully with those computers where you can type and then project the computer image onto a big screen. So you could hook up the four computers and the audience could see everything you're doing while you're doing it. They wouldn't have to wait until it was read out loud. Everyone could see the process.

PS: I'm interested in this notion of a nation consciously trying to build a multicultural society. So much of *Tripmaster Monkey* is about that. One thing I hear a lot from students when we talk is the idea that we have an *obligation* to build this inclusive society, but not that we have the *opportunity* to do this—that our whole world will be more exciting when we think of ourselves this way.

MHK: Yes. In Australia they want to consciously head off some of the horrible problems that we have here. Their history is so similar to the U.S. They do have a lot of racial problems. They wiped out their aborigines. Terrible things. They have had an all white immigration policy. But right now they've decided to open their country. They have a government policy to try to figure out how to have a harmonious multicultural society. There's lots of propaganda on television. And they have symposiums, and courses, and their politicians are always talking about it. There's a lot of silliness and a lot of rhetoric too. But they're at least trying to do something. I was just watching television and they would have these thirty-second propaganda ads on "Let's get together multiculturally!" They'll have a little scene that looks like a beer ad, and it will have all these people of different races in there laughing and drinking together and they're having a good time. And then it'll say "Let's get along," or something. I mean in one way it's embarrassing but in another way, they have to do this, they have to do these propaganda things because we aren't giving it to them in literature or in the movies. Artists aren't doing them.

PS: One of the things I've been surprised people have not talked more about is the inclusive quality of your multiculturalism, and your allusions: not just the presentation of America as a place that includes Chinese legends and particularly the Monkey King saga, but as a territory where Rilke's language meets Barbie dolls and B film plots. *Tripmaster* is such a culturally scattered and accumulative book. Part of what impressed me was the way you insist on that manacling of everything—that all these different worlds have to start talking to each other. It seemed daring to take a chance on that with the kind of unspoken injunction in our culture not to allude to things people might not know.

MHK: Yes, that's a problem, with good friends saying that *Tripmaster* needs an appendix or footnotes. Even from the beginning though, from *The Woman Warrior*, I had reviewers who wanted me to explain more. The problem of course is that most readers in America know nothing about Chinese American culture and so I easily could have tried to explain everything, but then there would have been too much exposition. It was even more of a problem when I was writing *China Men*, because that really is a history book, and I had to think about exactly what I could expect a reader to know, and how much could I expect a reader to go to the library and look up. And I had to be provocative enough in the book so that people will go to the library and look things up. I was constantly choosing, constantly thinking, "Does that break up the rhythm of saying?"—thinking: yes, that would be a good place to do it. I just stuck that "Laws" chapter right in the middle because I thought that if I put that chapter at the end people would skip it so I thought that if I put it right there people would have to stumble over it one way or another. So I've had to come up with tricks, even changing the structure of a genre, to try to compensate for people's ignorance and encourage them to do research.

PS: One of the things I like about *The Woman Warrior* is how much you use the dictionary yourself as a narrator/character. It's a great tool for a teacher, because you can point to the narrator's own need to study the world she comes from.

MHK: Yes. In a way, having been a teacher for so long, I can't keep that pedagogical spirit out of the books. Reviewers have said that too, that it goes on for too long, that sense that I'm trying to educate a reader. Maybe that's got to be part of the novel too. Why not also teach? One of the most wonderful feelings is when you learn something.

PS: And along with that there's the moment when you realize that you're confused, and interested enough to want to figure something out.

MHK: How do you know? How do we acquire knowledge? One of the ways is go to the dictionary. One of the ways is go to the library. One way is to talk to the old people. Another way is to confront people who are difficult and keep your eyes open.

PS: The other thing I thought you did so wonderfully, and do so frequently, is to change stories, especially in your juxtapositions. To say, "I can't just take something from the past and repeat it; it has to become my story. But this is what I grew up with, this is how I heard it," and then to put those stories of your growing up against other stories, from different literary traditions.

MHK: Juxtaposing different stories is very exciting. Putting all that Rilke, that beautiful, elegant translated Rilkean language next to this Chinese American language calls all kinds of things into question, such as what is beautiful, and what is understandable, and what do you aspire to.

PS: Some graduate students in my class did brief response papers as they were rereading *The Woman Warrior*, and one was a piece in which a woman set quotes from *The Scarlet Letter* against comments from "No Name Woman" in *The Woman Warrior*, explaining how reading your story in relation to Hawthorne not only changed *The Woman Warrior* but changed the Hawthorne novel as well.

MHK: Oh, that's wonderful, to see that happen before your eyes. That's what deconstruction is for, to help us see how new knowledge changes the past. You can't see anymore in the same way that you had. Someone recently was telling me about seeing *Help*, you know the Beatles' movie, after reading *The Satanic Verses*, and how he realized that all the villains that are chasing the Beatles are wearing headdresses and Beduoin clothing and dark glasses and are vaguely Indian-looking people. All from the experience of seeing how Salman Rushdie writes about England.

PS: You have a very strong sense of your—I don't want to say obligation, but—place in the world as a writer. Not that you can change the world yourself, by single things you say, but that you should be there speaking for the right rather than the wrong? You've talked in some interviews about needing to grow up to be wiser in order to write a wiser book, and you argue that it requires a good, humane person to write a good book.

MHK: That's just an idea that's come to me recently. I used to want to get away from any political discussion because I thought it was important that the writer writes anything and there shouldn't be any usefulness to what we write. We do it for the fun of it and for art's sake, and should not think about constraints. But now I'm beginning to see that it may be the obligation of artists to have a vision of a future. We need an idea before we can create who we are and what our society is. It seems to me there's a horrible emergency right now. We seem to be on the brink of destroying everything. And it seems I have this power to envision a healthy society, healthy human beings, and I need to maybe create new myths.

PS: It's interesting to hear you say that because so much of the way people seem to read and write about the first two books is that in them you've created a vision of the past—changing your relation to the "no name woman," and changing your relation to the mother in *The Woman Warrior*. But that's also a way to create a vision of the future, by creating a past to live on, move from.

MHK: It's about building a human psyche and how to get straight with parents and ancestors and then become able to intuit, to realize yourself as a human being.

PS: One of the things I was struck with in *Tripmaster* was your tribute to your friends. It seemed an essential part of the book to me. As you told where you got the material for many of the stories in the novels, it was like saying that though these stories are my stories, they're my stories because these people surrounded me with their own stories. That the book came from everyday relationships that in turn help create the imaginary world.

MHK: I'm glad you like that. It just struck me as such a right thing to do, putting that list in. It's more than just an acknowledgment; it's the admission that we're part of something, that when we're alone writing we're not alone— that the imaginative life and the real life intertwine. That's my community. Some people have used that in a negative way. There's some Asian American critics, there's been a couple articles that say well it's obvious this is nothing but a *roman à clef*, and here's evidence. Oh, you're reminding me that my British publisher took that list and put it in the front of the book. And at first I thought that this is very strange. But now I think it was a mistake because it gives away so much of what's going to happen. It really belongs at the end, when the reader knows about the adventures, images, and jokes, and then they see where they come from.

The stories come to me in lots of ways, you know; a name on the list doesn't just mean that they tell me a story that I later write down. Sometimes I watch them and it sets off something. Sometimes, they give me an opposite emotional reaction than the one I'm supposed to have and I've got to argue back with them. Or I don't like what they say, and I have to tell them what I think—disagreements trigger a whole lot of active creation. Another way is that someone does an action out in the world, an antic, that is just so perfect. Somebody will do something that just fits what I want and I've prepared myself to see it because I've started out writing this book. People will come up with just the right gesture, just the right thing to say, just the right clothes. That happens all the time.

PS: It seemed to me that it was the parallel for you as a writer to what Wittman was trying to do by putting the community into the play and insisting that there was a place for everyone. And it underlined what you said in other interviews, that you wanted people to write stories about the stories you write—that *Tripmaster* should be an urging to other creations.

MHK: Yeah, that's what I mean by a fake book, that it should be all-continuing.

PS: We were talking before about how the world is changed by certain experiences which alter our sense of the past. Do you get that sense yourself, as a writer, that by your writing your own sense of the world has changed, or your sense of how the world is perceived and understood by your readers changes?

MHK: Do you mean do I think that writing has an effect out there?

PS: Out there, but also inside. In writing about your family, in writing about San Francisco in the 1960s, has your sense of those worlds altered for you?

MHK: Oh, yeah. I think that I change and the world changes as I work. As I write I see that this "I" pronoun that I began with—I was thirty years writing in this first person—and in the last fifteen years or so I've grown so that now I'm writing with an omniscient narrator and have a much larger view. I am much less concerned about one small self. And I think I can trace the enlarging vision from the beginning to now.

I also see myself changing the language out there. Just as one example, when I went about publicizing *China Men*, so many people would say "chinamen." They'd read the cover and see "chinamen." And I would have to correct them and explain that I made it two separate words because that's the way Chinese language is: it's all these monosyllabic single words. And how the capital C and capital M add dignity and it doesn't slur. I'd have to explain all that to people. And now nine years later I find that when people introduce my titles, they say "China . . . Men," and I see that I've changed the way their mouths work. So I've straightened up the language a little bit. You know maybe writers have to do that one word at a time. I feel a lot of triumph in just that one word.

PS: Does it feel different to be living in California again after your years in Hawaii? Is there a particular sense of place that you have here that you did not have in Hawaii?

MHK: It feels like being home. I understand things here. I feel I can say "we" and I don't have to worry—I mean I know who I mean when I say "we." Whereas in Hawaii I was always a stranger. The Hawaiian culture cultivates that. Because the Hawaiians are a beleaguered people, or a colonized people, they make up all kinds of defenses. And I think one of the defenses is that they have a wonderful secret culture that is the heart of Hawaii. And the rest of us can never know about it. And then of course you don't push to know about it because they lost everything: they lost the land and they lost the monarchy. Are you going to take this secret or myth away also? So you don't want to do that. Which means that I as a writer come to a place where their main stories are not mine, and people are saying that there are stories that you can't know about. Actually, it's all right not to know about them, but on the other hand I can't ever say "We Hawaiians think this or that."

PS: But you felt that you could speak for others as a resident of Stockton, where you grew up? I've often wondered about the dense sense of place I feel in all your writing. Is this issue of place one you think about a lot, one you've reconsidered because of your time in Hawaii?

MHK: The sense of place has to do with everything. One of the mottos that has given me a lot of help and inspiration is remembering that somewhere—I think it's in *The Tempest*—Shakespeare said that one of the goals of the writer and the artist is to give to airy nothing local habitation and a name. *The Tempest* is a play about a place, about finding a Brave New World. And it's about human beings maybe getting another chance again and going off to an island where they could figure out what it means to start community, or find out what it is to love.

So, that phrase—to give to airy nothing local habitation and a name. I've decided that what that means is that abstract ideas and values are nothing. They're invisible, they're not dramatic, and they're not interesting unless you can localize them, can give them physical manifestation, can write about an actual place. You have to ground your ideas. We have to embody ideas in our characters and act them out in life. Ideas about altruism or a vision about a Brave New World. In art, what I think he's saying is to write about an actual place, write flesh-and-blood people, give them all ideas and standards. And then see whether they can take the test of a physical place, see whether their ideas hold up as they try to live in real life.

I feel that my years in Hawaii taught me a lot about local habitation in many senses. In the Hawaiian language and in Hawaii, there's a word, *aina*. It's a common word, it's part of the state motto that we respect the *aina*. A simple English translation for it is "the land." But it's more than the land because when you talk about *aina*, you also talk about the spirit of the people. So this is very political. We're talking about native peoples who believe that a human being is alive because of a relationship with the land. The land has a spirit, it has energy and power and we grow out of it, like trees. When the people lose the land, they die. Native Americans believe this too. If your roots are cut off then you die, you're nothing. I think that this explains why the young Hawaiians and the young Native Americans die in all kinds of ways—suicides, accidents, the drinking and all that.

I think maybe it's unclear to us, this connection with the land—to us urban people. Coming from Stockton, an agricultural place, this is the way I under-stand it. If you eat grapes that are grown on a piece of earth, then you know where it is and what's it like and know the taste of grapes from there. And then you try the grapes or the plums from another piece of earth. You will see, you will taste, a completely different taste. Each piece of earth produces fruit that just tastes the way it does because of that land. Your tasting of it is your knowledge of what that's like—it connects you.

I think urban people, we don't even know where the grapes come from. But we have a chance, because we do live in agricultural country. Just try how it tastes very different. The *people* that are grown on a piece of land are very different from the people who are grown on another piece of land. This is because there is a history and a myth and a connection to land. You can look at it in property rights terms. You can think of the war in Israel and the Left Bank. That all has to do with people who are grown in a land and people who have a theoretical relationship to the land—different kinds of ownership.

PS: And Stockton?

MHK: I come from Stockton. A lot of writing has not come from Stockton because Stockton is not one of your famous cities. It's not Troy, it's not New

York, it's not a lot of things. But what is it? It's an accident of birth, that I was born in Stockton. And then I have all kinds of ambitions to be a great writer. OK. Then I think, how am I going to be a great writer when my material is Stockton? But I am formed by Stockton and I came out of that soil. Somehow who I am is in relationship to that earth. It became my task to figure out what Stockton is and who I am in relation to it.

I think that there is a lot in Stockton that is anti-beauty, anti-intellectual, even anti-life. All my life, I've lived in and around Skid Row in Stockton. I say all my life because even when I went away to school or I went to live in Hawaii, I always came back to Stockton because that's where my parents are and my roots and my brothers and sisters, and my Chinatown. I keep coming back, and it's anti-life and anti-beauty. When I go to my house, my parents' house, I walk through devastation. There are all these stoned people, hoboes, dealers, and criminals. There are people lying there and I don't know whether they're alive or dead. It's dangerous. I have to think of ways to walk through there without getting hurt. That forms my personality. I have to think of altruism, do what I am going to do about these people. So, though there is a lot which is against life and against beauty and the intimate, maybe it's the best place in the world for a writer to grow up because those are the hardest problems that face humankind, right there in front of me. And I have to figure out how to live—not just survive that, but how to make beauty out of that. How to make sense of that? What are our social responsibilities? And then the big question—how do you make community out of that? There's just so many Stockton stories, and it's a matter of knowing them and knowing that they are significant, that I don't need to go to New York for my stories.

PS: Do you still feel this strong identification with Stockton as a source of stories, as a place—this sense that the beauty in your writing has to start from there?

MHK: Yes. There was an amazing Chinatown in Stockton which is the one that I write about in *The Woman Warrior*. The Chinatown in Stockton is very different from the Chinatown in San Francisco. The Chinatown in San Francisco is seeable. It's defined. We know pretty much what it is. It makes us think that that's what we look for when we look for Chinatown in Stockton. But the Chinatown in Stockton looks nothing like the Chinatown in San Francisco. The people are spread out. There is a communal spirit just because it's spirit, but not because of a place. It's only one small block that was the place and then they built a freeway through it and wiped it out. So, what is a community when it doesn't even have a place? I connect this a lot with what Zionists were arguing: is Zion a physical place on the earth and should it be? Or is it a place of the heart and the spirit, and our job is to maintain our community with our imagination and with knowledge and history—but not with a place. I understood that well from Stockton because our Chinatown was just a block and then the freeway wiped it out. It was such an insult, because they didn't finish the freeway. They just made it go through China-town and it stopped right there. They ran out of money or politics or zoning or something, so for years and years and years it was just like that, stopped right there. So it wasn't for cars, it wasn't for anything. Then you get this paranoia. But we all knew that our community didn't have to be a place, so we continued thinking of it as a very strong community connected by its rituals and memories.

It becomes the task of the writer to find the beauty that's there. Ever since my books came out and I've gotten famous, Stockton keeps trying to figure out, how are we going to capitalize on this so we can make Stockton a place where tourists might want to come? For awhile, they had a lot of hope. They think that I wrote something beautiful about Stockton so maybe people would come there to see the land of the Woman Warrior. Some people have tried this after reading my book. They try to find some wonderful, beautiful place that I have in my books. Then they go to Stockton. They can't seem to grasp it.

There's another Stockton writer named Leonard Gardner who I think writes the true Stockton in *Fat City*. It's the Skid Row, it's the Filipino socie-ties with a boxing ring in the back. It's all these people fighting for their lives as they're boxing. It's revival tents. There's a big revival tent outside of Stockton and Jesus is supposed to come on a motorcycle. Stockton gives out these arts awards every year but they just won't give it to Leonard Gardner because he keeps reminding them that what is wonderful about Stockton is the Skid Row and the hoboes. I lived across the street from places like Catfish Row. There's a liquor store where all these black men are sitting talking story all day. Then once in awhile one of their wives would come and yell and scream, or make them come home. So, I could see that there's talk-story going on everywhere, it's not readily seeable by tourists who come from the outside with the eyes that are trained for the Chinatown San Francisco kind of stuff.

PS: So one of your purposes was, like Gardner, to give us a true Stockton, not a stereotyped San Francisco Chinatown imposed on a Valley world, and not some exoticized romantic image.

MHK: Yes. All of this has to do with a being good writer. A true historian or sociologist or writer who would go in there, learn to see, and learn to discover and find things that other people don't know about. There's all kinds of secrets in these wonderful Valley towns. So, one of my goals in writing *The Woman Warrior* and *China Men* was to get that idea of the San Joaquin Valley into the books and let the world know of that amazing life that takes place. That agricultural life, that is sort of like cities, but closer to the earth. There's all kinds of people there—characters formed by the land. I find it a mission for myself to get people to break through stereotypes that say that New York is the center of America and the rest of us are not the center of our own lives. So, I set out to discover the stories that are not in literature and to give them local habitation—to let us all know that that's universal, that we are really at the center of the universe, even though we're local. As I say that word—"local"—that's another really political word in Hawaii. A "local" is a person who looks like me. It's a fight against colonialism. Hawaii's already been colonized by England and by the U.S. but there are people who refuse to accept that, who want to bring back the monarchy. When you're colonized, it means that they take away your local stories, your local customs, your local identity—takes away your land, your *aina*. This is why all the surfer kids, when they say they're local, fight for their surfing spots, calling them local. The forces against being local are immense—urbanization, the wiping out of talk-stories by the print culture and the television culture, wiping out the myths. The missionaries came in and outlawed the hula and its chants. Taking away the hula took away the most local thing of all—the use of your own body. Your whole body remembers the movements of your ancestors and the chants. That's your voice, that's your breath. That celebrates your ancestors and your relation to the land. You're doing that dance on the earth, barefoot and moving like the trees, like the wind. You are there, you are so connected to everything. So, when the colonizers came and took all that away, it took away everything. And when Hawaiians say they're being local, the way Shakespeare said be local, they're trying to reconnect their roots to the earth and their roots to their ancestors.

It's the strangest thing. You know, if you live in California, you're a Californian. If you live in New York, you're a New Yorker. But if you live in Hawaii you can't say, "I'm a Hawaiian." That word only belongs to people with a certain blood. It's not just blood, but people who know the music, and who know the stories. So that was a very interesting relationship to place.

And I could live with that tension forever, I guess; it was very interesting.
But Stockton is where I grew up. Stockton is my soil. Coming back to California is more like fish in water. It's not exotic. It's no big deal. But it's
home.

Kingston at the University

Paul Skenazy / 1989

In November, 1989, Maxine Hong Kingston spent a week at the University of California, Santa Cruz, as a Regent's Lecturer. She read from her work, attended classes each day, and met with groups of faculty. The classes ranged from courses in American ethnicity to writing for re-entry women; from introductory sequences in Women's and American Studies to graduate Literature seminars. In each, Kingston responded to a range of questions with grace and generosity.

The interview that follows offers a condensation of that week's interchanges. Previously unpublished, it ranges widely, reflecting the varied contexts and questions, and the way Kingston herself would move off into story or idea in response to her questioners. Questions from students and faculty have been conflated under the common rubric "Audience," though exchanges were often far more conversational than that word implies.

Audience: Can you talk a little about the "No Name Woman" chapter in *The Woman Warrior*? We've been arguing a lot about what really happens to her and what it means.

Kingston: It seems a lot of readers want to know what happened to that aunt: was she raped? Did she have an affair? Was she terribly promiscuous? Was there one lover? Did she manage to live a sort of free love kind of life, even in the constraints of that village, or was she just a victim of history and social circumstances? I think the reason they ask is because I ask. I am the one that put the questions out there. I use my imagination to make up what could have been the possible ways that her life was. Given the conditions of those times and that culture, and the ways of a small village, those were the only ways that were open to a woman. And I meant to show that maybe her character was very foolish, or maybe very rebellious, or maybe brave and she took her freedom, regardless of the consequences. I gave you all the knowledge I know. I don't know which one of those things happened. That's why I put so many questions and doubts into the story.

But there's also a doubt about whether any of it happened at all, whether she existed at all. Maybe this is a story my mother made up just to scare me, one of those cautionary tales. It could be one of those rite of passage stories where I am going into puberty, and I could get into big trouble. She's saying, "Look at all the consequences. Everybody is going to turn against you and your family, and you will commit suicide and the kid will be killed." So maybe none of it ever happened.

Audience: Did it?

Kingston: Well, my sister, who is a social worker and works with foster children at a placement program in Stockton, wanted to know the truth. She's braver than me because I am indirect, I write about it, you know. She just faces everybody. Some of the paperwork that has to be done for the placement program for the foster kids is to take the genealogies of the biological parents. So she has all these blank sheets of genealogies and family trees from the welfare office. She brought these to my parents' house. Then she said that for the sake of her own daughters, she would like to have a genealogy from the horse's mouth, you know. And so my parents said, "Oh, OK," because they understand that "for the sake of your children," they understand that. So she starts interviewing them. We get my father and all his brothers, and then they went on to the children of the brothers. And then my sister said, "Oh, wasn't there a sister in here somewhere?" And then my father, he didn't say anything. My mother, at first, didn't say anything either, but then she said, "Oh, go ahead and tell her." And then he said, yes, he had a sister. So that makes me feel that the whole story is true. But that's as much as I know. He did not say what became of her. And just by his silence, I assume that what I surmised is so.

I think that that is a very terrible thing to do to a human being, to punish her by saying that we will act as if she never existed, strike her name from the book of life. And she will just disappear. It's a most terrible kind of murder—to take her out of memory. I now realize that what I did by writing down her story and giving it my concern and care and finding the words for it, is I have saved her. I realize now that this is the power of art. I gave her a life, I gave her history, I gave her immortality, I gave her meaning. Maybe that's the important part. I think the things that happen in life and on the planet are phenomena. It's just chaos, nothing, unless we can find its meaning. And by finding her meaning and giving that meaning to all of us, I retrieved her from the no-nameness, the nothing, and created her again. And I do feel that your reading it finishes this act of creativity. She lives because of your having read that story and having questions about it.

When I wrote *The Woman Warrior*, I thought that the first chapter is dark, and the second is happier, like sunlight. And I thought why not do the bright, happy, high chapter first, because then it will bring everybody in and then I can hit them with the hard stuff later! But then I thought, "No, no, no, that's not the way I lived it." That's not the way I am, not the way my life is. And so I decided I would lead off with this very difficult story, and people will just have to work through it. And then they can get to the rewards and the dessert later on. I also saw it as like the way creation works, you know, first there was the darkness, and then the next day God did the light.

Audience: When your sister questioned your parents about the aunt, did your parents feel better or more at ease about talking about the story?

Kingston: No. All that happened was what I told you. I think my father, just by saying yes, he had a sister and she belongs on the family tree, showed that he had made an acknowledgment. I don't really expect any more. Sometimes just one gesture shows a lot, you know.

Audience: So your family never accused you of betraying them?

Kingston: No, they never spoke to me about betrayal. My mother and father read my work in the Chinese pirated translations, with ready-made forms, like soap opera. I think soap opera has sort of a fake passion and fake revelation, which satisfies a lot of people. My mother, whose favorite book is *Gone with the Wind*, thinks that I wrote something really terrific. I don't think they realize the amount of anger and passion that I put into the book, the vehemence with which I write. Also, they're sort of overwhelmed by my success. Everybody else says its OK, so she thinks it must be OK.

But I know that this is a demand of many mothers. It's all these taboos, these horrible taboos. They come up over and over again. James Joyce talks about the cunning of the writer, and Toni Morrison said that when she was a kid, the women would be at the dining room table, you know, with a table-cloth that came almost to the floor, and she would hide underneath it and listen. All these women's thighs around her and their talk, and she soaked it up. But, again, this cunning, this hiding. You know, when I wrote "The Brother in Vietnam," I wrote it as real as I could, and then I met with my brother and I gave it to him. I said, this is what I wrote about you and you may do with it whatever you want. If you say don't publish it, I won't publish it. If you want to change it, change it. What he did was he gave me these amazing images, for example, of how Vietnam looked in the morning.

There are other people that I was worried about. Do you remember Crazy Mary? She was someone who just didn't survive culture shock. She's alive, but not mentally. I actually was pretty thoughtless about her. There are people that you knew when you were a kid and you feel that they belong to you.

You forget that they have their own existence. It never even occurred to me how thoughtless I was until I went to the Stockton mental hospital, to an art show. And there was a painting, with her name under it. That was the first time it occurred to me: "She's not mine. She's not just a product of my imagination. This is a real person."

And I kept worrying about it. But not too much later, I got a letter from a student at one of the colleges in Southern California, inviting me to come speak at the university. And then the second paragraph said, "I am Crazy Mary's nephew." What it said was: "Thank you for describing my aunt with such compassion. You have made me understand my family." It confirmed what I believe about art: that if you write and really concentrate and try to understand something, it does come through. If you try to understand things from other peoples' point of view, then you can arrive at being able to love the people you write about and resolve the angers.

Audience: I think probably the darkest part of "No Name Woman" for me is where in the raid, women took part and were equally as violent against another woman as the men were.

Kingston: Yes, and that reminds me that the people who did the foot binding of the little girls were women. Women did it to other women.

Audience: I wanted to ask you about the place where you say you told on the "no name woman," and that drowned ghosts were particularly formidable. Do you ever see her?

Kingston: Do I see her? Oh, only in the way that maybe you see her as a reader, you know. She haunts me as an injustice. And I get very upset about the waste of a human life. I don't understand how the Chinese set up a culture in which there was slavery, and the slaves were other Chinese—the women. I find that very perplexing. Those are the kinds of hauntings I get from that story, and in that sense I see her.

Audience: In the first chapter and the last, where you are giving voice to that which has been held silent, was this the liberating part of the writing for you?

Kingston: A writer is always contending with a great silence. The silence is all that's not human. I'm working against the silence of people who try to forget huge chunks of history. We get all excited about Tiananmen Square, and then a few weeks later it's gone. We have this amnesia, you know, that's the silence. And we have to constantly be awake and remember our history.

In every culture, there are all those strictures that say your voice is not your own, don't create yourself with your words. So I guess in all of my work, but especially in that one, there is this struggle against the silence.

Audience: What kind of writing experiences came before writing this book? And how did writing this book enable you to go on to the next two books?

Kingston: As far back as I can remember I was a storyteller, and before I could write, I was inventing stories. I don't know whether I was born that way, or whether it was the way I was raised. But I was raised in a storytelling culture, and one of my first memories, which I wrote about in *China Men*, is of the sound of horses outside. My uncles had vegetable wagons that were pulled by horses. They were old renovated stagecoaches, and I loved the rhythm of the hooves. My mother took me to the window, and she and I invented a song to sing to the uncles. She called it teasing. She'd say, "We're going to tease them," and then we'd sing the song for them. So she always raised me with, "Let's invent a song."

And I learned to talk with the chants of *The Woman Warrior*—she chanted it, and I just copied whatever I heard. And so I had that beginning of hearing and inventing songs and poems and stories, and reacting to life that way. But I started writing, actually writing, when I learned English. I have all kinds of miraculous feelings about the English language. I don't understand why I wouldn't write in the Chinese language, but it was when I learned English that I started writing down the stories. At first it was poetry, and it always rhymed. Oh, I just thought it was a miracle. It was almost like I heard it and wrote it down. And I just kept writing from there, trying all different forms. The stories in *The Woman Warrior*, but especially the ones in *China Men*—I had already seen visions of those stories. And I tried to write them over and over again. But it wasn't until I was in my thirties that I found the form. So by the time I got to *The Woman Warrior*, I'd been writing for thirty years because I had started when I was so young.

Audience: When you were talking about how your mother told you the "no name woman" story as a cautionary tale, I started thinking about the contradictions between her on the one hand silencing you, and at the same time giving you that legend, naming the aunt in a way and bringing her life. And the contradiction between giving you the inheritance of telling stories, but telling you cautionary stories.

Kingston: I hadn't thought of that before, but it wasn't me that started breaking the silence about the "no name woman." My mother did it; she's the first one that said, "Let's remember this story." And actually she's even the one that gave it a meaning, but then her meaning was just don't fool around or you're going to get pregnant and get in big trouble. But she broke the frozen ice. Then the struggle on my part was to say no to that meaning.

Audience: I was really interested in your mother's life as a doctor and then coming to America to raise a family. What was she like as a person before, with her life in China as a doctor?

Kingston: I quite often try to remember, or try to imagine, what she must have been like. Her medical education was western medicine; it wasn't acupuncture and herbs. She was taught by European doctors. But she does know so much about herbal medicine, and she has all kinds of rituals that are very different from a western medical education. So I know that the woman I see now is very different from the woman then. I have various ways to think about how she is. Lately, I don't know why, but she brought out from hiding somewhere, out of boxes, this wardrobe that she brought over from China, all these clothes. Even her clothes from New York. And she's been wearing them. She's lost weight so she fits all the clothes that she bought when she first came to this country. But then she also brought out all her Chinese gowns, and *I've* been wearing them. And what I've learned by wearing my mother's clothes is that she's so small. She's exactly my size. And all this time I thought my mother was enormous, you know, much taller, much heavier, much bigger in every way—bigger soul, bigger personality, bigger everything. Just being able to fit into her dresses is a kind of demythologizing. Not only that, but they're so pretty. And I look so good in them!

Audience: When you were writing about your mom, did you actively seek her out and talk, or did you rely on memories that you had from her talk-story over the years?

Kingston: I did the latter. I have a very hard time with direct confrontation. And so quite often I feel very sneaky. It's almost like the Heisenberg theory, where if you even look at something, you change its nature. And there's part of me that thinks I've got to pretend I'm not looking to see what happens. But when she read the book, she said, "This is so accurate. How did you know?"

Audience: It says a lot about her abilities to tell stories.
Kingston: Yeah, and my ability to hear and listen.

Audience: You talk about the writer making private space for herself. I wondered if you could contrast that with Virginia Woolf's concept of a room of one's own. When I teach that piece I have students, women of color students especially, who say "What does this have to say to me? I don't have a room, the women around me don't have a room." But you often talk of the writing itself as providing you with space.

Kingston: In most of my life, I've never had four walls and a floor and a roof. I have found that it really is perfectly adequate to have a corner of one's own. I thought it was the most richness when my parents had a pantry and I rearranged all the cans and preserves and everything so that I'd have a shelf of my own. I put my books and papers there and then I cleared out a space and I put a table in there and a chair and I locked the door. That was the most space that I had for a long time. We had a basement in my parents' house. My brothers and sisters, we would play city, and we would pretend that we had a town. Then we'd take chalk and divide up the space. So I took chalk and made another section of the basement and said that that was my room, and of course you hear the voices and there's a lot of people running around, but you can really concentrate and shut out noises and enter other worlds. There's another little spot—I used to get up in a tree and sit there. I had a little cigar box and put in my secret diaries and I'd sit up in the tree and write. Of course my brothers would read everything I wrote. But no, I don't think you literally need a whole room.

And you also have to know what you want, you have to know yourself well enough to know how you work best. I was very impressed at Jane Austen's house where she lived pretending that she was not a writer. In her house, to keep up this pretense, there was not an office or a room. Her table was just a small writing table, and it had a crack in the middle. This was in the living room, and they say there was a squeak in the door and if she heard the squeak, she knew someone was coming, so she'd put away her papers. They'd come in and she was just sitting there, sewing or whatever. So people have their spaces in the strangest places. Some writers even seem to prefer not to have a space, so that they can act as if nothing's going on. It also changes with different stages of your own life. Maybe in reaction to not having a room when I was young, I now have a bedroom and a computer room. I've got two writing rooms and then I don't even write in them all the time. I spread myself all over the place. In fact, I even have more than one house.

Audience: One kind of pressure I feel as an Asian American woman has to do with family expectations of me. I'm not supposed to want my own space, or want to be a writer. My parents still want me to be a nurse or a doctor, you know, to bring honor to the family, but I've come to the point where you just have to do stuff for yourself. You can still respect the elders, but you also respect yourself. My parents think I'm crazy for all that, but they don't say it to me anymore like they used to. They have to respect me a little bit, because I've come this far, and I've stuck to it.

Kingston: This reminds me of a horrifying story: it's morning, and everybody's starving to death and so the good son or daughter comes and cuts his or her finger off and puts it into the soup to feed the aging parents. That's a metaphor for martyrdom. Just recently I went to Europe and I noticed how many paintings are about martyrs cutting off an arm or leg as a blessing. Getting boiled in oil, covered with arrows, drawn and quartered. I've decided that is not a martyr tradition I want to be associated with. The only way you're really going to be able to give is if you have a lot inside of you, you know; if you're hollow inside, you're giving yourself away.

Audience: Did your family approve of your going to college? Did you feel supported?

Kingston: Yes, but at Berkeley, for the first time I had to learn to live without a family and a community. It was very hard. I started as an engineering major because I wanted to be practical and I wanted to find a way to make a living. When I went into the English Department I felt frivolous, like all I was doing was having fun. I was going to read and talk about books. But the education was in critical theory, and what was happening to me as a writer was that no sooner would I create something than I would criticize and destroy it. I kept thinking maybe I should be in a writing program. I think my standards were too high. But I used to go to the tennis courts in Berkeley. I just saw how faithful the tennis pros were. They just kept practicing and practicing, and they didn't take breaks all the time. I'd have my typewriter there and I thought, "I'm going to be just like them." And then I began.

Audience: Was your writing your primary creative outlet?

Kingston: I also sewed my own clothes most of my life. This is what I learned from my mother; I guess coming from a farm and being poor, if you're going to have any clothes, you'd better make them, including your underwear. And so I saw that as a very creative outlet, the sewing. And I remember clearly giving up the sewing when the writing was going very well.

But mostly there was painting; that has been very important to me. It makes me see. I am very visual. The visions, the images, come first. I find the words for them afterwards. I'm not an ear writer, the way I think James Joyce is a sound writer. But there's a narrative impulse in me, too. *China Men* started out, for example, when I kept seeing an image of a white triangle. I didn't know what to do with it. But I learned what it was because of something my father kept mentioning when he talked about stowing away on a ship from Cuba to come to New York. He was in a crate. He talked about looking through cracks when he was hiding, and he could see this triangle of white trouser legs. As a painter, all I would do is draw the triangle, but as a writer, I get to talk about how he came from China and got to Cuba—the story part.

I took a lot of painting courses when I went to Berkeley, but now what I do is sketch in pencil, which is the same way that I write. I write in pencil because I don't have to commit myself right away. You can write really lightly, too. You can have all the shades, so it's almost not there. And you can say to yourself, I'm not really writing anything!

Audience: Can you talk about your time teaching in Hawaii? Did you develop any special approaches to your teaching, especially to issues of how to encourage writing?

Kingston: There have been two ways that I try to approach teaching writing. One of them is that I want the students to be free to write about what they want. I then come at them with form and don't even touch the content. That's something that's theirs, that's personal. I tell them, for example, that all I want is a hundred pages of anything by the end of the semester. I did not grade on content or even style, but just quantity. I thought maybe that after they got bored with pages and pages of telling me what they ate every day, and what classes they took, that they would go more into their feelings and personal lives. The way I graded was a hundred pages was an A, 80 was a B, 60 was a C, 40 was a D, and 20 was an F. Actually I've had some wonderful, true writing, because some of them would be uninhibited and try to get through this as fast as possible, so just by going fast and putting down as much as they could, they were breaking through some kind of block.

Then I would doubt this method because I wondered if I was teaching them concrete things. When they get to college they don't even know how to shape writing. Also, teaching high school students, there was so much content that dealt with their personal lives, their emotional troubles as people. So it seemed like forms of therapy instead of class. Then I felt like I should be telling them what to write because they have to be taught to see a life. They think it's so ordinary. They think it's boring. They have to be taught to see the drama of their own lives. So I started developing exercises in which I give them experiences and I take them for walks and tell them what to look for. And improvisational exercises, as they might do in the theater department, where they take on characters. I set up scenes and they would improvise these scenes on their own.

In Hawaii a lot of my students were Japanese American, and a lot of what they enjoyed writing was love stories. Their love stories were always about blonde people, white people. These are the looks that are worthy of love, as they see it. This is all they see, so I would spend a lot of time correcting that. Mostly it was just a matter of asking them, well, what if this was a love story that had a person in it who looked like you? Can you just change it and see what happens? And I found that a number of things happen, because then the story had to open up to what happens when you bring this lover home to the family, and their reactions. And so it became more real, bringing in the social consequences of this relationship. I think this taught them to see the beauty of their own looks, and to break out of the stereotypes.

Audience: Were there specific issues about language and dialect that arose while teaching English in Hawaii?

Kingston: I taught in Hawaii for about seven years. They have a highly developed, wonderful pidgin English. Many of the problems of teaching English there are that both the Hawaiian language and pidgin are non-written languages. So as an English teacher it's a matter of coming in there with a form that is so rigid and codified. Spoken language changes so quickly, and it depends so much on voice that the most highly developed music on the Islands is chant and songs. And of course when you chant, your body also changes. The highest form of that is the hula. So then you come in there with a written language in which you don't need to move your body. I had so many problems of feeling like a missionary. We have 35 states that have an English-only law, but in Hawaii, the law is English and Hawaiian. They have two languages. I made many, many mistakes teaching, and sometimes when I run into old students I feel so guilty. I guess the best discovery was to think that I musn't just go into the classroom and tell them that English is the cash language and so, let's just learn it, and then you take care of pidgin on your own. That doesn't work because you need to also bring them along in pidgin. You need to be able to show them your respect for it, and teach them how to use pidgin better than how they do it. Pidgin has a very limited vocabulary, so I tried to teach them to write in English and pidgin. I wanted them to discover how to spell these sounds. That was very difficult. So I showed them that pidgin has its own syntax.

Audience: Did this approach help your students become more engaged?

Kingston: Yes and no. Discussion itself was a major problem because many of the students come from traditions where the kids don't talk. The silence can be so hostile, so hateful. Talking is what haoles do. In Hawaii, if you speak, it has to be true. But the kids had to pass a test in standard English even to get into grammar school, some of them, so the kids are sitting there asking, do we have to speak standard English?

Audience: Did it help that you yourself grew up speaking two languages?

Kingston: It probably helped me in the long run because I could see how students struggled with English, but maybe I'm also very unsympathetic, too, because there weren't any ESL programs when I was young, and I was just put into school where I flunked kindergarten, where I was given a zero IQ, and where I had to sit in the corner. There was no understanding of me as a student, and yet I learned English and I can use English in a very poetic way. So, in spite of everything, maybe I learned English and use it better because I had such a difficult struggle, and it made me try so hard. Sometimes I don't believe in techniques of teaching language, you know, ESL; maybe you don't even need it, maybe kids just kind of pick it up. But on the other hand, maybe I was a different kind of kid, and maybe there's more merciful ways of learning. Part of my education was also that I went to Chinese language schools. Six hours of American school and then three hours of Chinese school, so I learned the languages as two separate things, and there was no bridging or getting them mixed up.

Audience: How long did you go to Chinese school and what did you learn about Chinese literature? How did that background help you?

Kingston: I went to Chinese language school for seven years. The education is very archaic in that the method is the same as in classical times, which is to memorize. They didn't explain anything. It's just rote memory and learning many words that you don't hear used. At about the 6th or 7th year they began giving you literature, but in the beginning, almost everything is taught in forms, so everything was a kind of poetic language. Seventh grade is just barely beginning to be able to read real literature. It's just about ready to read the newspaper and I couldn't go on. But my parents gave me classical poetry. They sang it. They told classical sagas. In fact, *Robinson Crusoe* I got orally. I thought he was a Chinese guy. And Doctor Doolittle. I didn't know they were English literature. When I got to college I started labeling all this, and I thought, oh my gosh, I have had a real education in classical Chinese literature. Berkeley legitimized all that stuff for me.

Audience: You said you always knew you were a writer. Was the writing easy for you from the beginning?

Kingston: Oh no, no, no. I had all kinds of strictures to myself about "no name woman," of don't tell, just don't tell. Because these are shameful things. The first thing that freed me was that I thought to myself, "I don't need to publish this. I'll just write it for myself." And so I could be as ungrateful and ugly as I wanted to. I could put down forbidden emotions and thoughts. But then the next thing that happened was that the form of a short story, the form of a poem, the form of a novel, guides you to confronting all kinds of things and having characters confront one another. And then it guides you toward resolution, guides you toward climax so that you're going to say the forbidden and take the consequences.

As I described people, I found that I understood them more and more because I gave them so much attention. I even began to see things from their point of view, why they did some of the things they did. And then I thought, "These are loving portraits." So by the time I got through—and this would take about ten drafts—I thought, "What I've written isn't a lot of embarrassing gossip. I've made a piece of harmony in the world." And then I thought, "Yeah, now it's ready to publish."

What I'm hoping by saying this is that you will realize it's OK to write about the very worst people in your family and worst feelings that you might have about your loved ones. The writing process and the form itself will guide you to what it all means. And then inside of you resolution takes place, and you are at peace with all of that. And what you publish is showing human beings how life took place, and how life and love and positive things came out of the negative.

Audience: I just had a writing workshop and one of the things that came up for three or four different students was that we would talk about their papers and then they would say, "But is that interesting to you?" They were worried about being interesting to me, the teacher, and interesting to the other students. So I wanted to ask about when you discovered that there's something interesting about the world as you see it and the world you come from that is worth someone else knowing about.

Kingston: I think that if a person is young or in the early stages of writing, you just have to understand that the life that is yours, the family that is yours, is unique. Those are gifts, special gifts. Nobody else has those feelings and thoughts and people and your personality and the way it feels to be in your body. The hell with what is interesting to somebody else! It doesn't matter! The life that is given to you—you appreciate it and you play with it and you suppress it and you put it into words. If you're going to work to get other people to like it, you start to lose yourself because what you're doing is looking at it from another person's point of view. You're looking at someone else's standards of what's interesting and not interesting and then you start distorting just to be interesting. It's very necessary in order to live your own life that you yourself be interested.

Audience: When you look back at *The Woman Warrior*, are there things you wish you could alter or expand on?

Kingston: I guess it's been about twelve years or so since I've written it, and during that time I usually think that I perfected it. But new information comes to me. In the end of *The Woman Warrior*, for example, the girl knows that the older generation calls the younger people Ho Chi Kuei. In the book I say, "What does this mean?" I have the girl look the words up in the dictionary. There's a whole page in there. Now, Chinese being a language of homonyms (many words with the same sounds but maybe different tones or sometimes even the same tone) you can only figure out meanings from context. So when she tries to figure out what Ho Chi Kuei means, it seems to have myriads of meanings.

When I finished writing it that was all I knew. My hope was that readers would write and tell me. The first letter came and it was a person who said, "I know." Then I got really scared, as I always do in the presence of knowledge. This first person said that Ho Chi Kuei means "good earth papers," in the sense that you belong to this earth and you have the papers to prove it. Then they wrote the Chinese words, and I said, "OK, this is it. I have the answer now."

But then another letter came, and that letter said Ho Chi Kuei means "a good child ghost." That makes perfect sense too. It fit all the tones in the words. OK. So after awhile I get enough letters, each one with a different answer, to make me realize that I wrote it right in the first place by saying I don't know. So it's good that I left it open-ended.

Audience: What about the myths you use in the books?

Kingston: Yes, there are things that I wish I had been smarter or wiser about. In all my books, I take the old myths and I play with them, show how the myths change. And when they change here in America they become American myths. But now I'm feeling bad that there were whole chunks of the original versions that I left out, and I don't know why I didn't include them. Maybe it's because when something is all around you and is evident you don't always see it. Maybe fish don't see the water, you know, or we don't see the air because we're of it and we can't detach ourselves to see it.

One of the things that I wish that I had said about Fa Mu Lan, the Woman Warrior, was that she was a weaver. This is one of the first bits of knowledge I ever learned. The chant starts off with the sound—"chick-chick-chick"—of the loom going through the shuttle. "Chick" is also the word for weaving or knitting. To make a woman character a weaver is so wonderful because that is a woman's art, something that women have done through thousands of years, in all cultures. It's important to know that the Woman Warrior did women's work; she wasn't just a military hero. Also, I love it that the word "texture," which has to do with weaving, comes from the same root word as "text"—"text" in writing. So weaving and writing have a connection.

Another thing I would include is a different ending to the Woman Warrior myth. In the original chant, Fa Mu Lan finishes the war and she comes home to her village. Her whole family is still there. She's a general and a military hero. She gets off her horse and she tells her army to stay there for awhile. She goes inside the house and when she is inside she takes her armor off, puts on a beautiful gown, does up her hair and puts flowers in it so she is very beautiful and very feminine. Then she walks out and reveals to the army that she's a woman. And they are struck by her beauty and her femininity, and of course, they are shocked that they had gone through a war led by her in disguise and had never known. Maybe the reason I left that out was that when I was writing the book I wasn't ready for a mythic heroine who was so feminine. In this book I was still searching for an inspirational figure, an archetype of a woman who had masculine powers, because I needed so-called masculine powers to live the life that's in the book. When I was writing this book I was very troubled by feminine powers—they seemed like weaknesses. Remember there's a woman in the book who is stoned to death because they think that she is a spy for the Japanese? She has an ancient old-fashioned headdress with mirrors coming out and the people say that she's signaling the Japanese airplanes. That woman was very feminine. She had bound feet.

Her powers were in charming people with the way she walked and her nice clothes, her beautiful hat. In a terrible emergency such as the Japanese invasion, all she could do was put on her prettiest clothes. That's all the powers that women have had in many societies for a long time, and that woman has to die. As a writer I killed her off because we don't want to be that kind of woman anymore; it's not useful to us. Another character like that who dies is Moon Orchid. Moon Orchid has no working skills. She doesn't know how to do anything. She can't type. She can't even speak English. But she knows how to dress well. She has high heels, she's very pretty. So she dies, OK? The women who don't die are the powerful peasant types like Brave Orchid. She can figure out how to work in the fields and in the cannery. She finds for herself the kinds of powers that will help her make a life in America.

I left out the traditional ending of the Woman Warrior chant because I rejected that ending when I was younger. But now as I look back, I think it would be a great delight—a delight like Fa Mu Lan herself had—to show the soldiers that a woman is capable of everything. If the soldiers never knew that she was a woman, then it would be just another example of a great masculine military hero. So of course the right thing to do was to take her out of her disguise so that we women can get credit for everything that she did.

Audience: What about the title, the whole idea of the Woman Warrior?

Kingston: Yeah, I have often regretted calling the book *The Woman Warrior* because I have become more and more of a pacifist. Even as I was writing *The Woman Warrior*, I was finding a lot of dissatisfaction with having a military general as a hero. So I end the story with another mythic woman, Ts'ai Yen. I like her a lot better. Her important contribution was that she went into this tribe which fought with bows and arrows. They put a whistle on the arrows so that when they went through the air there were these death sounds—the music of battle. Ts'ai Yen took the same reeds that they made the knockwhistles from and made flutes. That's like beating swords into plowshares. Did you know that it was a fad after World War I to take empty shells and make flower vases out of them? People would squeeze the vases almost shut and then open them out and put flowers in them. Ts'ai Yen did something like that by making the flute. Then she composed music for that flute. So I like it that I ended the book with her. She's not as famous as Fa Mu Lan.

But there were also things that I left out of her story. She was far from

home and she was lonely among the barbarians, and she would look at the
geese going by. In China they call them "home flying geese" because they
seem to form words—when you look at the geese they do look like Chinese
words. She made a song that the geese are writing letters home for her and
they are taking her letters home. That is so beautiful. Sometimes life is so
evident and ordinary that you fail to recognize something special, you don't
see it.

Audience: I'm interested in names and naming. It's interesting how you
wrote about no name woman; I could sense how important it was that she
have some name in relation to her identity. Can you address that issue?

Kingston: That's wonderful, to connect up no name and naming. In "No
Name Woman," remember I talk about me and my sisters playing in the
sloughs? Stockton used to be filled with waterways and sloughs that were
filled with grasses and reeds and birds—and also with people who lived in
them. They were people with no community who lived alone. When we were
children, we would go in the sloughs and we would look for signs of these
strange people. One of them was a Chinese woman. I kept thinking she was
a witch. She had red rouge on one cheek and black on the other, and she had
wild hair. She always carried bunches of the river grasses and the tulles. I
was obsessed with her for a long time, and terrified. We kids had strategies
about how we would get away if we ever ran into her. Sometimes when you
saw the tulle grasses blowing, you thought: "Oh, my God, she's coming!"
She was a wild force of nature. And then my brother named her. He called
her Pia Na, which are just words he made up. But I think that his instinct was
that if you could name her, you could contain her.

OK. That's naming something fearful in the outer world. But naming the
self is also very important. In many cultures, including Chinese culture,
throughout your life you give yourself new names. You recognize new powers
in yourself. You're a new person. You recognize that and you honor it by
giving yourself a new name. I think that self-definition is very important. Did
you notice that the narrator of *The Woman Warrior* doesn't have a name? Her
name isn't Maxine; that's my name. I see this as a literary text that's very
separate from myself. Throughout, nobody calls her anything. The point is
that she is still in search of her name, she's still trying to find her powers,
she's still trying to find out who she is. And by the time I got to the end of
the book, I still didn't feel that I wanted to put a name to her. There would
be still more quests and struggles to go through.

I think it's also very interesting that we've just discovered this kind of naming here in this country. For example, when black people said black is beautiful—redefining what beauty is—a lot of black people found a new name. Like Cassius Clay became Muhammed Ali. And a lot of people put X into their names; many women also put X into their names during the feminist movement. It was saying I'm going to be free of father and husband. Many women would pick out a new name. In Chinese culture, though, I think it's very interesting that it was usually the men who found the new names. Really successful powerful Chinese women keep their names, like my mother. She said that if you become a professional woman, like a doctor, you keep your maiden name. Even when she came to America she kept it. I think what she's doing there is hanging on to her own identity, thinking: "I'm good enough already. I'm not going to change. I'm going to make this name the one that's admirable."

Audience: When you went to China, did you learn things that surprised you?

Kingston: There was a crisis for me when I went to China for the first time. We have a lot of immigrants and they will give you their memories of China—which means that they invent a China. There were memory villages; people actually made replicas. But the memories and the models were not the same as what's over there. In our imaginations we build our own versions. I wanted to describe the mythic China in my books—just record that and then go.

OK, so I recorded it and then I went. The fear was that when I got there I would see something so different that it would invalidate everything that I had written. But I went to my parents' villages, I went to the rooms that are described in "No Name Woman." I saw the well where she drowned. And I felt really good because I found that the China I had imagined is very much like the China that's there. The trip gave me a lot of faith in the power of my imagination. And I was also affirmed in my belief in talk-story—that the ancestors and my mother had passed on a tradition that's thousands of years old and yet entirely accurate. I had all kinds of affirmations.

At the same time, I was shocked at what close quarters the people lived in, how small the rooms are. I didn't describe the village right in "No Name Woman." I was imagining an American farm, with land, a farmhouse with a barn, and outhouses. People would come across the field from one farmhouse to another—remember when the mob comes? The way it really looks is like adobe huts, just like the adobe of the American Southwest, where house is added on house. Houses have common walls, and every family is adjoining and abutting every other family. There's vertical space and lofts but everything is very small, with dirt floors. And the lanes between the houses are so small, like alleys. And then there's something my parents call the great front door. Their great front door was even smaller than one of our average doors because in China they have raised thresholds, like on a ship. You step over them and then you enter a dirt floor. If I had known all that, I would have made all the spaces closer together, even more claustrophobic than the way I've written it.

But seeing it did make me understand much better why what the "no name woman" does was a great explosion in that village. When there is a huge family that lives in one room and then the other branch, the cousins and uncle and aunt, live in the next room, anything anybody does has significance for everybody else. Being there, I saw how anything you do changes the whole village.

Something else I saw in my father's village was the community life around the well. The well where the "no name woman" drowned is right next to the Hong family temple, the largest, grandest building in the village. (That was interesting to me too: in my father's village the center of the communal village life was a religious temple. When I went to my mother's village, the largest building—the one that had tiles and ceramic signs—was a music building. It made me realize the difference between my mother and my father. She was the one that came from a place that centered around performing for one another. She says that they stored all their drums and horns and musical instruments in there and every once in awhile the whole village would get in there and jam together. I just really love that about my mother's village.) But my father's village is the one I write about in "No Name Woman," and the center is the Hong family temple.

So I took pictures of it. I took pictures of a lot of things because I wanted to show these pictures to my parents when I got back and see what they remembered. I took pictures of the mountain behind my mother's village, for example, because I figured probably villages and huts change, but a mountain—that's not going to change. So I took all these pictures back to show my mother, thinking that I could provoke more talk-story from her. And she looked at the mountain, and she says: "Oh, is that still there? We were going to level it."

I found her college. You know the medical school I describe in the book where the ghost sat on her chest? Oh, the power of talk-story! A careful and wonderful reader in China read that my mother went to a medical school in Canton. I wrote down the name of the school, and this woman found it for me and took me there. When we got there people in the courtyard tried to kick us out. I said, "There was a medical school here." And one person said, "No, there was not a medical school here." She was a cadre leader. Then this old woman came up and she says, "Oh, I remember there was a school here and I remember the President"—she said his name—"and I remember the students." I knew then that I had found the school, so I took pictures of the neighborhood. I tried to show my mother those pictures but she didn't want to look at them, because during the Cultural Revolution the Red Guards had gone in there and killed the President and chased all the students out and closed the school. She somehow thought she was going to see pictures of dead bodies or blood or something.

But when my mother and father saw pictures of the family temple they told me that an activity for young men was to hang around on the steps of the temple, because the girls come to get water out of the well. The girls have these earthenware jars for the water, and the game was for the guys to whistle and harass the girls to see whether they could make them drop their jugs. My mother started telling me how she just hated going to get water because of the guys. She didn't tell me what they said to her, but once she got so shivery that she dropped her jug and went home and everybody scolded her.

So I got this new story and I got the placement of the temple, the sacred next to the profane stuff that was happening at the well. I wish I had had that for Chapter One, because it shows a lot of the sexual mores of the village. That kind of story would have helped modern American readers identify. It would have fit all the themes of that story too, which is about sex, human relationships, and the bondage of women. There's the lighthearted aspects of just whistling, but then there's the rest of the spectrum—the suicide and the illegitimate baby.

Audience: Did you have opportunities to speak about your writing in China? What kind of responses do you get?

Kingston: Oh, just amazing. I'm so gratified that in China they see me as a Chinese writer. I work really hard to be part of the American canon, so I was surprised when I got there that they had decided that I was part of the Chinese canon. They saw me as a hope because they are still coming out of the Cultural Revolution, and they are trying to repair some of the damage by having what they call roots literature. They are aware of Alex Haley and the roots writing that we've had here. And they thought that I had been working in roots all along and under wonderful, free circumstances. So they saw me as not only retrieving roots, but maybe pointing the direction in which they might go.

Audience: My question kind of splits into two parts. I really liked the "White Tigers" fantasy. When I was a kid I used to fantasize a lot, but I've had the most important writing experiences in essay form, which feels very direct to me. So I wondered, on the one hand, if you could talk a little bit more about what the fantasy meant to you as a child, and also, a little bit about your essay writing?

Kingston: I sympathize a lot with what you said about the essay form being direct. I think that my writing life as an adult has been shaped by the essay. With my Berkeley education, what I learned to write was the essay. I found essays very wonderful for thinking. "No Name Woman" actually started out as an essay, because I wanted a form that used reason and the mind. The stories seemed totally chaotic, this mob coming, suicide, and people behaving irrationally—that's a mess. But I wanted to approach it rationally, so I set out to write an essay. And as I wrote and rewrote, I found that the essay is really flexible in that it had this frame, this scaffolding, that I could hang on to. Having this structure gave me the ability to handle all of that irrational material. I framed it. The essay form is miraculous in how far you can stretch it. Within it you can tell stories, you can explore that ghost-like world, you can have an entire narrative. You can write all kinds of confusing things and then come out in another paragraph and tell people what it means.

Audience: What about the fantasizing?

Kingston: I'm just now beginning to realize how much of my life I've spent in fantasy. Probably it has a lot to do with having so many brothers and sisters and being the oldest. I never felt that I had room, and the way I made all the room in the world was to create a fantasy world. I think my main psychological problem is that when I have a problem, instead of dealing with it, I will go inside a fantasy world. I will make up all kinds of things about it, and I will even write a wonderful book about it rather than deal with it! One reason that I stopped writing this year is I just decided to be in the real world—to just face problems. I don't like to confront people, but I'll confront anybody now, people in the grocery store line, anything. It's my way of getting out of the fantasy world.

Audience: I was interested in the image of the white tiger. Can you talk about that a little bit?

Kingston: First, there really are white tigers, OK? There's a whole bunch of them at the Cincinnati Zoo, if you want to go see them. So this is a physical reality in our universe. Second, it is a myth in China. There's a constellation in the sky that's the white tiger, and there are legends about people who go on various kinds of quests who encounter white tigers. There's a sanctuary and a haven that's called the Mountains of the Two Dragons and the White Tigers, or something like that. There are 108 bandits who live at this place. There are many mythic places that they say the white tigers go. These places are like quest places. When you go searching for whatever you're meant to find, you go to these dangerous places; you go through all kinds of psychic and spiritual adventures of life and death. And if you do things right, you will see a white tiger and then you will come home and you will tell people about it. I always feel that that's the end of the quest—the quest is the going out and the finding and the coming home. The end is not just finding it, but it's the coming home, bringing your knowledge back to your people.

I also think of the white tigers as a joke, because in *The Woman Warrior* the little girl is saying that it's really dark out there, it's dark and it's snowing. She thinks the white tigers are all around. Maybe she's found them. But it's snowing, see, so you don't know if you've seen a white tiger. If the white tigers come to you, you have to be able to recognize them. But there's a lot of doubt sometimes. Doubt is one of the things we have to fight with inside of ourselves. Have I found something of value here? Is this it? Or is this just a figment in the snow?

Audience: In the very last chapter in the book, you speak of this beautiful song that the woman sang when she was out in the desert, and you say that "Eighteen stanzas have been handed down to your people." I wonder if they exist.

Kingston: The songs have been lost. I keep writing about things that are lost because I think that readers will find them. There were three books of peace that they say existed in China, but they're lost. Maybe we can find them by writing them, by envisioning what was in them. But what's wonderful is that even though the songs are lost, there's paintings of her, and there's a scroll that's in the Metropolitan Museum of Art. The scroll is golden because of the sand. It shows the tents of the barbarians, and it shows her and the flute.

Audience: You mentioned earlier your conflicts about using a metaphor of war in *The Woman Warrior*. I wondered if you could talk more about the impact that the 1960s and 1970s and the Vietnam War had on your writing?

Kingston: There are a lot of places in *The Woman Warrior* which bring people up to the present. It's not just a story about the ancient, mythic past, nor is it just a story about a present time of childhood. I remind people where I am at the moment that I'm writing the book, which is the early 1970s. The Vietnam War is just over, and there's still a lot of fallout from it. Many of the events actually take place during the Vietnam War in the Sixties. I place each of the events in war. I think it's pretty terrible, but in everybody's living experience, there's been a war, whether you've actually fought in it in another country, or whether you were here suffering or participating in another way. So the childhood sections of the book begin with my earliest memories, which were World War II. It's a child's view of World War II. There's watching the parents put up the blackout curtains, going to my first movie and being really horrified because it's a war movie. I remember it was black and white and it seemed like color had gone out of the world. The war's there in the movie as a lot of noise, a shooting scene that showed these soldiers who were screaming and people bleeding. I thought it was real. I started crying and had to be taken out of the theater.

Then there's another section about the Korean War. That war seemed very far away, even with the maps we would see everyday of the DMZ. The place where the Sixties and the Vietnam War showed up in *The Woman Warrior* is the chapter "At the Western Palace." I guess most people remember that as the story of the husband, but actually that is a war story, too. Maybe you noticed that the story begins with the scene at the airport. Soldiers and sailors are being shipped out to Vietnam. And Brave Orchid remembers that her son is on a ship and might be in Vietnam. I think that's very symbolic of the times, the migrations of people. During the Vietnam War, there was a darkness, a pall all over the world. I saw it. I could physically feel it. When I was in it, I'd forgotten what it was like to not have that. So I really didn't notice until after, in the Seventies. Of course there's other wars, like the Japanese invasion into China that Brave Orchid lived through. Lately I've been thinking about her in the way that we think about Vietnam veterans, as a victim of post-traumatic stress syndrome. We were in Stockton driving on the freeway through a very nice part of town, and there were all these trees and she said, "Oh, the reason they plant all these trees here is so when the Japanese bomb us, they won't be able to see our houses." After all those years, it's still there. It doesn't end.

I myself was not seeing clearly about war and peace. But now as I look back, I see that *China Men* picks up on that same topic more clearly, by actually having a whole chapter on the brother in Vietnam. I also feel that I continue that theme in *Tripmaster Monkey*. This one really is about the Sixties and being draft-age, and I lay down the options. You can go to Vietnam. Or you can get married and be a Kennedy-husband—that's what people called them. One of my brothers did that, the only one who didn't go to Vietnam. There were two who were in the military. And another one went to Canada. I have since met some amazing women who stayed at Niagara Falls and escorted men across the border. Niagara Falls is, of course, a honeymoon place, so you could go and pretend to get married and then go across the border for the honeymoon, but really she's escorting the man to safety. And then these women would come back across the border and take another one.

Audience: What kinds of reactions have you gotten to *Tripmaster Monkey* since it appeared?

Kingston: The last week or so, I have heard from three or four of my friends who told my husband that they don't like *Tripmaster Monkey*. They think Wittman is very obnoxious. They say, it doesn't feel good to be harangued by a wannabe Berkeley head for hours at a time. They say that there's no feelings, that it doesn't make them cry. I've been feeling a loss of confidence.

I wanted Wittman to be a human being whose mind is made up of all that he knows, all that he has read. And loaded with all of those ideals and values that he learned in the English department. He graduates and he thinks to himself, how am I going to apply this in the real world? So, I'm asking a really important question: what use is a liberal arts education? What use are those values? What kind of human being does it create?

When I was writing it I was thinking of Emma Bovary and Don Quixote, both of whom are people that were created by books. Both have tragic lives and I was thinking, I don't want this to happen. I think literature has wonderful, true ideals and values and visions and we embody them. Those are our burdens—the knowledge that we find at the end of the quest, and it's our task to bring it out into the real world. I thought I would write a book on what happens to you in the 1960s. It puzzles me a lot that my friends who struggled with these problems during the Sixties now look back on Wittman, who represents their youth, and say they don't like him. I'm trying to figure out why.

Audience: I'm one of those people who can only take Wittman in small doses. Especially at the beginning of the book. I felt like he was just this loner who wasn't seeing the people that were outside of himself. But when he started putting together the play is when I really started to take an interest in him. So I thought maybe you had done this on purpose—made us experience this kind of distance, and then changed our attitudes.

Kingston: Yes. I'm so glad that you found that. At the beginning of the book, I felt that I was writing in the tradition of the alienated young American hero, and some critics never saw past that. But what I wanted to show was that, yes, we, many of us, are alienated, troubled loners, but we really have to figure out a way to be in community. But community and families are falling apart. So, we have to make it up, each one of us. The book is actually a struggle against alienation into community.

Audience: To go back to your friends' reactions? One of the things that's difficult for those of us who lived and did college in the Sixties is that that is a hard time to identify with our own selves. Most of us have had to do what Wittman is resisting and that is compromise our principles. And I also think that Wittman's arrogance is so symptomatic of the Sixties. And that's not something I want to admit or enjoy thinking about.

Kingston: But you must be arrogant to say, "I am going to change the world." I mean that is so arrogant and yet you ought to say that.

Audience: That's a difficult thing, especially now, where the emphasis is on community. When Wittman creates community out of this arrogance, there's something saving about that. But it doesn't make him any more fun to be with.

Kingston: But also there was a huge paradox in the ending, where he joins his community by delivering a monologue. A lot of people like him the least when he's doing that. Some people feel very uncomfortable with it because they feel scolded.

Audience: I think that has to do with how you position yourself as a reader. A lot of us talked about how there is also a loss of guidance in our culture now, the family's fragmenting, and sometimes we do need somebody to talk to us as Wittman does. And Wittman's "I" is not totally alone. Whenever Wittman's getting out of line there's always someone else to push him back in line—community people do that.

Kingston: Yeah. They actually put on a marriage for him at the end. They give him a reception.

Audience: And that's what surrounds his soliloquy. So *Tripmaster* doesn't just end with "I I I I I." When he brings his script to the community, it changes. One of the things that I keep looking for as a reader is a model for reading. And it seems to me that one of the models for reading in that speech is the imperative to harangue *Tripmaster Monkey*—there's a certain responsibility for us as readers, insistence even, that if we want to join the play, we have to start writing an answer to Wittman.

Kingston: Oh, terrific. Because you see, I am not completely resolved either about Wittman. He has an idea. He's going to create community by putting on theater. He will use an artistic form, create a communal ritual. But that's not enough. The war is still going on in Vietnam, the civil rights marches are still going on, he has not solved the world's problems by putting on one show! There's gotta be another one and another one. This is why I wrote the show and then I wrote the speech, coming afterwards, because he's saying he's not satisfied yet. There's more work to be done. You need to answer his answers.

Audience: Monkey doesn't sit still.
Kingston: No, he doesn't. No, no, no.

Audience: I have a different set of complaints, or concerns, about *Tripmaster*. Do you have an intended audience for the book, or is it the same audience as for *China Men* and *The Woman Warrior*?

Kingston: You know, I'm not like some writers who are very specific about their audience. Cheever talks about looking into the woods and he sees somebody walking there and he's writing for that person. My sense of an audience is very wide—maybe people in the distant future—in a sense, the universe. My audience is not limited to the living. I am not just thinking of Chinese Americans or white Americans. I've spent ten years of my life being a high school teacher, and I feel such an impulse to educate and enlighten. When I stood in front of high school kids, I felt that everything I said had to reach every one of them—the kid with the lowest IQ and the genius kid, and kids of all racial and economic backgrounds. As I read the reviews for *Trip-*

master Monkey, though, I began to feel that I had left some people behind, which I never thought of as I was writing it.

Audience: That's exactly my concern. I think it's pretty much only available to very literate people. It seems to me that *Tripmaster* leaves out people who don't know how to work with the allusiveness of those opening sections.

Kingston: An educated audience would get more out of it in that they would have the fun of puzzling the allusions out. But I'm hoping that readers who weren't English majors would get something out of it too. They don't have to figure out that some remark came from Beckett or Joyce. There's a substance there anyway, I was hoping, so even if they don't get every single layer, they get the essence.

Audience: Well, I come from an uneducated family. I'm the first member of my family to go to college and I came to college late. I always feel like everybody else knows something that I don't know, which I realize a lot of people feel like, but oftentimes in my case it turns out to be true. I put my foot in my mouth all the time, and it's one of the reasons I talk very loudly and very aggressively because people that way don't argue with me. I know that there are allusions going on in this book and I know that I'm missing a lot of them, and so I feel challenged. I feel like if I don't get all of them, I'm ignorant, and so the book gives me an inferiority complex as I'm reading it.

Kingston: But *The Woman Warrior* also has a lot of allusions that I know a lot of people did not get. And yet, people don't seem to have that same kind of frustration.

Audience: They expect it more. And there's an access. You have a way of drawing us into it.

Kingston: I'm your guide.

Audience: Yeah, and it really reaches that child in me, that deep level of a child that's lost in the world; that's part of the power of that book. In *Tripmaster*, we don't have that emotional rush to help us across the chasm.

Kingston: I just assumed that this was for the common reader. There is a theme of being inside and outside, being alone or being in community—the struggle to break out of isolating delusions and social circumstances and communicate with another person. And that means how to be inclusive as a writer who works with material that people often see as exotic or strange. Exotic means being pushed out, otherness. That's something that I struggle with, wanting not to be exotic. And yet exoticism has a lot to do with mystery and beauty and we don't want to throw out the baby with the bath water.

Audience: The thing about *The Woman Warrior* is that the places where one would feel excluded, it's easy enough to chalk those up to ethnic differences. At least if you're not Chinese American, you don't have to feel like you should have known the allusions that are there.

Kingston: Oh, but in this one I've got Western allusions, which you guys ought to know, because you're born with them.

Audience: This connects to a more general problem for me of what we do with unknowingness and difference. What is our response to cultural confusion, especially in a multicultural world. What do we do when we don't know the code systems of any social occasion, whether it be a reading occasion or a multicultural one? When do we feel our ignorance as a test we've failed, and when do we feel it as a challenge—"I can handle this,"—and when do we feel it as a privilege or right—"There's no problem, I've been trained for this all my life."

Kingston: Oh, you've said so much. I guess as a minority person in America, and with a lot of perceptions that English is not my language, there is a lot of leaving me out of this culture. So a lot of my work is appropriation. I'm going to appropriate this job and these books and this language—the American language. I'm going to appropriate this country. So a lot of the allusions are to say that the Joycean soul, this Rilkean romantic poetic soul, is mine. But the way that you're all talking, it seems like I put those allusions out there to give you pain and trouble. I meant them to be fun; that was my whole point. Maybe the greatest joy of my life is to read. I love it, it's pleasurable, it's sensual. So the allusions were just my playing with my books, you know.

For me, writing *Tripmaster* was such a great relief. In the first two books, I felt that I was translating a culture for everyone. I not only had to translate the people's words, but I had to translate a whole world, all of China and its myths and history. It felt like a burden to me. And, there was a big part of me that just wanted to use everything that I know, to use the language at the hardest level that I can work it, the American language, the language that I hear and speak. In *The Woman Warrior* and *China Men*, I kept putting it aside. Then suddenly it was like, oh, I'm going to be free, I'm going to put anything I want in this. So with *Tripmaster*, I said I'm just going to play with all the books that I read and it felt to me like an outpouring of things that I had been holding back and denying. I felt some really exciting things were happening with the language in the Sixties because people were finding that vocabulary for psychedelic states or visions or social action. But as I was working with that language, I saw too how it had its roots a hundred years ago in Whitman. So if it goes back a hundred years to Whitman, then it goes back thirty more to Poe. I feel very much in that tradition, showing people how 1960 was using language of the 1860s. Because we don't remember. Walt Whitman said, "Look to the East, that's also your motherland." He already had that idea that our myths are not just from Europe, but from Asia. So I'm saying, "Look at Asia," because we already know that we come from Europe. For a long time when we say classical, we meant Greek and Roman. And I'm saying, "Look, there's more classics, more."

Audience: How do you respond to the attack on you and other Asian American women as emasculating men in the community?

Kingston: A lot of Asian American history is masculine history, because the women didn't come until very recently. For 100 years Chinatown was masculine—men founded and lived in Chinatown, and all the work that was here was done by men. It's only been in the last 40 or 50 years that we've had any feminine history in this country. Okay, so what happens when all our writers are women? The men critics say, "You have feminized our history, and you emasculate us when you do that."

But it's not just a literary argument. In *Tripmaster*, I'm dealing with a relationship between Asian American men and women. And in real life it's really bad, just like what's going on between the masculine critics and the feminine writers. Seventy-five percent of us marry people of other races. We'll do anything to get away from each other. This is what's going on in my book. Nanci, who's a Chinese American woman, is very beautiful, and Wittman and her are about that far apart all the time. But there's another Chinese American girl that he meets on the bus. They can't stand each other. It's a physical aversion that they have, which has a lot to do with not appreciating your own beauty, with not understanding the great message of the 1960s, the "black is beautiful" lesson. So the only girl that Wittman really gets it on with is Taña, who is the stereotype of the white beauty, the California girl that you see in all the ads. Wittman's been brainwashed to appreciate that type. So they have a relationship, but look how distant it is. It's not great, passionate love. *Tripmaster* doesn't have that kind of warm, passionate love scene. And it's because of shortcomings in the characters and shortcomings in our society.

There is something else I want to say here about how men and women are inside of myths. A few years ago, I got a contract to begin making a movie of *The Woman Warrior*. In getting ready, we interviewed a lot of actresses. I think I know personally every Asian American actress in America, in the world, and it upset me that it was really easy to find the Moon Orchid character. There's a lot of delicate, feminine, pretty women that are sort of beautiful but flighty. Everyone wanted to play Moon Orchid, and nobody wanted to be Brave Orchid. Nobody. Here is this strong peasant woman with big feet who talks loud. We can't say this is just about Chinese stuff. This is about America. There is a standard of beauty going around in America that you have to be weak and delicate. And there isn't the other type, this strong type. People don't agree that that is beautiful. These are myths that we buy into, and the question of how we get out of them is the question of how we are going to get free. I just went to this series of Buddhist retreats, and there was one with just Asian women. Just Asian women for three days and we could not see anybody else: no TV. We were at the studio of a painter who paints Asian-looking goddesses. Big paintings, so I was surrounded by the paintings and by Asian women for three days. And by the end of the time, I had rediscovered the beauty of Asian women. Most of the time, the TV is showing blonde people, Barbie dolls, and advertising that says you are worthy of love if you look like this.

And that's part of what I'm struggling with where Taña and Wittman fall in love. The politics of love. I mean, people seem to fall in love with somebody and they think it's personal. Just that special face and person and body. But it's not personal. It has to do with all of your history, with human history that conditions you. When I say that seventy-five percent of Asian Americans marry people of other races, it has to do with being assimilated, it has to do with visions of what's exotic and what's not exotic, it has to do with wars and migrations. It surprises me how much thought, philosophy and values actually do influence feelings, may even cause feelings.

Audience: Is Wittman trying to free himself from the politics of love by saying, "You can set your mind to loving anybody out on the street"?

Kingston: Yes, that's what he's saying. He sets himself up to say, "I can love anybody." But then he manages to pick this gorgeous woman to say, "Oh, I'm going to really try to love her."

Audience: I want to switch subjects. When I was reading *China Men*, I got interested in some of the problems with language in the book, with translating and the devices you used to express ideographs, as opposed to English. If you think of language as sort of the filter through which you organize your relationship with the outer world, some languages, like English, operate by difference, to establish that this is one thing as opposed to something else. But from everything I could gather, Chinese seems to work to organize reality in terms of relationship. Like this is a chair because it's wood and it's cloth—additives.

Kingston: And by context. Yes, it's just like that! But then Chinese also gets the smallest particles too because each word and each sound are just one. It works in small particles in the sense that one word is one sound. I feel really fortunate that I have those two languages of Chinese and English because they really develop both sides of your brain. And another wonderful thing that happens in Chinese language, not now maybe, but in classical times, was a poet is somebody who can write and sing and paint his poem. See how integrated that is? All those parts of your body are connected. You're not fragmented. Even now, the poets still do calligraphy. When I was in China they would paint these beautiful poems and give them away as presents. And another aspect of Chinese language is the music, because it's a music of homonyms. You can have a sound and then maybe ten words are the same sound, but the way you get meaning is by the tone, the pitch. And the other way that you get the meaning is context, meaning does come from relationships, which are not just linguistic but familiar as well.

Audience: I have a question before I have to go. I've been teaching *The Woman Warrior* and I'm about to move to *Beloved*. Do you have any sense of the connections between the two of you as writers?

Kingston: What a good question! Toni Morrison and I and Leslie Marmon Silko traveled through China together five years ago, with Allen Ginsberg, Gary Snyder, and Francine du Plessix Gray. And during that time Toni was working on *Beloved*, and I was working on *Tripmaster Monkey* and Leslie Silko was working on this novel that is almost finished, *Almanac of the Dead*. I felt that we had the burden of these novels. I especially saw it in Leslie because she has a vision of a war between North and South America, which means that that war was going on inside of her psyche. Toni Morrison talked about her method of writing—she saw the novel like a big painting, all black, and then there's orange over here and blue over here. So she thinks about various incidents in color terms: because maybe we have some blood red over here, we've got to balance with some more over here. Like a painter. But what amazed me about this trip was the connection between us all. I knew I was going to look for my roots. I went to my village, found my family, and I found places that I was writing about. And I felt that Toni Morrison understood me completely. We would be going down a river and there would be a woman out washing clothes and Toni would stand there by the boat and say, "Goodbye, Maxine!" Like if it weren't for certain circumstances, I wouldn't be a famous writer, I'd be over there. She understood history.

As the trip went along, I felt like we all found our ancestors in China. Leslie Silko traveled a lot wearing her Laguna Pueblo clothes. Then we got up north, and everybody found these Mongolian rugs and Leslie pulled out this rug with the same design on it as on her poncho. And so she just knew there was a land bridge and people came across the land bridge. And then Ginsberg and Snyder are Buddhists. Gary Snyder had that book, *Cold Mountain Poems*, and we went to the Cold Mountain Monastery where he presented the poems to the monks that were there. And there was a painting on the wall that was the same painting that was in his book, which he identified with. And it felt really good because though the Chinese have wiped out the temples, his temple was still there. Allen Ginsberg went to a monastery that came from Tibetan teachings, and found symbols that he recognized, especially some kind of old bone that he worshipped. And Toni Morrison kept encapsulating us in various stories. The Chinese gave her a peasant hat which she wore throughout. She was very interested in what people did for a living, and she was there among the communes, the workers.

Those are the kinds of things that Toni Morrison picked up on. In *Beloved*, she is getting for the black people alive now, for all of us, she's getting the energy from the ancestors. The way you get energy from the ancestors is you find out the truth about them. Some of her images—putting a gag in a slave's mouth—that has to do with silence and voice and freedom. By writing that book she takes the gag out.

Toni is so important. The Chinese have had a lot of help remembering ancestors because we have a whole religion around it. But there's been all kinds of attacks against blacks to take the history away, take the voice away. That's what it means to put that gag on. Toni is someone who can tap into her ancestral memory, her collective unconscious.

Audience: Do you think people approach you differently as a fiction writer than as a nonfiction writer? I mean, there's this impulse, I think, to not separate an author from her work, and I was wondering if you get that kind of reaction.

Kingston: You're right, it is in the culture. And I can see it in the publishing business. They keep telling us that nonfiction sells, that fiction does not. People have very little faith in the imaginary world. I understand this impulse is also because we want to integrate many things—the moral stance of "I do what I say." This is a good side of what people want when they want a nonfiction writer.

Audience: And in an age when there's so much inauthenticity, to have any thread of authenticity connected between the work and the person who created it is important.

Kingston: Oh, good. Yes. But if I have this impulse to write autobiography in which I describe people in terms of their dream life, I didn't make that impulse up. I want to credit my ancestors for *The Woman Warrior* and *China Men*—it's not as if I made up these forms. It's because I am open to hearing talk-story. It's part of my culture. This is what my family does. I hope you see that talk-story actually reverberates. These stories don't end, they didn't have a beginning. I just wrote down parts of them. In talk-story, every time you tell a story it changes, it grows. In writing it doesn't. I hope you see that these stories live on, they generate other stories, these people have a life that continues. It makes me feel good to have an opportunity to continue the stories orally like this with you.

Audience: One of the things that strikes me is that you use the word "integrate" a lot. But in the type of integration you talk about, there's a great deal of insurrection, which means that it's not just the facts and the stories that you're talking about. It's also doing something to them that's going to change people.

Kingston: I like your word "insurrection." Most of us most of the time see the world as just the facts. But facts are hard and frozen, implacable. The artist comes in and breaks up the facts, breaks up the stereotypes, breaks up the static way that most of us look at the world.

Audience: Is it the reader's job to put facts back together, or are you going to do that for them in these books? Once the writer scrambles the facts in his or her imagination, then what do you do?

Kingston: If the writer has done a good job, they don't just scramble the facts; they transform them. You can't put them back together. If you tried, it wouldn't make sense any more. This is what I mean about the writer demythologizing, then making the new archetype. Not all writers do this. There are a lot of writers out there that remake certain myths over and over and over again. Like true romance stories. There's a significance to the fact that there are thousands of modern romances and thirteen *Friday the 13ths*: what they're trying to do is to keep those myths and not let you break out of seeing the world like that. There's a lot of satisfaction in those genres.

Audience: I was wondering about the ways you keep breaking down a reader's comfort by altering stories in *China Men*, jumping from myth to legend, family story back to myth story. And also, in *Woman Warrior*, with the self-questioning at the end of every chapter. You talked about these stories as dreams, but the dream's almost boxed into each of those stories, and the box is a series of introductions and conclusions in which you argue with the very dream you dream.

Kingston: Yes, I do that. I test those dreams or ideals and see how strong they are. I test them with my doubts and with my criticism.

Audience: Where do you find the source for that questioning of the story-telling?

Kingston: Well, I think that that was a very important part of my education—they taught us how to doubt. That's part of the western mind. I'll give you a metaphor or a story about this process we're talking about—of the implacable facts and what we can do to change them. At the last Buddhist retreat that I went to, I went in with a lot of problems. We began when the leader told us to draw a circle inside an outline of our own body before we went to sleep. He then guided our dreaming by saying, "Tonight, dream a mandala to draw inside the circle." So that night I did dream my mandala—it was a rifle site, the scope of a gun. And I thought, "This is the mandala of the 20th century." But what am I going to do with that? It's fact; it's not just some crazy nightmare. And so I was horrified by this all day. And then the next night I thought I would go sleep in the living room. I dragged my sleeping bag out there. I wanted to do it because I thought I saw a huge mountain out there, hovering over the house. But I hadn't seen the mountain at all when I first came.

So I put my sleeping bag under it. That mountain was scary and for me it symbolized the implacable facts, the way there are some facts in life that you can do nothing about, like war—those horrible conditions of life. And during the night I kept waking up. Sometimes I'd see lights by the mountain, and I thought, "I didn't know there was a trail up there." And all night, every time I woke up, it seemed like there were more lights. At the same time, I began thinking about war and peace and conflict resolution. And it was like this big problem began to break up into its aspects. And by morning the mountain had disappeared. It wasn't a mountain; it was trees. It was just that the light wasn't coming through. But I understood that as a process—thinking about the implacable facts, facing them, breaking them down into the various problems, handling them with imagination. All that breaks down the shooting at each other. All these complicated kinds of thoughts seemed to be the complicated trees that I was looking at, rather than this implacable mountain.

Audience: That reminds me of your comment that you created the notched arrows you saw in the museum. That in writing the book and imagining the scene of Ts'ai Yen in the desert, you broke down the way that we had perceived reality, and you rebuilt it. Your imagination keeps giving you more world views than you, or us as readers, had before.

Kingston: It's really strange the way creativity sees the world. I think what happens is that you set out to see something, and you've already made up an idea of what it is you want to find. You've already set yourself up to find it because you have the image of it. But then on a larger level, I think that we can actively control this by making up a vision of a better society, by making up a vision of what it is to be a good human being. And when you make that up abstractly, that gets you ready to find it out there, or to build it out there.

Audience: And ready to figure out what needs to be done to make it.

Kingston: Yes, and that means to plan all those steps to get from unreality to reality, all those steps on the way.

Audience: Someone showed me a wonderful trick with ink dots and a piece of paper, where you're supposed to connect these nine dots in three lines and the only way you can do it right is to go outside of the dots. Most people won't go outside the dots because the dots are the framework you've got, so to go outside of that, you've got to stretch the boundaries of where you normally would think.

Kingston: So there are two different ways to handle that implacable mountain. One is that you find all the little steps along the way. One thing I did during the day, before I made the mountain melt away, was I made ceramic mountains with little steps going up, and I made little holes going through—just like in *China Men*. So that's one way, to make all the steps. And then the other way is to get outside the dots and look at the bigger picture. Instead of drilling, you fly overhead.

Audience: I had a question about another one of your transformations. In *Woman Warrior* I noticed that you referred to a lot of people as ghosts—the milkman ghosts and the meter reader ghost. I love the humor of that. It also made a lot of sense because we know so little about the inner reality of people who do ordinary things and yet sometimes have a great deal of impact on us. But then, in *China Men* all those ghosts have become demons, so I wondered if there was a change in the way you saw things? Or is it how the woman writer as a child defines outsiders, as opposed to how the men define them?

Kingston: I guess for the first five years of my life I never saw any white people unless they came as a milkman ghost or welfare ghost. And as long as you don't know the true humanity of a person, they're just a ghost. That's a translation of the Chinese. Pearl Buck said "white devil"—she did it like that. I did "white ghost." I think in *China Men* they became "white demons" because the men actually worked with white men, they had a relationship with them that was harsh, whereas the women hardly ever saw any, and so they're ghostly. When you do translation, you can do it different ways so that it works out.

Audience: But aren't there also the larger ghostly presences? You subtitle *The Woman Warrior* "Memoirs of a Girlhood Among Ghosts." So there are other ghosts—your memories, your history.

Kingston: Yes, there are also the ghosts of history and social responsibility that haunt you. When you're little and helpless, or if you feel helpless, then they merely haunt you and make you feel guilty. But as you develop as a strong and effective human being and political being, then you can do something to change history. You become an actor in history. We take up our social responsibilities, and then they aren't ghosts anymore. And you don't feel guilty anymore.

Audience: Is this your definition of a meaningful life?

Kingston: For me, a meaningful life is one where you are becoming a humane being. I don't believe that we are born humane beings. A humane being has all kinds of values to embody and put forth in the world. One of my values is that we be able to form a community, a harmonious, non-warlike community. Which means that you have to be a human being who can take action. You are able to form bonds with other human beings and figure out a way to love each other. And we have to make those communities all the time. It's to make the family a good community; then you won't have to leave that family. When you go join that corporation, you transform that corporation into a loving community. I think to live like that would be a meaningful life.

Audience: You said your mother can't fully understand the meaning of your book. What does she think of you growing up as a child? I'm thinking of the part of *The Woman Warrior* where you wanted to tell her all the things that were on your mind, say one thing a day, or two things a day, or whatever. Did your mother understand what you went through? Could you explain it to her?

Kingston: No, I don't think she understands. I think the best way I had to explain it to her was to write it in this book. I find myself still trying to explain all that when I go home. I've given up on doing 102 things, but I still think this time I'm going to tell her such and such. And then I try it again and again. But she's not open to listening. Take that passage: "I have 102 things to tell you, ma." How mistranslated can it get, right? In any language that must be pretty straightforward. She *read* it. And she didn't respond to it at all. It's a continuing human task for all of us, to constantly work to get close together, to communicate in a loving way. It's really hard. In *The Woman Warrior*, the girl was very childish to think that she could systematically do each thing until by the time she got to 102 it would all be done. It's never done. As long as my mother is alive and I'm alive, there will be the constant effort to reach each other. Just when I think I've done it there's something else, you know? Which means that we just keep growing.

Audience: Do you think you make progress?

Kingston: Sometimes I think I make progress, and then we slide back. I'll give you one example. The other day I went home and I tried to make tea, and my mother only had a teapot with a broken handle. It was a lot of trouble. Then I was out shopping and I saw a teapot. It was for sale, it was from China, and it was really cheap. I didn't think about it; I just bought it and I brought it home and I said, "Look, I got you a new teapot." Well, she just exploded at me, just yelled at me. "What a waste of money! How much did it cost? Six dollars and ninety-nine cents? How can you waste money like that? I have a perfectly good teapot. Why do you do this to me?" I just looked at her and said: "Gosh, mom, all you have to do is say thanks!" And she just stopped. She said, "Oh, thank you for the beautiful teapot." Human beings work on automatic so much. We are so afraid of letting in new things. My mother freaks out at getting presents because a present means a surprise and then you're out of control. So she fights by yelling at me.

Audience: Reading about your mother made me wonder how your relationship with her has affected your other relationships, like the one you have with your husband.

Kingston: I think that I am a classic case for any Jungian or Freudian psychologist. I married a man who is just like my mother. I didn't think that I could ever do such a thing. My husband is Caucasian, so of course he doesn't look like my mother. And he doesn't talk like mother. He has a very English-major Berkeley style of talking. So of course this isn't my mother. But you know what? I give him a present and he freaks out completely. And that's it. I married Brave Orchid.

Allen Ginsberg wrote a Kaddish for his father and a Kaddish for his mother. And in the Kaddish for his mother he writes something about his mother running down the street, around the corner and into her arch-enemy: grandmother. Mom and grandmother are arch-enemies? These are the people who are supposed to love each other the most! Same thing with mother and daughter, same thing with husband and wife. It's a life-and-death struggle, a love and hate struggle. And as I said about telling my mother the 102 things, it continues. It just continues.

Audience: Is there any hope?

Kingston: As long as we're still alive, there's hope. I did get my mother to say thank you, and take the teapot. And then you know what she did to me? She gave it back as I was leaving the house. She waited a week, used it for about a week. Then she wrapped it up and gave it to me. And I said thank you.

Audience: Can you say something about how your father has responded to your work? Was it different than your mother?

Kingston: Well, as you know from my work, my father is a very silent, strong type. Most of the ancestral history I got from my mother; my father just doesn't say much. There's a line in *China Men* where I say, "I'm just going to tell your stories, and you just have to speak up if I've got them wrong." It was a way of provoking him into doing something. So when a Hong Kong pirated edition of *China Men* came out, my father read it.

My father has a beautiful calligraphic hand, and when he was younger he was a poet, and has a lot of classical poetry memorized. He quite often draws his poetry, paints it; he also often says, "I don't know why the poetry doesn't come to me any more. I love poetry so much. I wonder why it doesn't come to me any more." I find that incredibly sad, as a writer, that he waits for

poems to come and they don't. And then my mother—and you know my
mother—she says, "Well, you *used* to be a poet." That's her way of inspiring
him, you know. She's a really hard woman. But so my father read *China Men*
and he wrote in the margins—responses, corrections, additions. Little things
throughout. The most wonderful was that for the sexist parts, he would write
something wonderful about women in the margin. Isn't it great? It shows he's
come a long way, improved.

Audience: He let you read what he wrote?

Kingston: He told me some of it. But what makes me feel really good is
that this is communication between me and my father, and maybe this is the
best and only way that we will ever communicate; maybe it serves us right
because we're both writers. We're not going to get that kind of communication where we talk and hug. But another thing that's really wonderful about
it is that it's right in the literary tradition of China. What they used to do in
the old days is a poet would write a poem and then another one would do a
response, or one would do part of a poem, somebody else finish it, or you
write commentary on various texts. That's an art in itself, to write commentaries. The Bancroft Library collected some of my papers and they were
going to give a reception and put all my papers on display. So I thought,
"I'm going to contribute this copy of *China Men* with my father's writing
and put it in the collection." I invited my parents to the reception, but I didn't
tell them that I'd done this. The Bancroft Library put my father's book in a
glass case and open to a page that had lots of writing which he had done in
red. So I take him to the case, and I say, "Look," and he looks and he's
really surprised, wide eyes, big smile, and this joy, this joy, and he starts
turning around to all these people and he says in English, "My writing, my
writing!"

Audience: I've heard people say that *The Woman Warrior* internalizes
stereotypes of Chinese Americans, that it confirms the stereotypes for readers. Do you feel that at all?

Kingston: I've heard people say that and I've read those articles too. What
do you think they mean, because I don't actually know, and they don't give
examples.

Audience: I guess it's thinking of you as representative of something, and
using your book as representing a whole culture.

Kingston: Now that I understand really well. Some Chinese American will

read my work and say, "That's not me. I'm not like that." I have some white
friends who just read *The Woman Warrior* and will say, "Now I know all
about you." I think the problem has to do with not having enough books. If
there were lots of books about us then every book wouldn't have to carry the
burden of being representative. Then everyone would see that since there's
such a variety in the way that we write, there must be a variety in our people.
The situation is really correcting itself in a miraculous way this very year.
Amy Tan's book, *The Joy Luck Club*, is a nationwide best seller. There's two
anthologies of women's writing: *Making Waves* and *Forbidden Stitch*. A man
named Steven Lo is going to come out with a book called *The Incorporation
of Eric Chung*, about the adventures of a Chinese American in Texas. Jessica
Hagedorn, she's Filipina, is having some fiction come out in the spring. I
don't know why it's all happening right now. Chinese Americans must really
be at a center of some well of creative energy. So this problem of each one
of us causing a civil war every time that we publish a book—maybe that will
not happen any more.

Audience: At the end of *The Woman Warrior*, you talk about paradox and
opposites and being caught between cultures when you were growing up.
Can you say more about the idea of opposites?

Kingston: As Chinese American children, all our parents are so different
from everybody else, and all our beliefs are so different—we believe in
dreams, they believe in facts. I mean, just the smallest things, like chopsticks
and then going to school, and the first time I ever used a knife and fork. The
way the language works is opposite, the way we look is so different, we have
assumptions about an integrated way of thinking versus a linear way of thinking. And so I had to invent the kind of mind that says, "I can do opposite
things all at once. I can chew gum and rub my stomach counter-clockwise
all at the same time!" Maybe the reason I used that word "paradox" or
"opposite" is that culturally Chinese and western culture really are so different. We are actually at opposite sides of the planet. And I don't want one of
them to destroy the other one. I don't want to become an American by wiping
out all my Chineseness. Nor do I want to stay Chinese and never participate
in the wonderful American world that's out there. So instead of destroying
part of myself or denying some of reality, to me there has got to be a way to
have it all and to do it all. And I'm still at that phase of thinking of it as
paradoxes. I now see that there can be an amalgam, that the next stage is—
what do they call it in music? Fusion, yeah. At the end of *The Woman Warrior*

I realized for the first time how opposites work in Chinese customs or Chinese manners. If somebody tells you you're really pretty, to be really polite, you say, "Oh no, I'm just really ugly." Or, "Oh no, I'm so ugly, but you should see my sister. She's really beautiful." And then my sister would have to say, "Oh no, no, no, I'm so ugly." The girl in *The Woman Warrior* actually internalizes all this, so she really does think that she's dumb and ugly. And then at the end, by confronting the mother and saying "Oh, you just think I'm stupid. You think I'm ugly," she sees that it's a joke, and all this time she didn't know how to play! The more pretty and the more smart she is, the more the mother has to tell her she's not, to keep her from getting a big head. But then you see why I have to, for self-preservation, believe in paradoxes.

Audience: That reminds me of the opening of F. Scott Fitzgerald's *The Crackup* and opposing ideas in your mind at the same time.

Kingston: That's right. I identified a lot with that book as a high school student, and I wrote my college entrance exam on *The Crackup*. I totally identified with it on the psychic level. He's trying to keep himself from cracking up, and I felt all kinds of schizophrenic things about being Chinese and being American.

Audience: Are you talking about a special kind of chaos that comes from being bicultural? And having this kind of lifetime border experience?

Kingston: The idea of a border seems so nice and neat, whereas I hardly see it as neat. Things exist, wild phenomena, changing right before your eyes so you can't even figure out where they belong. And it's not that as you grow older you accept them more. That's not the way it works. I think that you dont have to be a biracial or a minority person to experience all this, either. This is the way life is. There was a big bang and everything's been exploding ever since. So it's our task as minority people, as all people, as artists, to order, to figure out meaning, to figure out beauty. One way is through art and writing, thinking and sorting out, making steps and looking at the big picture. You look at it, and if you are a good, brave person, then you work with it and create something out of it. Somebody wanted to know what does a dried umbilical cord look like because I mention that in *The Woman Warrior*. Well, that's like one of those chaotic things that are floating around, right? But you have to look at it, and after you look at it, you find amazing significance. It has to do with how you came into the world, how you came into existence. It has to do with your people. My people had a ritual for the umbilical cord which honors your coming into the world, as opposed to some other people we know who throw it into the incinerator with appendixes and cancer. It's like any little particle, it just amazes me. Nothing is unworthy of your attention. You look at each particle of that chaos and see what you can make out of it.

Interview with Maxine Hong Kingston

Shelley Fisher Fishkin / 1990

From *American Literary History* 3:4 (Winter 1991), pp. 782–91. This interview was taped in the spring of 1990 for *The Feminist Forum*, a television program sponsored by the University of Texas chapter of the National Organization of Women. Reprinted by permission of the interviewer.

SFF: In a recent article you wrote in the magazine *Mother Jones* called "The Novel's Next Step," you explore what the novel of the future might look like—perhaps a sequel to *Tripmaster Monkey*. Among other things, you note that your hero's wife, Taña, will have to "use the freedom the feminists have won. These struggles have got to result in happy endings for all, and the readers must learn not to worship tragedy as the highest art any more." Are you suggesting that feminist writers need to write out of power and pride rather than anger and rage in the future? How can they build on "the freedom that's been won"?

MHK: I think that feminist writers *have* been writing with power and pride, but I am suggesting that we have to invent new images and ways of power. So far the world thinks of power as violence, that power comes from a gun. We must create a new kind of drama in which there *is* drama, but it's nonviolent. And this has barely been thought of. I'm saying that women especially have a duty to work in this direction. I felt really appalled when Miss U.S.A. said women ought to have every right to go into combat. I see that as women trying for power by being as good as men are in violent ways.

SFF: In *The Woman Warrior* you counter the stereotype of the silent and confident Woman Warrior, and in *Tripmaster Monkey* you counter the stereotype of the Chinese man who came to make money—a story you explore in *China Men*—with the image of a Chinese man who came to play. In fact, one of your characters says, "What if we came for the fun of it?" Do you think that these wonderful new images of confident women and playful men can help *shape* a new reality?

MHK: Yes. I hope when artists write new characters, we invent new archetypes and they are visions of ways that we can be.

SFF: So the stories we tell about who we are can shape who we become?

MHK: Yes. What we need to do is to be able to *imagine* the possibility of a playful, peaceful, nurturing, mothering man, and we need to imagine the possibilities of a powerful, nonviolent woman and the possibilities of harmonious communities—and if we can just *imagine* them, that would be the first step toward building them and becoming them.

SFF: You've occasionally alluded to the power of the imagination to create reality, to embody truth, to make something exist that may not have existed before—not just in a psychological sense, but in an almost tangible, real sense. You describe, for example, the whistling arrow that you saw in a museum that was exactly like one you had imagined in your book, and you wrote, "I felt I had created it. I wrote it, and therefore it appeared." Do you think that your imaginative vision can generate reality and can generate truth?

MHK: Yes. It was wonderful that I saw this whistling arrow in the museum, but the point of my story was that this heroine took the arrows and turned them into flutes, and then she composed songs for these flutes. My idea was that we can turn weapons into musical instruments. It's sort of like plowshares from swords, and, again, I'm saying that the first step is to have that kind of consciousness that can create the world and save it. We have to change human consciousness and that's a step towards changing the material world.

SFF: I was thrilled to find out that the main character in your novel was named Wittman Ah Sing, because ever since I read *The Woman Warrior* I was convinced that Whitman had to be close by lurking somewhere in the shadows—Walt Whitman—

MHK: Oh really? Walt Whitman? After reading *Woman Warrior*? Oh, that's wonderful! Am I glad! I'm touched!

SFF: It showed. Everywhere. I wondered if he's been an empowering influence for you?

MHK: Oh, yes, yes, yes. I like the freedom that Walt Whitman was using to play with and shape the American language. Especially in writing *Tripmaster Monkey*—I just lifted lines from *Leaves of Grass*. You would think they were modern Sixties' slang—"Trippers and Askers" and "Linguists and Contenders Surround Me"—all of that—"Song of the Open Road," "Song of Occupations"—I just took those for title headings for my book. I like the rhythm of his language and the freedom and the wildness of it. It's so American. And also his vision of a new kind of human being that was going to be formed in this country—although he never specifically said Chinese—ethnic Chinese also—I'd like to think he meant all kinds of people. And also I *love* that throughout *Leaves of Grass* he always says "men and women," "male and female." He's so different from other writers of his time, and even of this time. Even a hundred years ago he always included women and he always used [those phrases], "men and women," "male and female."

SFF: What other writers have helped inspire and empower you to come up with your voice as an American writer and as a feminist writer?

MHK: I found that whenever I come to a low point in my life or in my work, when I read Virginia Woolf's *Orlando*, that always seems to get my life force moving again. I just love the way she can make one character live for four hundred years, and that Orlando can be a man, Orlando can be a woman. Virginia Woolf broke through constraints of time, of gender, of culture. I think an American writer who does that same thing is William Carlos Williams. I love *In the American Grain* because it does that same thing. Abraham Lincoln is a "mother" of our country. He talks about this wonderful woman walking through the battlefields with her beard and shawl. I find that so freeing, that we don't have to be constrained to being just one ethnic group or one gender—both those writers make me feel that I can now write as a man, I can write as a black person, as a white person; I don't have to be restricted by time and physicality.

SFF: At one point the narrator of *The Woman Warrior*, who is totally exasperated with her mother's stories, complains, "You won't tell me a story and then say 'this is a true story,' or 'this is just a story.' I can't tell the difference. I can't tell what's real and what you make up." How do you respond to questions like that about your work?

MHK: You mean when the audiences ask me, "Is it real?"—when students ask that? I think people ask me those things because I put the question in their minds. The people give me back the question I give them. I know why they do it. I meant to give people those questions so that they can wrestle with them in their own lives. You know, I can answer those questions, but then that means I just answer it for me. And what I want is to give people questions (which I think are very creative things)—and then when people wrestle with them and struggle with them in their own minds and in their own lives, all kinds of exciting things happen to them. I don't want people to throw the responsibility back to me.

SFF: The first line of *The Woman Warrior* is, of course, "You must not tell anyone, my mother said, what I am about to tell you." And then you go on to tell the chilling and terrifying story of "no name woman," your aunt. I wondered about the theme of silence and silencing, of not telling and not talking. How did *you* manage to break through the silence and put this experience into words?

MHK: All different ways. Sometimes I get really tricky, like a lawyer, and I think, "My mother says, 'Don't tell what I am about to tell you,' " and I think, "Well, I'm not going to 'tell,' I'm just going to write." Or she says, "Don't tell what I am about to tell you," and she tells it in Chinese. But what if I told it in English? But more seriously, what I have told myself was that I will write those stories because I have to, and there's no real way of stopping that, but I won't publish. And that freed me. It made me feel all right to write whatever way I pleased. And then as the years went by and I wrote more and more perfectly, and I wrote with more and more understanding, then I saw that I really needed to publish, and it was all right to publish, because in that story about the "no name woman," that punishment that happens to her is very terrible—all these villagers are taking a living creature and saying, we're going to wipe her out of the book of life, we're going to forget about her—she never existed. I realized that by writing about her I gave her back life and a place in history and maybe immortality. And then I thought, it's a duty of mine to save her in this way. There's a redemption that takes place in art, and I had resolved questions that would not resolve in life. So of course I had to publish. I feel that I constantly deal with the "don't tell" taboo—I think we all do. There's a lot in society that says, "Don't tell this secret, don't tell that"—or "What you have to tell is not beautiful, or unacceptable, or too crazy." We're constantly told this. "It's blasphemous." It's not as simple as a First Amendment right that says we have free speech, a free press, we can do anything we want. The taboos continue in all different forms—psychologically and socially. The artist has to constantly figure out how you're going to "tell."

Audience: What do you think the value is for women, especially women of color and ethnic women, of telling the truth?

MHK: It's always important to tell the truth because if you don't, there are all kinds of terrible social and psychological consequences. There are implosions and crazinesses that take place when you keep important energies and forces locked up inside of yourself. I think that some of our truths are things that are not dealt with in standard autobiography. I think that dreams are very important to women—and important to everybody's psyche—and to have access to those dreams is a great power. Also visions that we have about what we might do, also prayers—that's another "silent, secret" kind of thing. I think part of what we have to do is figure out a new kind of autobiography that can tell the truth about dreams and visions and prayers. I find that absolutely necessary for our mental and political health. I think the standard autobiography is about exterior things, like when you were born and what you participate in—big historical events that you publicly participate in—and those kinds of autobiographies ignore the rich, personal inner life. I feel that it's a mission for me to invent a new autobiographical form that truly tells the inner life of women, and I do think it's especially important for minority people, because we're always on the brink of disappearing. Our culture's disappearing and our communities are disappearing. One of the ways to keep ourselves alive is to recognize these invisible forces that are very powerful in ourselves.

Audience: Cherríe Moraga, one of the coeditors with Gloria Anzaldúa of *This Bridge Called My Back*, a long overdue forum for the voices of Third World women in America, said about that book, that one thing about books is that books can get places that bodies can't. How do you imagine your books going places where your body can't?

MHK: One of the first things I ever noticed and loved about reading is that words can get through all kinds of barriers; they can get through skin color and culture. It's so easy to read and go through all kinds of struggles with an author. I love the way, when we read, we actually take on the mind of the person that we're reading. Notice I say "mind" or "vision"—it doesn't have to do with "bodies." I travel a lot, and I know that I communicate very well in person, on one to one, but the books say things in a better way than I can get verbally, and also it works so efficiently, with those books getting out all over the world. Anaïs Nin used to say that every time one of her books was translated into another language, she'd conquered another country.

Audience: Do you feel there are elements in your writing that will speak to readers in the twenty-first century?

MHK: Probably. I think that it's already a miracle that—I wrote *The Woman Warrior* about 13 or 14 years ago, and just now I found out that it made the 1989 trade paperback bestseller list. Given the way the world is in the twentieth century, a 14-year shelf life for a book is a miracle. It's right up there next to "Sixty-four Ways to Tie Your Scarf, Your Most Versatile Accessory." The trade paperback list is full of how-to books like that one and how to cook and garden, household hints. *The Woman Warrior* is one of the few literary books on the list. Another one is a William Kennedy book. I've thought about how come my work is up there. What does this mean about American society? And I think it's because I do write about "how to"—my books *are* "how-to" books—"How to Live," "How to be Alive," "How Not to Give Up," "How to Understand One Another," "How to Cut Through Silences," "How to Break Through Blocks in People so that We Can Truly Communicate With One Another," "How to Keep the Family Together." I guess maybe my books *will* last to the twenty-first century, because you can get 20 "how-to" books in one.

Audience: Some readers—in fact, some minority women—have complained that all the men in *China Men* are fools or clowns. How do you respond to criticism like that?

MHK: I've also heard people call *China Men* a "heroic epic" when people try to assign a genre to it. That's sort of an opposite reaction to "clowns." And that has been typical of reactions to my work—very extreme reactions one way or the other. Oh, by the way, the person who said it was a "heroic epic" does not like heroic epics. Quite often I feel forced to write against the stereotype. As much as you would like to ignore the stereotype, saying it's totally irrelevant, actually you can't. It impinges on your life a lot, it impacts on your work, and I know that quite often I write against the stereotype and I react against the stereotype. One stereotype of Asian Americans is that we're really serious, and we never have any fun, and we have no sense of humor. When Shirley MacLaine made an early trip to China and then she came back with a documentary, one of the things she said on the documentary was that "they have no sense of humor," and "we told all these jokes and they didn't laugh." I think I might overemphasize showing how Chinese and Chinese Americans are the most raucous people: they laugh so much, they're telling jokes, and they're always standing up and performing for one another. They're *so* outgoing. And so in *China Men* and in *Tripmaster Monkey* I really go overboard to emphasize that part of the character. I also think that being able to laugh and to be funny—those are really important *human* characteristics, and when we say that people don't have those characteristics, then we deny them their humanity.

Audience: Some readers—again, particularly Asian American readers—have complained that you reinforced certain stereotypes of females in *The Woman Warrior.*

MHK: Yes. I have heard it before. And it often comes from younger people, who are so afraid of the stereotypes when their parents' generation, or maybe a recent immigrant generation, speak broken English, or when they have traditions that seem to be very similar to stereotypes. Some of the traditions of course are exotic. And the accent seems so close to what they see in the movies. And then right away they say, "Well, that's a stereotype." What's so horrible about stereotypes is that sometimes they will be superimposed onto a real person who *does* act like that, and then you push them away. And then you say, "Aw, that person's an 'Uncle Tom'—that person's buying right into the stereotype." I translate Brave Orchid's name. This was something that Pearl Buck did in her novels. She would translate the women's names. But they would be, like, "Peony" and "Lotus Blossom," and all that. I think that when I translate Brave Orchid's name, I am doing something *really* against the stereotype—for *who* has a name like that? It's so different from "Plum Blossom." It's so powerful. It's so odd. And yet, by translating the name itself, people will say, "See, she does that same thing. Translates a name instead of using the Chinese name and just putting that out there." Then people will say, "She *didn't* translate the name, and see what an exotic effect it has." Stereotypes do all kinds of very complicated things to those people. And I think when those young people think I am doing a stereotype, they don't realize that they are blinded in certain ways. I've also heard people say, "Why don't you write about rich, successful Chinese American people? Why don't you write real role models?" I think I *do* write about the great emotional, psychological struggles. I'm not that interested in writing Horatio Alger stories. I think of myself as somebody who's been given a gift of an amazing literary voice, and so I want to be the voice of the voiceless. I'm not that interested in being the voice of a wealthy, corporate Chinese American executive.

SFF: What made you choose to be the voice of this wonderful 23-year-old male Berkeley graduate in the Sixties? What made you decide to become a man, or at least have your character be a man, and then keep your feminist voice for the narrator in that novel?

MHK: Well, he sort of seemed to come to me out of nowhere. I just saw this person and I liked him a lot because I could see him and I could hear him. What I liked about him the best is that he's got this wild, inventive Sixties language. And this is what I loved about growing up in the Sixties— there was this new language that people were inventing for new psychedelic states, and spiritual states, and for political activities—you know, street theater and things that they were inventing—and so I wanted to write about that. But I did think to myself, "Why not a woman? Why not 'Wilma Ah Sing'?" And part of it is because women did not have such exciting lives in the Sixties. A man had a much more dramatic life. I think about the literary scene in the Sixties when I was writing, also, in Berkeley. You'd go to a party, and what I'd love about the party is that the poets would get up and read, would entertain one another with poetry—but it was always the guys that would get up and read, and the girls were always in the back listening to the poems. And so to write about that time, even during the times of the demonstrations, the men had all the exciting jobs. Even Bettina Aptheker complains about having to run the mimeograph machine. And then also, men had a more dangerous life, too, because they had the draft. They were always susceptible to having to go to Vietnam. So there's that dramatic story that they had that the women did not have.

Audience: Are your books read in China? Are they translated into Chinese? Do you get feedback from China?

MHK: I've been published in China in many various translations. There must be at least four translations. There are Hong Kong pirated editions, Taiwan pirated, Taiwan legal, plus Beijing Language Institute, which does a very careful Mandarin translation, and I felt very happy when they sent this to Canton University. Canton University said they were going to retranslate and do Cantonese dialect. And so I have a place in the "canon" of Chinese literature. I learned this when I visited China. They consider me "one of them." My name in China is Hong Ting Ting. They feel that they cut off all their roots during the Cultural Revolution; they got rid of everything, their roots to the past and their roots into the future (in fact they try to write something they call the "roots" literature). They see me as one who was put in a very privileged position and continued writing on "roots," and they feel that I saved some of their roots for them. They teach my work in China. And then some of those young people will say, "She made these myths up, we never heard of them, this isn't so." And that just shows that they got rid of a lot of the myths. It surprises me because I never thought of myself as a

Chinese writer. I feel that I descended from Walt Whitman and Nathaniel
Hawthorne and Virginia Woolf, and then a Chinese man told me how much
Tripmaster Monkey reminded him of the *Dream of the Red Chamber*—and
so they showed me that I have my roots in Chinese writing. I think that's
good, that's very nice, to have roots that spread all over the world.

SFF: Do you have any thoughts about some of the other plants that have
sprouted from these roots, the boom in current Asian American writing? Are
you cheered by the writing you helped inspire?

MHK: It's amazing. In the last year there have been six novels that have
come out by Chinese and Japanese Americans, and then there are going to
be two more. Jessica Hagedorn is publishing a new book. It's called *Dogeat-
ers*. It's just been amazing. This coming year I've heard of at least three
Asian American novels and I've heard of a couple of anthologies. There's a
new kid on the block whose name is Holly Uyemoto; she's 19 and she
dropped out of high school at 15 and wrote this novel. I guess she must have
written it between the ages 15 and 16 and just recently at the age of 19 got it
published. There's been an amazing flowering. And I do think I probably
helped inspire it.

SFF: In *The Woman Warrior* you have one wonderful passage in which
you talk about the very intricate and complicated knots that the knot-makers
in ancient China used to make, and that there was one knot that was so
complicated that the knot-maker was blinded by it and the emperor had to
outlaw it. And you said, "If I were in ancient China, I would have been an
outlaw knot-maker." I'm wondering if, in fact, that's what you've become,
as you weave these incredibly intricate knots of fiction and fantasy and history and myth.

MHK: I wrote that a long time ago, but I think it was prescriptive and
predictive in that forms of what I write are all intricate inventions. I think
that in every one of my books I had to create a new way of telling what I had
to say. And I feel that I break through pigeonholes of what's fiction and
what's nonfiction, of what an autobiography is. My next thought is trying to
figure out a way to integrate fiction and nonfiction. So I think that I am
constantly experimenting in new literary forms and they are very complicated.

Maxine Hong Kingston

Donna Perry / 1991

From *Backtalk: Women Writers Speak Out*, ed. Donna Perry (New Jersey: Rutgers University Press, 1993), pp. 171–93. Reprinted by permission of the interviewer.

I met Maxine Hong Kingston in May 1991, the day after she received an honorary doctorate at Brandeis University's commencement exercises. Again she was being honored for her ability to speak to us all.

Q: Do you consider yourself a political writer?

A: I do now. When I was first publishing I didn't want to be called a political writer because I saw it as a limiting category. I thought it meant that my writing would be defined by outside events and standards, and I wanted to write a literature from personal emotions and peculiar circumstances. I didn't want aesthetic standards and socially relevant standards imposed on me from other people. So I didn't want to talk about politics or to look at my own work in terms of politics. I really resented Marxist readings that came at art in a narrow political way, saying, "If this piece of art doesn't fit our propaganda, then throw it out."

But I now think that I am a very political writer in that I want to affect politics and I want to have power through the means of art. I feel that I am playing for political stakes and I want to change the world through artistic pacifist means.

Q: What do you mean by "artistic pacifist means"?

A: I want to make the world a more peaceful place. I want to help prevent wars. I feel very much a failure at this Persian Gulf war because if I had been more effective ten years ago, twenty years ago, then this may not have happened in February [1991, four months earlier]. Many people will say, "Well, where was the peace movement in January?" But that's too late already. We had to have been working a decade ago. So now we have to create a climate to prevent a war ten years from now, twenty years from now, or seven generations from now.

Q: How does the artist change the world?

A: An artist changes the world by changing consciousness and changing

168

the atmosphere by means of language. So I have to use and invent a beautiful, human, artistic language of peace. This has rarely been done. The shape of the novel and the short story is violent because we have violent confrontations—[then] a denouement where things explode. You especially see this in movies.

Q: Have there been books that have had that kind of impact?

A: Art is so indirect that it's hard to pin down exactly—now here's this book and it prevented this action—because if we prevented the action we don't know that we did it. Maybe no one book can create an atmosphere of peace because no writer can ever be that powerful; but if there were many books and many readers we could do it.

I've been reading William Saroyan's short story "Cowards" [1974, reprinted in *Madness in the Family*, ed. Leo Hamalian (New Directions, 1988)], a wonderful story about a man who hid under the bed during World War I. It's just the right short story to read right now in the aftermath of the Persian Gulf war . . . [The characters] are Armenian Americans . . . in Fresno, California, but they are Americans, and they are all going off to fight in Europe during World War I. And now we are fighting again, all in different configurations.

The story asks, "What is cowardice?" Is it a refusal to fight or is it just going in to fight? But that's just one little short story, and it didn't stop World War II, but maybe evolution is longer than that.

A Native American speaker I heard once said we should think about the effects of what we do in terms of seven generations. How wonderful if in our energy policies we would think ahead seven generations instead of, "What are the gas lines going to be like next week?" Art is like that, too—maybe there is an impact . . . [down] seven generations. Maybe there isn't, but you've got to keep doing it.

Q: There's a connection here with the Chinese books of peace.

A: Yes. The Chinese have this tradition that once upon a time there were these three books of peace that had all kinds of directions on how to have nonviolent communication. The myth is that these books were burned, and so we don't know what was in them—we don't know their effects. So I think of it as, that's what I have to do. I have to rewrite them, to try and figure out what was in them, to bring them back. You see how rare these things are.

Q: At the end of *Tripmaster Monkey*, Wittman launches into an angry diatribe against racism during his one-man show. Yet he becomes a pacifist. What are you saying about anger here?

A: Even though Wittman is ranting and raving and is verbally violent, he doesn't do anything about it. His explosions aren't even explosions—he implodes quite often. He cuts his own hair. He burns his own socks. But he never hurts other people. And I'm very aware that he never does racist name-calling. It's very hip right now, as it was in the Sixties, to call people by various racial names, but he never does that, even though he has a hip kind of language.

I'm working with [the question], Is it possible to get all the anger and the hate out verbally? And, if so, does that turn a person more peaceful? It's the same question that Wittman asks at the beginning: "Does playing football make you more violent or less violent?" Does it mean that you get all your violence out, and football players then become the most peaceful of men because they realize that the violence is just a game and they are not out there to kill anybody, and then it's over with and everybody goes home? Or does it aggravate it, and then you become more and more violent? What does letting the anger out do?

Q: Which is it?

A: I'm not sure that I answer that, except that my narrator comes in and says that he [Wittman] becomes a pacifist. It's more like her hope and her blessing for him rather than really knowing that it would happen. That's why I'm taking the book into a sequel now in which he is going to become older. Right now he is idealistic because he hasn't been tested yet. He's been a little bit tested—he managed to put on one show—but to truly be a realized adult man he has to continue. There have to be more shows, he has to have more nonviolent acts. In my next book he is going to become middle-aged and older, so that I can show a whole life of lived, involved, pacifist ideals. He's just barely even decided that he's going to try to be a pacifist. He's still reacting; he hasn't created himself yet.

Q: I got the sense that you wanted to get everything into this book.

A: But it's still not enough. That's why I want to do the next one.

Q: In *Tripmaster Monkey* you make more demands of your reader than you do in the earlier books. Were you writing an unfinished book on purpose?

A: Yes, this is a fake book [a term from popular music describing a book of melodies with, perhaps, only a hint at what the accompaniment should be]. I'll throw out a few things, and you improvise and finish it in your mind and imagination and life, and then also I, myself, will finish it in a sequel.

Also, I think it is demanding because an educated audience—one who has read a lot—will get more out of it than somebody who is not a reader. It is a book for readers. And it is about a reader. And the people in the book read. And I read. When I was writing it, I thought, I'm going to enjoy myself in this book—and my greatest enjoyment in life is to read. In my conversation I make literary references all the time and in my head I make them even more—I can hear Joyce and Shakespeare and Rilke. So why can't I use this in my writing? It's such a delight. It makes me really sad when there are so many readers who think it is off-putting to do allusions like that.

Q: You mention these literary presences. Did you have any specific literary models in mind for the novel?

A: I did in a really subconscious way. *Tripmaster Monkey* was going in all different directions. Chaos. Then, at the end, I thought, It will all come together when I do a monologue. That will pull the whole book to a point into one person. I thought I had really invented this wonderful form. And then my husband said, "Oh, that's exactly what Joyce did in *Ulysses*. That's just Molly Bloom doing her thing" [she laughs]. And so I didn't invent it, but I didn't consciously have Molly Bloom's soliloquy as a model. Subconsciously, having read Joyce, it was there.

Q: The whole novel reminded me of *Ulysses*. I felt that, like Joyce, you were writing a comedy that would include everything—in your case, about being Chinese American.

A: The *New York Times* critic [Le Anne Schreiber] also said that *Tripmaster Monkey* was like Joyce, but she made the comparison as a criticism [23 April 1989]. She was saying Wittman was like Stephen Dedalus, and it was as if Stephen Dedalus took the book away from Joyce. I was thinking, Isn't that good, to sound like Joyce? Isn't that a *tour de force*? She made it seem like an accusation.

Q: Is the writing of fiction different from that of semiautobiographical stories?

A: Those categories were done by the publisher. I never categorize my work. It all feels like one long flow, and the process is not that different, although the first two books are based on real people and then I imagine about real people. Then, in *Tripmaster Monkey*, those [characters] are not real people. I make them up. But then they come to me in my dreams. They walk up to me. I can see them. They say things to me.

Q: Did Wittman take over the book? Did he write it?

A: No, it's me writing the book because I could always see a distinction between him and the narrator. The narrator is more myself, although Wittman is myself, too, because sometimes the narrator's voice and his voice come together and sometimes they are very separate. Even by the end of the book, when he [Wittman] is going on and on [in his soliloquy], the community comes in and they give him a wedding reception, and she [the narrator] at the end pulls his ear. She is often doing that.

I think also that the relation between the narrator and Wittman is the relationship between us and God. Sometimes God or Goddess is very close to us, and then sometimes we are being an atheist and she dies. Then, when she dies, his [Wittman's] voice becomes very strong and it takes over and it's very different.

I'm teaching Dickens now in my English class [at Berkeley], and the narrator is always an even distance away from the other people. The nineteenth-century God is not that far away—he is not right next door either—but he keeps an even, middle distance away from people. But my narrator comes and goes. And sometimes God is dead, and then the characters run wild as their voices take over and they become solipsistic; then other times she returns and there is great joy. It is also a play of yin and yang [and a play] of the feminine spirit, which is dead quite often in this century.

Q: From what you are saying in the novel, I had the feeling that Wittman had to be a man.

A: So many feminists are mad at me.

Q: Pat Barker said the same thing when she left writing about women to write about a male character in *Regeneration.*

A: *Ms.* gives me a bad review, and I meet women who say that I wrote the first one [*The Woman Warrior*] and have been going downhill ever since.

Q: In a television special on you and your work, the actor Victor Wong talked about the humor in your books. He said that in order to get everything in *Tripmaster Monkey* you probably have to be Chinese. Is that true?

A: Wasn't he great? Wasn't he just such an alive person?

Q: Yes, he really was.

A: Well, he did say that. No, you don't have to be Chinese American, but I think that you probably can get more out of it if you are. I think that I have written it in a way that just the average reader would be able to get a lot out of it. But if a person knew a Cantonese language they would get some more out of it. If a person knew village dialect, shtetl language, they would get even more out of it. I was very gratified by what Victor said because he was born and raised within miles of me [in San Francisco], and so that means he got that out of it, being another village home-boy. I've gotten letters from people like a Filipino American who said, "You wrote about my father's store, which was on the corner of such and such." He wrote me all about his store and the other store across the street. Now he got something really special out of it that nobody else could get because he knew that store and I knew that store.

Then there are my brothers and sisters, and there are a whole bunch of brother-and-sister, private, in-jokes that they got. They all think that *Woman Warrior* is a hilariously funny book. My brother said that it's the Chinese American *Portnoy's Complaint*. I think that you have to be my brother or sister to get that out of it. So there are many layers.

Q: Talking about humor, I'm surprised that more reviewers haven't discussed the humor in *Tripmaster Monkey*. Do you laugh as you are writing?

A: Sometimes I laugh, and sometimes I cry. I have a lot of feelings. I think there are probably more people getting the humor now than when the books first came out. But people come to them, as they come to any book written by an ethnic American, with too much reverence and respect, trying to be politically correct and thinking it's wrong to laugh at a racial joke. So maybe that's why people don't get the humor. It's like being in the audience at ethnic movies. At Wayne Wang's movies I've sat with audiences that were mostly Chinese American, and everybody is laughing and falling in the aisles. They just think this is funny. And then I sit in another audience at an art house, and there are scholars and anthropologists and liberals, and there is such reverence that either nobody laughs or they are not sure what to do.

Q: So reviewers of your earlier works have missed the humor?

A: *Woman Warrior* had some weird reviews from people in places like *The Atlantic* or *Harper's*, one of those magazines with no sense of humor [she laughs]. They said, "She has a quirky sense of ethnic humor that is questionable," or something like that.

Q: So you read reviews?

A: Sometimes. I read them less and less now and care about them less and less. But I used to read all the reviews. I don't like to read them when they make me feel bad because the reviewers don't understand. I think there were lots of reviews of *Tripmaster Monkey* in which they did not understand, and it hurts me because I think communication is life. Communication is love. And I often see people as refusing to understand. There is a denial. Because I think that I am writing very strongly and it's not that I don't say it well enough. My part of the communication is done well. It's the other end of it.

Another reason I don't read reviews lately is that I discovered that the reviewers aren't reviewing the books that the readers get on the shelf. Publishers send out these bound galley proofs [to reviewers]. Well, on the bound galleys it says, "This is not the final thing. Have it checked before you quote," but I rewrite my bound galleys completely. I rewrite the whole thing.

Q: That must drive your editors crazy.

A: Oh yes. Knopf charged me a thousand dollars. They reset the galleys. In fact, they sent out a new set of galleys, which I think never caught up with the reviewers. They reviewed the bound galleys and wrote about the ending of *Tripmaster Monkey* as being tedious, but I rewrote the ending. I thought it was tedious in a previous draft, and I made it much more dramatic by the time the book came out, but they had read the previous one.

Q: Why do you wait until it's in galleys to make these final changes?

A: [She laughs.] I can't help it. That is my pace. This is why I try not to give them my books until I do think they're ready, because I think that the various drafts are like building a tower. When you get to the top you can see visions, and you can see further, and you can see higher. Sometimes it's not till I get to the galleys that I can really see up there. I don't mean to rewrite; it's just that, as I'm reading it, I see what I ought to do.

Q: So it's a matter of seeing it as a final version, set in type, justified right column?

A: And I think, There it is; now I know what to do. Then I rewrite it [she laughs]!

Q: Would you rewrite your earlier books if you had the chance?

A: I am going to do it. I am going to rewrite them, but in a different way. Not go back and pull those other books and do them over again, but, in the next book, say all the things that I didn't say earlier and correct myself. But I would make it a new theme in the new book. I would put things that I left out before into a sequel. Like this next one won't just be a sequel of *Tripmas-*

ter Monkey. It will be a continuation of everything, so everything you make grows with sequels.

I've been really appalled that there are a lot of students now who are writing dissertations on my work and it looks like they just read one book. They don't write about it in the context of everything, which they should do because I think *China Men* is a sequel to *Woman Warrior*. I see each book as building on the last one. It's almost like I do the rewrites and then the next book is another rewrite.

Q: *Woman Warrior* was so successful, particularly among women. Has the popularity of that book been at all a burden?

A: Oh no, no. They all want me to write a sequel, but I just have to go where the compass points and where my interests are. I think to be a good feminist means that first you realize who you are yourself as a woman and, when you become a strong woman, then you face the Other. Whatever that Other is, whether it's men, the rest of the world, people of other races— whatever to you, in your psyche, the Other is. And so, when you become a strong woman, you also face the yang, and so, of course, the next book has to be about men, that's the other half of the universe. So to me it's profoundly feminist to write about men, to be able to create men characters, and to understand what I previously could not understand.

Q: You've said in other interviews that you wish you had downplayed the warrior aspect of Fa Mu Lan in *Woman Warrior*.

A: Yes, but that's okay because in the last story of that book she is less of a battle-ax-type woman. She is more of an artist. There are some things about Fa Mu Lan that I left out. I forgot that she was a weaver. I don't know why I left it out; I guess I didn't understand, as women do now, that sewing quilts is an art. I wish I had remembered because it would have connected her with Penelope and with Spider Woman and weavers in the sense of the text. So I should have done that. And then there is another scene [in the original version] where she comes home and becomes a woman again—a feminine, beautiful woman—with makeup and with flowers and with silk clothes. So I think I could have included that. But then I was at a different stage of feminism at that time [she laughs].

Q: Would it have been as effective to downplay her being a warrior? I know a young Chinese American woman who was quite inspired by that.

A: And that is the correct way to remember the myth or legend because that is history and that is what happened. She was a knight in armor, and so to take that away would be to distort history. But it was also part of history that she turned back and had beautiful hairdos and makeup and all that. And I like that ending a lot because it shows that any of us can come back from war and not be like Rambo. Rambo never comes back from war. He just stays that way. Whereas she [Fa Mu Lan] comes back and she becomes a soft human being again. She is not brutalized by war. So it's good for me to bring in that ending, too, which the ancient people had.

But see the whole thing is part of the continuing problem of how do we tell the story of peace and how do we imagine peace and how do we live it? We still think that peace is boring—we think that peace is nondramatic. And if there isn't going to be a war, then what are we going to do with ourselves? After I leave here [Brandeis], I am going to Omega Institute in Rhinebeck, New York, to do a Buddhist retreat led by Thich Nhat Hanh, who is a Vietnamese monk who led the Buddhist delegation to the Paris Peace Conference. One of the things he says is that we don't know how to feel peace. We don't understand the joy that is peace. We think that it's boring. And that is an aesthetic and a social perception. He is dealing with many of these same problems we are facing, and I just know he has some answers.

Q: My students all want to know where you got the courage to finally speak, how you broke the silence you talk about in *The Woman Warrior.*

A: I don't know. I guess I never thought about it as courage. I think of it as secrecy—well, maybe it is courage. You know James Joyce said [in *A Portrait of the Artist as a Young Man*] that he would forge the conscience of his race with "cunning, silence, and exile," and I have always thought that those were very weird things to say because how could you do it with silence? But maybe he means secrecy, because as far back as I could remember writing—I guess I was eight or nine years old—it was my secret thing to do. I'd hide my work and I would pretend I was doing something else, and I would write all the things that were forbidden to say. And then I just kept that up forever. I was very clear from a long time ago that I didn't have to share this with anybody—so that makes me very brave. I can always write it, throw it away, and I don't have to publish. But I do have to say it. Everything has to be expressed.

Then, when you write well—with an understanding of people and situations from their own point of view—the writing becomes beautiful. At that point I thought, Well, now I can publish it because everybody will see how beautiful this is. It works out very well that way, but it means continuing with the secrecy and the working out of things inside until they become a very beautiful thing out in the world.

Q: Were the first things you wrote family secrets?

A: The first things I wrote were very much like the things I write now. So I think that I've been working on them for forty years because I began writing them then, but I didn't have the vocabulary yet. I didn't have the skill. So I just kept doing it over and over and over again until I had the understanding and the wisdom and the beauty of it. I began as a poet—I always had the rhythm and rhyme of language—but it would get bigger and bigger and bigger. I think that's the direction of all the work. It always seems to get longer and longer [she laughs].

Q: You begin *Woman Warrior* by telling a secret; that's a great way to open a book. How did your family react to your letting that secret about your aunt out to the whole world?

A: Well, I think the way I told it is okay. You see, my parents have only read my work in Chinese translation, and the translations are pirated editions and the translator works with ready-made forms, soap opera forms that don't have the power and the anger of the English. And so when my parents read that, I think they just see it as a nice story. So they feel good about it. They never talk to me about, "Oh, we told you not to say this and you did." My mother says, "Oh, everything is so accurate; you described China so accurately." I guess she just feels fine. Maybe when she says that things are accurate, it is like saying that it is the truth and the truth is always right.

I do have a cousin-in-law who is Caucasian who said, "I only read the first chapter because it's just terrible for you to say things like that." She just never gave me a chance by reading the next chapter where things begin to work themselves out.

Speaking of secrecy, did you notice that Alice Walker and Toni Morrison both began books with almost that same sentence: " 'You must not tell anyone,' my mother said, 'what I am about to tell you.' " Alice Walker's novel [*The Color Purple* (Harcourt Brace Jovanovich, 1982)] begins: "You better not tell nobody but God," and then Toni Morrison [in *The Bluest Eye* (Holt, Rinehart, and Winston, 1970)] has the line, "Quiet as it's kept. . . ." You see everybody has that same line; it's the same struggle to break through taboos, to find your voice. It's that same "exile, secrecy, and cunning" that Joyce was talking about.

Q: My students found *Woman Warrior* a painful book, especially one woman who is the daughter of Irish immigrants. She said your parents could have been her parents.

A: That's fine to let pain come in. I get lots of letters from women and from people of different ethnicities. They come from all over—Finland, and a lot of Jewish people—so I know that I am telling a human story. Even though it is very specifically Chinese American, it is also everyone, and I know that the people are feeling their own pain. Some people resist feeling by trying to understand my work as a Chinese book: the Chinese people are like that. And they understand it intellectually that way, but I see that as a sign of a person who's denying their own identity and their own feelings.

Q: Reviewing *China Men*, Mary Gordon said, "Mrs. Kingston's success at depicting the world of men without women must be the envy of any woman writer who has tried to capture this foreign territory" [*New York Times*, 15 June 1980].

A: She's such a fine writer. I remember her writing that. When I was working on *China Men*, I remember reading a critic who was praising the great male writers, like Flaubert and Tolstoy and Dostoevsky and Henry James, who were able to write great women characters. I don't remember if they said women had done men in this way or not, but I remember thinking that to finish myself as a great artist I'd have to be able to create men characters. Along with that, I was thinking that I had to do more than the first person pronoun.

Q: Did the things you tell in *China Men* really happen? Did you hear the story about your grandfather yelling his secrets into a hole because he couldn't say them out loud, for example?

A: Yes, I hear about those people from my mother. I met most of those men, but not all of them. But they were still a real presence. I never met my grandmother either, but they were [all] so real that I know, through my mother's stories, that they existed in real life. So they exist in my imagination. In fiction, there are people who I think about and I hear their voices, and then they are embodied in people who walk up to me and say things that are lines, exactly as I need. So the line between imagination and reality is not a sharp one.

Q: I like the history of U.S. discrimination against Chinese that you put in the middle of *China Men*.

A: Yes, isn't that a weird thing to do? [She laughs.]

Q: It gets the reader angry—there in the middle of the book, when we have come to know these people, to see the horrors of U.S. immigration policy.

A: Oh good. Those are the effects that I wanted. Also, I put it in that way because I found that readers don't have the information. OK, so where are you going to put the information? Do I do an appendix? No, they'll skip the appendix. Do I do an introduction? No, they'll skip the introduction. Do I do footnotes? No, because that's too scholarly. Can I trust the readers to be interested enough to go to the library and do their own research? No [she laughs]. So, I'll put it right in the middle. I have seen Bibles with the Old Testaments and the New Testaments where, if you open them right up in the middle, it's the psalms, and I thought of that. If you open that book right in the middle it's like psalms; it's like commandments. It's laws that are implacable. So I was reproducing things that are set in stone.

Q: The language shifts there, too.

A: Oh yes. I wanted to say, "There's poetic language and there's legal language." I was contrasting the language of feeling, where you could make friends with the characters and feel for them, with this formal, distanced language. Actually, I didn't even write that part. My editor, who was a correspondent in Asia during World War II, wrote it to make it sound really legal, journalistic, and not my language.

Q: One thing I admire about your work is that in each book you seem to be taking new risks, experimenting with different voices, not replaying the same thing.

A: That's right. I was talking to my husband about that last night. How we, all of us, just have to complete ourselves by doing the next thing, and I'm not doing *Woman Warrior* over again. It wouldn't occur to me to do it over and over again. Isn't it interesting that a lot of poets lately seem to be writing prose and prose poems, and then you see short-story writers who are writing novels, novelists who are writing nonfiction, nonfiction people who are writing fiction. It's because you just want to continue with the other forms. I have been reading Henry Miller's [*The Paintings of Henry Miller:*] *Paint as You Like and Die Happy* [ed. Noel Young (Capra, 1982)], and he had this whole other life as a painter. And Gauguin was a great writer and I just read *Noa, Noa* [1900], and Van Gogh wrote the most amazing autobiography [*Dear Theo: The Autobiography of Vincent Van Gogh*, ed. Irving Stone (1937)]. So there are genres within literature, but if life is long enough, then I'm going to paint some more.

Q: Did you ever think of writing plays? The pull of drama is all over your work.

A: No. I think about it, in that these books have been optioned for movies and for plays. Everybody keeps thinking why don't I do it, because the play-wrights haven't been able to adapt or translate right, but I don't think about it mostly because the next book is coming.

Q: You mentioned that it will take Wittman Ah Sing into adulthood. What else?

A: It's going to have everything in it. Right now I'm going to go to the J.F.K. Library [in Boston] to read the manuscript of *The Garden of Eden* [Scribner's, 1986]. That was Hemingway's last book. The published version is not the whole thing; it's only 250 pages. There are two thousand pages of manuscript. Hemingway was trying to find a language that was about rela-tionships and about community. In some senses he failed because now he is known for shooting all those animals, for bullfights and his suicide. But he was reaching for something else. He didn't burn the book; he just left it there. But he wasn't strong enough to see it through to publication. A lot of it has to do with sexual roles, and so I just want to see what he was aiming for. He's got a map of the shape of a novel, and I expect him to take me so far and then I'm going to have to go the rest of the way. This has something to do with this next book. I need some sort of a map, in the way that I had *Ulysses* for a map although I didn't know it. This time I'm more conscious and know that Hemingway has got something going there, and I thought I would take a look.

Q: So reading Hemingway is for you—not necessarily for use in the book per se?

A: It's for me, but it's also for use in the book. I may even write about it and write about the whole process. You see, this next book is going to be fiction and nonfiction. The fiction part will be to show Wittman Ah Sing growing up, and then the nonfiction part is the mind of the self that is creating it—that will be how my head works, which is to think about Hemingway. I mean, he is our father. He is everybody's "papa." He told us he was, so I guess he is [she laughs]. He left some kind of a map. Like I say in *China*

Men, my grandfather left the railroad as a message. Well, Father Hemingway left *The Garden of Eden* manuscript, and I want to find out where I'm going next.

Q: What role do readers play in your writing process? You've mentioned your husband. Does he read what you write?

A: He reads the last draft, when I think that it's perfect and there's no more to do. After he gives me his criticism and feedback, I do another draft. He also reads the galleys. The other role he plays is being the person who lives with me; I constantly bounce things off of him, and sometimes I don't even know that they are related to my work. It's just life perceptions that you exchange, and I'm sure that's very creative.

Q: Is he your best editor?

A: Yes. I wonder if that happens all the time? I know a lot of people say that.

Q: Jamaica Kincaid said that, too.

A: I wonder why people feel that the spouse is the best one? Is it that they really, objectively, are the best one, or is it an illusion that they are?

Q: Maybe it's the trust you have.

A: Or maybe they understand you and they would anyway, even if you were not a writer. And so, if you accept that they understand you, then they must understand the writing. Which I think they do. My husband does.

Q: It sounds like you are pretty private about what you do until that last point.

A: Yes, because everything is so invisible, and I'm just bringing it into visibility, and anyone can tell me that there's something wrong with it. I can see that it's not complete and there's so much more. I'm getting less shy about that now, though, because things are coming out more finished now. The early drafts are more complete and almost perfect. So I've been reading pages in progress to audiences and telling them that it's a work-in-progress.

Q: Do you feel that you are a better writer than you were twenty years ago?

A: Oh yes, much better. *China Men* is a better written book than *Woman Warrior*. The language is more lucid. The sentences are smoothed. The rhythms are more interesting. The way I can tell a story is more dramatic. And I had much more control of narrative form.

Q: In an article on your influence on other Asian American writers, you said that you've talked to people who say that they get "Maxine Hong Kingston rejection letters" that tell them to read *Woman Warrior* and *China Men* and get an idea of how they should write.

A: Well, I was just quoting what I had heard from them, and I'm not sure how these publishers said this to them. It could have been said in a really condescending and racist way that made these young writers feel pigeonholed and discouraged them, making them feel that what they had to say has been said and, "Go away!" But it could also have been said in the way of a teacher to a student or an older person to a younger person: "Know what your tradition is." In a way like older feminists could say to the young lawyer who thinks that she's done it all on her own: "Know your history; be grateful to the people who went before." Also, you don't have to reinvent the wheel [she laughs]. I hope that it was said in that way and that the young people could receive that and take it seriously and, yes, go back and read.

Q: You once said you were "not a good person" because you knew people would not like your stories and you told them anyway. Several writers I have interviewed have talked about feeling a sense of responsibility to their racial or ethnic group, but it sounds like that didn't bother you at first.

A: Another way of thinking was that for about the first thirty years of my writing I wrote in the first person singular, and then at a certain point I saw myself as very selfish and solipsistic and narcissistic. I thought that surely I've got to be able to put another person into a scene, that I should be able to use the other pronouns. I saw it as a great failing as a human being and as an artist not to have a larger world. It's not enough to have a rich interior world because then I'm missing everything else out there. So then I struggled very hard to take in the rest of the universe, and I think of that as being a good person: to consider all of the other people and everything else, not just one's self.

Q: One critic wrote that despite recent gains, "Asian American writers often are expected to play the roles of cultural ambassadors, to speak for their race." Also, because their history has been largely untold, some feel they must "shatter stereotypes and honor the historical record with a religious fervor" [Edward Iwata, "More Asian Americans Suddenly Are Winning Mainstream Literary Acclaim," *Los Angeles Times*, 11 September 1989]. Have you felt any of this pressure?

A: Yes. This is the same thing that I have heard so many black writers say that they have to take the whole responsibility of race. Then, at the same time, there are people of our own community, other Chinese Americans, who will say, "Well, how dare you speak for us? Who voted for you? How can you make fun of us?" I had a short conversation with Philip Roth as we were walking up from the Brandeis commencement ceremonies. I thanked him for the writing that he had done after *Portnoy's Complaint* [Random House, 1969] in which he faced the reception of some Jewish people who accused him of making fun of them and of his mother and all that. I told him that he said it, and all I had to do is take out where it said "Jewish" [she laughs].

Q: So you get attacked on both sides: You get attacked if you try to break down stereotypes and if you don't.

A: Oh, yes. That's right. There are people out there who are just trying to say, "Stop it, don't even do that. Don't write." It's sometimes from a masculine-feminine point of view. So many minority men are angry at minority women for saying anything, especially among Chinese Americans. For some reason, most of our writers are women, and most of our critics are men. And the men are saying that we [the women] have feminized Chinese American history because our history is mostly masculine. There were mostly men who came here for one hundred years, and yet there are women who write. So these critics are saying, "How dare you write it?"

Q: I know that the writer Frank Chin has criticized you for this. Describing that dispute, San Francisco writer Edward Iwata wrote, "The struggle between Frank Chin and Maxine Hong Kingston is a literary battle for the soul of Asian Americans" ["Is It a Clash over Writing Philosophies, Myths, and Culture?" *Los Angeles Times*, 24 June 1990]. How do you respond to this?

A. For a while I just thought, Why doesn't Frank Chin just shut up and go home and write? The only way he's making a literary reputation is to attack me. He doesn't have anything else going for him. That's his career. And by doing that he is destroying himself as a writer because he is just wasting his words.

This idea of writing for the soul of Asian America—maybe there is something there. I no longer read Frank Chin, but I hear that the latest works are an attempt to find Chinese American manhood through a violent, warrior mythos, trying to find an identity with killers, with knights from the past who solved things by going to war. He says that our history is one of battle, of blood. I know that he has battle cries and one of his mottoes is, "War." He says it in Chinese.

I am going in the completely different direction. I am looking for a language of peace. I am trying to rewrite a book of peace. And so maybe that is fighting for the soul, not just of Chinese American people, but the human soul. I want the human soul to be one where people care for one another and where people cherish and nourish and value one another, and I am trying to think of ways of conflict resolution that have to do with talking or hugging or something, whereas his idea of conflict resolution is to kill each other.

Q: Where is this going to go? This is very true of the African American literary community too. Writer Ishmael Reed trashing Alice Walker for her portrayal of black men in *The Color Purple*.

A: It's just so horrible. It's the same thing. And Ishmael and Frank are friends. The guys are doing all this criticizing, and the women are just going about creating. In general, also, the women don't answer the critics. I go back and forth on that. Most of the time I don't answer this. Frank does terrible things. He tells me when he sees me at a conference he's going to beat me up. And I don't answer it because I keep thinking I'm transcending, I'm not being reactive. But then sometimes people see this as weakness and say, "See, these women don't have an answer." But we don't want to answer, because any little thing we do to them will destroy their manhood even worse because they are already so fragile.

Q: Is this inherent in men and women, or is it part of the acculturation they go through that leads to this sort of split?

A: I think it's partly that and another part is that it is aggravated among minority people because minority men have even a worse time becoming men than mainstream men, so the battle in the general culture continues back home. They say that wife beating and all cuts across cultures, but I have a feeling that it is probably worse among the minorities. When you face the frustration of not being realized as a human being, that human energy comes out in this mad way. I'm so upset that even literary people act this way. We should be more enlightened—after all, we have other means besides fists and guns. So why are we using these means for the men to beat up on the women?

Q: In terms of the conflict between men and women of color, I think the press plays right into this.

A: Oh yes, they love it. And there are plenty of black men and Asian men who love Alice Walker's work. And they love my work. And there isn't even a battle going on. It's Ishmael Reed all by himself. It's Frank all by himself.

But the press plays it up as if it's all these Asian men against me. I think that for a while Frank got so much press because the press didn't know who else to call. So every time a new book comes out, they call Frank and then he speaks as if he's speaking for everyone and says, "Oh, we hate Amy Tan; we hate Maxine." But it's just him; he doesn't speak for anybody.

Q: This raises another point: Who should review books by Asian American writers? Should it be a member of that community or not?

A: That's another one of those double binds because we all want it both ways. Everybody thinks, Well, if we get an Asian then that person really knows what they are talking about. And then, if they give a negative review, it's not from ignorance. On the other hand, they think, It's really terrific to have a white person review it because then it's being recognized by the canon-makers. And so people fight about it all different ways. A newspaper someplace in the Midwest—I think it was in Chicago—assigned *China Men* to the only Asian American they had on their staff. He was a sportswriter. He wrote about oranges. He said there is a whole tradition of citrus fruits that I didn't understand.

I was at a gender and ethnicity conference at Georgetown University where there was a great uproar started by a Chinese American young woman who was upset because most of the papers that were delivered on my work were done by Caucasian women and only one was done by a Chinese American woman. I thought that was a pretty good proportion right there, but I think that she felt that I was being coopted. But I think that if all the papers had been delivered by Chinese American critics, she could have been equally upset that we were ghettoized and not recognized by establishment critics.

Q: What would you say to all these people who are writing about you? What do you want them to bring to a study of your work?

A: I want them to read well and accurately. I don't want them to speed read or skim, which is a condition at college, I guess. I want them to have their hearts and their minds and their eyes open as they are reading it and to read with their feelings. It's not just an intellectual book. They have to let the images come inside of themselves for the images to do their work. Something amazing happens with images and metaphor: we see these pictures, and they go inside of our imaginations, and our imaginations change. So I hope that people will allow themselves to change as they are reading the books. I hope that they will become different people by the time they finish. Maybe this is why they resist it: they don't want to become different people [she laughs].

Q: You're back teaching at Berkeley, where you were an undergraduate. Does it feel strange?

A: I love teaching and being back after having been a student there. Some of the professors that I had are still there, and it is just so amazing being a colleague of theirs. I love talking to the students.

Q: You mentioned teaching Dickens earlier. What course is that?

A: It's called Reading for Writers. I'm teaching David Copperfield because it's the story of a writer and how he becomes a man and becomes a writer, and I wanted a book that was long so we get that sense of nineteenth-century time.

Q: It's a great book to study for narrative voice.

A: Yes. The older man who is the narrator will sometimes get very close and look at David and say, "Oh, that poor baby." Then, at other times, he's inside of David. It's really wonderful.

Q: What other authors do you like to read?

A: There are some people that are really special favorites. Right now I'm reading William Saroyan, as I said. I find he is just a great writer. I think [Toni Morrison's] *Beloved* [Knopf, 1987] is a great book, a very human, mythic, epic book. I expect a sequel because that young woman ought to grow up.

Q: You, Toni Morrison, Leslie Marmon Silko, Francine du Plessix Gray, and four other American writers went on a trip to China back in 1984 as guests of the Chinese Writers Association. Did you have the sense that you were seeing for the first time these people whom you had imagined?

A: I saw them for the first time, but also I felt I was seeing them again. And I know they were seeing me the same way because there was my picture and all the other family pictures at their houses, and then also throughout China people would say, "Welcome home," or, "It's nice that you've come back." They knew that it was my first trip there, but still they referred to it as a return. I think we all think that way.

Q: Harrison Salisbury, who was also on the trip, wrote that people were lined up to see you—that everyone claimed to be a relative [*New York Times*, 20 January 1985].

A: Oh, yes. All my relatives at the train station. God, it was so wonderful! That whole journey was a linguistic adventure, too, because we traveled from the north to the south, and the closer we got to my home village the more I could communicate. It was quite amazing. Harrison Salisbury is quite amazing. Here's this man in his eighties who could walk faster and do more than any of us, traveling with his typewriter that he had since World War II.

Q: You mention dialect differences. When you finally gave a speech you used a peasant dialect, didn't you?

A: Yes. Really, the only Chinese language that I have is the dialect that my parents speak. It is a real minority dialect in the southwest, and it is not even the main dialect of people who are here in the U.S. So here I was traveling further and further south and listening to the dialect changes and having translators coming along. At Chinese school we studied Cantonese dialect, but that isn't my parents' dialect, which is the peasant, village dialect.

So we came to these formal dinners where various ones of us had to give speeches, and they [members of the delegation] just kept poking me, "Okay, you speak, you speak, and do it in Chinese. You do it." And I thought, No, I just can't. I don't think I can give a formal speech in Chinese. I can't do it in Mandarin. I can't do it in Cantonese. Then it occurred to me, I'll just do it in village speech. And so I did, and I translated myself. I would say a sentence and then I'd translate it into English. And I realized that no one there understood me because the Chinese there wouldn't either. And it felt really good when I realized that I was being more politically correct than anybody because my class credentials were impeccable! I bet no Communist ever did this because they would do whatever the official national language was. Or, if they were really feeling peasant, they would do Cantonese, but they wouldn't do this peasant dialect [she laughs]. I just got such a kick out of it. I felt so at home [more laughter].

Q: I get a sense that you like to poke fun at the establishment in this trickmaster way.

A: First I feel really shy and awful and out of it and *declassé*, and then I get into it [much laughter].

Q: Do you think that you will write about that trip?

A: That is really interesting to me because no, I haven't written about it. It takes a long time for me to take things in and see what they become. And I notice that Toni Morrison and Leslie Silko haven't written about it. But Charles Wright has had some poems published already about the trip and Allen Ginsberg and Gary Snyder were composing as they were going along, so they have their China poems. I think everybody felt profound connections with roots, and so it is interesting to see the creative process of people. Some people are faster, some are slower, and maybe it will come out in their work in other ways. Maybe there was an image [from the trip] in *Beloved*. I don't know.

Q: Has there been a downside to your success?

A: The bad thing is that people recognize me and trap me. Just on this trip [to the Brandeis commencement] a young man trapped me. I was in first class, and he came through the curtain, and he started talking to me and pretty soon he was right up in my face [she moves forward to demonstrate]. He just wanted to tell me everything about himself, and he wouldn't stop talking. I couldn't figure out how to get rid of him [she laughs]. He introduced himself as a conservative, and then he had to tell me his whole conservative philosophy of life [she groans].

But then, in some ways, he's a character in my work. I've imagined him, and he appears. He was like Wittman, except that he's a right-wing Wittman. In another way, when he did that to me it's like he's saying "Here I am! You write about me and take responsibility for me." How are you, as a good liberal, going to answer that?

Q: I think I would say, "Go away!"

A: But he can't go away; he's another being on the planet.

Q: So what are the good things about your success?

A: There are lots of good things. Wonderful things. My father says that I'm living the life that he wanted to live. My sense of community has gotten so wide. I now know that I can go anywhere in the world and will run into a friend or I will make a friend. I actually have the power to make a family, a community, that's all over the world.

I'm having so much fun with the pronouns "we" and "our." When I say "my people" and "our people," I mean everybody [she laughs]. And I watch other people think that I mean Chinese people or Chinese American people or Asian American people or women. But, more and more, I'm spreading the meaning to mean every human being on earth, living and dead, because there are reincarnations, too—ancestors and root people. So I am feeling more and more like a Spider Woman. So there are all those good things, but also the responsibilities of all that kind of power.

Creating Peace Out of Pathos

Joan Smith / 1991

From *San Francisco Examiner*, 29 October 1991, pp. B1, B4. Reprinted by permission.

Maxine Hong Kingston, whose father died last month, who lost everything in the East Bay fire, including a book-length manuscript, family photos and heirlooms and art made by friends and admirers, answers the phone in her Texas hotel room, where she is attending a conference on dreaming, and says she has just been out for a walk.

"I found a stream and I just sat in it with my feet in the mud and I had a notebook and pen and I think something is coming to me. I think I'm discovering what to do next," says the bestselling author of *Woman Warrior* and *China Men.*

"I think everyone who has been in the fire ought to do it," she adds, laughing. "For balance."

When the fire broke out, Kingston was in Stockton attending the one-month anniversary ritual of her father's death, and she started hearing about it only as she was driving home at about 1 p.m., listening to the radio.

"I heard there was a fire around the Caldecott Tunnel area and thought, well, too bad, but that's a long way from my house. But by the time I got to Oakland they were saying that the fire had jumped over the freeway and that 150 houses had burned and that between Broadway Terrace and Broadway was on fire and that's right next to my house and I kept thinking, 'No, no, no, no, no.' "

The first two freeway exits were blocked, and when Kingston finally got into Oakland, "ashes were falling and the sun was all red" and there was a police roadblock at the first street to her house. She waited until the police were distracted, talking to other people, then parked her car and snuck past them to make her way on foot. But the air was getting smokier, burning limbs were falling from eucalyptus trees and she was finally forced to turn back.

"That was a terrible moment," she says. "I just thought, 'There goes the book,' and gave up."

But back in her car, Kingston decided to drive to another part of town where the air was better and try again.

"So I parked and went up the road, went and went and went, under the BART rails, which were red hot, and I got within a block of my house, and couldn't get any closer because the wires were down, there were wires all over, and I could see that the whole neighborhood was gone. It's the only time I cried during the whole thing.

"Then these two men came on bicycles and I said, 'I just lost my novel,' and one of them patted me on the head and said, 'It's up here and you're still alive,' and the other said, 'Would you like a ride on my handlebars?' "

And the diminutive 51-year-old writer, who says she just thought, "What a blessing, what a blessing," jumped on the man's handlebars for "a magical ride, a fire ride from Disneyland."

"Down the hill through this incredible wind, this hot wind, with logs and fires and fire houses, watching the flames go up all around and the ashes falling. It really taught me to live in the present because I was *really enjoying* that ride."

Kingston's husband, actor Earll Kingston, was in Virginia, performing Chekhov. So she went to stay with her friend, Bessie Chinn, and spent the next two days, with Bessie and other friends, sneaking through police lines to sift through what was left of her house.

"I just had to go up there. I knew the manuscript was gone but I had to look at its ashes, to find out what happened," she says.

"Did you know that when paper burns it is very beautiful?" she asks dreamily. "It's just amazing to look at a burned book. It looks like feathers, the thin pages and it's still book-shaped and you touch it and it disintegrates. It makes you realize that it's just air. It's inspiration and air and it's just returned to that."

Kingston says her new novel was "a book of peace" and that she had written 156 pages—"very complete pages of good writing because I had gone over it many times."

"In ancient Chinese mythology there were three books of peace and they were burned, in wars or fires or book bannings, so it's right on a kind of cosmic level that a fire came and burned my book too," she says. "It feels as if I am working with the forces of destruction and creation, so I am going to do it again.

"People have been calling to say they want to give me things, but I think it would be nice if they would help me rewrite my book. Part of the book is about Vietnam veterans, so if veterans could write to me about how they have triumphed over post-traumatic stress, or how they arrived at a peaceful life after going through war, or if people know anything about the books of peace from China, or if they know some mythology I never knew. I had lots of notes about mythical cities of refuge, where people could go during terrible times for sanctuary. Those are the kinds of notes I lost.

"I want people to help me retrieve a book of peace. I'm realizing that writing does not have to be solitary. You know, 'talk-story' (traditional Chinese storytelling) is a communal activity and I'm beginning to think that the reason modern American writing is so depressing and so alienating is because it's a solitary activity. And if I can turn it into a communal activity I bet I can write something very hopeful."

Reinventing Peace: Conversations with Tripmaster Maxine Hong Kingston

Neila C. Seshachari / 1993

From *Weber Studies: An Interdisciplinary Humanities Journal* 12:1 (Winter 1995), pp. 7–26. Reprinted by permission.

In November 1993, Maxine Hong Kingston was invited to give a convocation address at Weber State University on the occasion of the 10th anniversary celebration of *Weber Studies*. This interview was taped on Friday, 12 November 1993, in Kingston's suite at the Radisson Hotel, in Ogden, Utah.

Seshachari: Yesterday [11 Nov. 1993] at the Convocation Address at Weber State University, you said how in writing *The Woman Warrior* and *China Men*, and even *Tripmaster Monkey*, you left out the endings deliberately as not being important, and you proceeded to say how your new book in progress would include those. Thus, you will begin implementing your new vision with a book of endings, so to speak. Could you explain that vision, as well as your plans for the new book in progress?

Kingston: It wasn't that I left out the endings thinking they were unimportant. I left out those endings because I wasn't wise enough and I didn't know the endings. *The Woman Warrior* ending perhaps is the one I most deliberately left out.

At the end of the Chinese traditional chants, the Woman Warrior comes home and turns from a man, a general in armor, back into a beautiful woman, and then she presents herself to her army as a beautiful woman and sends the soldiers on their way. Now I had left that scene out of my version of *The Woman Warrior* because I was writing in 1975. I wanted a feminist book and I didn't understand the importance or why, in the ancient myth, you would have this strong figure turn into such a feminine person with make-up. The chant tells about her beautiful, long, black hair and how she wears it up and she puts flowers in it. She wears a silk dress and she's a classically beautiful

192

woman. I left that out because I didn't see the need for a modern feminist to wear make-up.

Seshachari: When I first read *The Woman Warrior*, I felt disappointed that Fa Mu Lan, after all her conquests, came home and subsided into a very docile and obedient wife.

Kingston: And I didn't even tell in that story the entirety of her makeover. But I want to include that ending now.

Seshachari: In a different voice probably?

Kingston: Yes, yes, and also with a different wisdom and understanding. I want it very much now to be a hopeful story about homecoming from war, one that shows how a war veteran can transform herself into a peaceful, nurturing, mothering, feminine human being. She becomes more human and humane.

Seshachari: If you had used a traditional voice, you might have made your readers feel that she became a thing, a possession, a wife. But your newer, wiser voice might bring out the actual sense of her being a partner in the family.

Kingston: Also, I am telling her story in a different context now, and I am writing about a different phase of human life. *The Woman Warrior* is still a story of adolescent growth. It tells the journey from being a girl to a woman and so there's just that rite of passage of a young person. But the way I want to use that story now is, I am writing about middle age, the middle of life and even the end of life. I'm talking about the end of a war. And here is not a knight setting out for adventure at the beginning of a *bildungsroman* but one who has finished the war. It is a story of how to come home, how to reintegrate oneself into one's family and community.

Seshachari: And how differently would you end *China Men* and *Tripmaster*, if this were a book of three different endings?

Kingston: I ended *China Men* when the brother returns from Vietnam. It ends on a very flat sentence, "OK, everything is OK." He did not kill anyone, and he was not killed. It's not triumphant, it's not heroic, it's just survival, and that was all the wisdom I knew. And now, 20 years later—I feel that 20 years is a period of time when we live through traumas, troubles come inside of us, and we process them, we live with them, we study them with the conscious mind, then we are able to put them into artistic expression. So 20 years later, my brothers have made lives for themselves beyond the war. They have come home, and they have been able to create peaceful, humane lives. And so, I need to continue "The Brother in Vietnam" past the adventure story and past the adolescent-young-man story into middle age.

Seshachari: Then would you want to change *Tripmaster Monkey* or continue . . .

Kingston: Continue, not change it. See again, *Tripmaster Monkey* ends during Wittman's late adolescence. Wittman is a boyish person and he has just gotten married but there's no commitment or understanding of what marriage is. Not enough time has gone by to test the marriage, to test the carrying out of one's values and principles. The story ends when he decides that he will be a draft evader. You know, for young people there are these instant decisions. But the real test of a human being is a long term carrying out of ideas, and so the next book is about Wittman becoming older and middle aged.

Seshachari: His is a memorable courtship, brief but very picturesque. It catches the sense of the Sixties very well.

Kingston: His wife Taña will be in the new book, so that we can see what kind of people they become. Is a six-month relationship a genuine relationship? What other powers are needed in the characters in order to sustain their love?

Seshachari: In "The Novel's Next Step" published in *Mother Jones* in 1989, you talked about the global novel, and I think you very wisely said that the time for the American Dream and the American Novel is in a sense over. We've got to think globally and include the chaotic elements in our lives but lead them to a nonviolent end. Are you going to integrate these three stories in terms of the ideals you talked about in that article?

Kingston: Yes, that article was in a sense my outline.

Seshachari: You called it your minimalist novel.

Kingston: Yes, what I wanted to do was . . . I was going to write against the minimalist novel in order to write a global novel. The reason I was thinking of a global novel was that I began to notice that every city that I went to anywhere in the world is a cosmopolitan city. You come to Beijing, London, anywhere, and you are surrounded by people from all over the world. Every country has had its diaspora and everybody is going everywhere, and so in order to write a story about any city, any American city or any other city, you have to be able to write characters from every cultural background. A story of a city is also the story of all the people on the entire planet.

Seshachari: You're saying in every city there's a microcosm of the macrocosm . . .

Kingston: There are really few tribes where there are people of just one race and one cultural background. Everybody is all mixed in together. Characters come from different linguistic backgrounds. I hear pieces of many languages. . . . If I write this novel in English the characters will have accents from all over the world. The novelist has to have an ear for the varieties of even one language.

Seshachari: Even in the United States there is no one single standard accent. There are people of so many cultures congregated here.

Kingston: And then of course there is Black English, which is so important and central to the American language. Any American novel has to have that basic sound.

Seshachari: And did it all come about—this vision of yours—because you negated or erased an end to the Fa Mu Lan story? Did that start you thinking you had left the family out, that you had left harmony and good familial cohesion out?

Kingston: I think it comes out of my observation of daily life and just knowing that in any one day or any one trip to the market, it feels like traveling around the world.

Seshachari: In "The Novel's Next Step," you also talk of the idea of social action. Now you have initiated some interesting group activities with Vietnam veterans. How did this idea of working with the veterans, exercising your social zeal for peace, come to you?

Kingston: It seems to me, like most of my ideas, it came gradually. There is of course the Vietnam War and my own peace activism at that time. Also my having two brothers in the service during the Vietnam war. During that time, like other Peace Activists, I tried to think of ways to help stop the war, to help pacify all of us. I had many adventures at that time. We were in Hawaii. We were some of the people who held a church sanctuary for AWOL soldiers. All during the Vietnam War, I could feel there was a darkness hanging over the whole world and it lasted for so long. I had a son and I was horrified that some day he would be drafted. All of these feelings of being a mother were very strong in me, and I felt very protective of not just my son but my brothers. And I didn't want my son to grow up in a world where there is going to be a draft. Those times were very interesting. People were trying to solve the most terrible problems. I have friends who also had children at that time and some of them had the baby at home without a doctor, thinking that maybe they won't register this baby. And if they don't register him, then he will never be drafted. And then the war ended so inconclusively. I was just looking through news clippings that I have of that period and soldiers were still trickling home in the mid-Seventies from Vietnam. So it was inconclusive—it wasn't an ending. And I was thinking, I want to make an ending. I want to be able to manipulate reality as easily as I can manipulate fiction. Do we imagine the world? If we imagine characters, can we cause them to appear in the real world? What if I could strongly write peace, I can cause an end to war.

Seshachari: Chaos theory tells us that the littlest flappings of the wings of a butterfly can cause turbulence someplace else. By the same theory, the beginning of an action by a visionary writer like you could just as well create a wave or a surge of yearning and action for peace.

Kingston: I love that [idea]—that scientists can verify that imagination can manifest a physical reality. So, I was thinking, the end to the Vietnam War is not just that they stop shooting and we stop shooting. That's not the end. The end has to be something very wonderful. The Vietnamese have a commune in France. Thich Nhat Hanh, a Vietnamese monk, has a religious commune in France, and I was thinking how wonderful if I could bring a group of Vietnam veterans to live in community with Vietnamese people.

Seshachari: And you went along?

Kingston: No, this is just still in the imagination. I'm thinking, that's the way I want to end a book. I want to raise the money to take a group and go there and then I can just witness the coming together of all these people. To me, that would be a true ending to the war with Vietnam.

Seshachari: You have already begun something here.

Kingston: Yes. I've begun all the intermediate things. One reason that I started these writing workshops with the veterans is that I got a lot of mail from veterans. They write to me about their experiences in war, and they ask me questions about, oh about all kinds of things, about ethics, about trauma, about how to write. I was gathering quite a lot of mail, a big stack, and I kept saying, Why do they write to me? It must be because they read my books or something, but I didn't know how to answer these letters, and I didn't answer them. I just kept putting them in a stack until I could come up with an adequate answer. What can I say to these people? And then it came to me that I wanted to answer them in person. I wanted to hear their stories in person and I wanted to give them something. And what I could give them is the best thing I know, which is the method of writing.

Seshachari: Yesterday you remarked how you were changing your traditional ideas about writing. You said how we all have this idea of writing as a solitary act and how you too went into your attic, you a petite woman, with the ceiling of the attic no more than two inches higher than your head. Since working and writing with the veterans, have you now come to recognize that writing can be a communal act? And, is your writing that takes place as a communal act of the same quality or better than the writing that took place when it was a singular act?

Kingston: I . . . hmmm . . .

Seshachari: Of course I do recognize that even when we sit in a communal setting, each one is writing one's own.

Kingston: Yes, I am a solitary writer even among the community of writers. I am not sure what the direct effect others' writing has on my writing. So far, when writing in community the work goes faster. I can feel our group energy pushing me to work better. Writing alone, I'm very slow. So that's one good effect. The veterans are writing the most wonderful, strong stories. We pull the stories out of one another with our intense listening.

Seshachari: Would you have been able to write one complete segment of *The Woman Warrior*, say "Shaman," in a communal setting?

Kingston: I do believe that our lives and our art go together. Who I am and what I write are the same. *The Woman Warrior* is about a young girl trying to come to an understanding of herself; she is still individuating, she is learning what is secret and what is public. I wrote with the privacy of writing a diary. What I am writing now is about public life and about communal life, and so I set up the outside world to be the same as my inside world.

Seshachari: So, when your subject matter evokes solitude and relies heavily on the solitary thinking mind, the emotive mind, it is better to sit by yourself in solitude and write, whereas, if your object is say global peace or a communal venture, then it might be better to write in a communal setting. Are you trying that out right now?

Kingston: Yes, and I feel that the writing process doesn't just begin when you are putting words on paper. It begins in the living that you do before, and I feel powerful enough now so that I can set up my daily living circumstances in order to support me and support my art. I do a lot of this by instinct, like bringing the veterans together. I don't figure it out until later.

Seshachari: Your instincts are marvelous. You were a trailblazer even in the early 1970s when you started writing. Nobody had written an "autobiography" like *The Woman Warrior*. I call it a "mythopsychic" autobiography, by which I mean it's a psychic autobiography which draws heavily on mythology.

Kingston: I like that. That makes sense. The way I've looked at it is that I want to write about myself and other people in the truest way possible. To write a true autobiography or biography, I have to know what the other person dreams and how her imagination works. I am less interested in dates and facts.

Seshachari: Asian women generally tend to be socially inhibited. The act of writing is an act of baring oneself, in the Eastern sense, without shame or shyness. But you write about your grandfather going down the basket in such surprisingly uninhibited ways! How did you shed your inhibitions to grapple so brilliantly with psychic realities?

Kingston: I feel that writing is also a very secretive act . . .

Seshachari: But it becomes public the moment it is printed.

Kingston: But that's later. Also, it's not really public in that, while people are reading it—and they are reading quietly and alone—you are still at home doing whatever you're doing in private.

Seshachari: But what about when your mother says, You wrote this about your grandfather?

Kingston: But she never did; she only said, Oh this is so accurate. I had an Asian American student, a Korean, and to pay her way through college, she was a stripper in North Beach. She was doing that at night, and in the daytime she came to school. In my class, she wrote a story telling about her thoughts and feelings. She didn't want to show her writing to other students because she said, I'm baring my soul. She felt embarrassed to exhibit her inner life. But I feel the opposite. I think that for somebody to read my words is not shameful because the communication is so complete. When the reader reads the first person narrative, the "I" becomes the "I" of the reader, so the reader becomes me. So how can there be public shame?

Seshachari: What a useful dictum for all writers! It's the most difficult thing to bare oneself and be genuinely honest from the depths of one's mythic racial memory.

Kingston: Yes. I have this motto which is, Pay attention and tell the truth. And in telling the truth, sometimes you tell it fictionally, sometimes you tell it nonfictionally.

Seshachari: When you were talking about the veterans, you told us about the meditation walk, where you felt you were in communion with mother earth and father sky and all creation including humans. How would you connect your inspiration for your creative writing with your communal solitariness?

Kingston: Well, I don't do all my writing in the community. Much of my writing is in solitude, but I feel that it's vital that periodically there be this gathering of communal energy. It inspires me and I go back into solitude. It's like a wave—you know the wave goes out and comes to shore. This writing in community is a new discovery for me. I've spent too many years carrying writing as if it were a burden that's only mine. I want to tell everybody, and young people too, that there are many things that we must do in community. I wish I had started sooner.

Seshachari: You remember the address you gave in San Francisco at the 1991 MLA convention just after the Oakland fires?

Kingston: Yes, I remember.

Seshachari: You had lost your manuscript in the flames.

Kingston: And I asked people to give me things. I asked them to give me titles or ideas on *The Books of Peace*. I asked them to find Hemingway manuscripts, Anaïs Nin pictures, Vietnam War stories, World War II stories. That's right, I remember that. Right after the fire I gave speeches asking people to give me things. What I was doing was saying, You are my community. I'm not going to write your book all by myself! Will you help me write it? You help me with the research and just send me all this material.

Seshachari: Did you receive a lot?

Kingston: A lot. A lot. Yes.

Seshachari: And are you going to make use of it in your new book? Is it titled *Another Book of Peace*?

Kingston: I think of *Another Book of Peace* as a subtitle; I'm also beginning to think maybe I'll call it *The Fifth Book of Peace* . . .

Seshachari: Since the fourth one went up in flames too?

Kingston: Yes, yes, so this will be a fifth one. People have sent me things . . . and of course I make use of everything they give me. Somebody brought me a teddy bear. A woman was sitting in church, and she said a vision came to her in church. The vision was, she remembered she saw me on television and I was using an Epson QX10 computer and she had an old Epson QX10 at home she wasn't using. A vision came to her in church, Give Maxine your computer. So here's this woman at the door. She gave me a computer. People brought me clothes, shoes, underwear . . . stories. Audio and videotapes of my readings from the work in progress.

Seshachari: And was that the beginning of your "communal" life?

Kingston: That could be. There was a fire, and then the very next couple of weeks I was telling people to help me with the research.

Seshachari: So you had to be deprived in order to gain . . .

Kingston: . . . to get this idea of community.

Seshachari: How wonderful. It's almost like a biblical or mythic story.

Kingston: One idea that I had too was that the only things that remained after the fire were the things I gave away. Literally so, because the gifts that I gave to people, the people after the fire brought the gifts back. So I was thinking, all that remains is what I gave.

Seshachari: How did you learn to accept the finality of that loss and proceed with your writing life as if nothing had happened?

Kingston: Oh, I haven't accepted the finality. If it were possible, I would not have had any of this happen.

Seshachari: But then you said you didn't want hypnotists to hypnotize you and have you regurgitate the lost book of peace from memory.

Kingston: No, no because that's only memory. I don't want to regurgitate. Writing should be constantly an act of creation and going forward into the new. But I've been thinking a lot about loss and memory because my father died just before the fire, so there was that loss of my father and then the loss of the house and the loss of the book. Everything happened at once. But everybody has losses. Working with veterans, I understand now that the mourning is never over. We will always have mourning after a traumatic event; after a loss there will always be mourning. We want it that way because we don't want to forget our feelings for that person or that thing. However, the mourning changes; mourning breaks up into different elements. We will mourn in different ways and one way of mourning, perhaps you pass a spot or you go under a tree and you remember a person that you talked to under that tree. That's his spirit visiting you. Maybe by that time you feel very happy because you remember. That remembrance and that happiness are mourning, too, transformed.

Seshachari: As long as a person is alive in the mind of another human being, that person is not truly dead.

Kingston: Yes, and that person is alive in you and in your heart. I am sure that our relationship with those people continues to grow and I will continue to resolve my relationship with my father even though he's dead. I can still think of things to say to him. It's too bad that he can't answer, but sometimes he can even answer—

Seshachari: It's a dialogue in the mind?

Kingston: Yes, because then you think, Well, he would have said this and this, and so his presence is continuing.

Seshachari: Very early in your writing career, in an interview with Timothy Pfaff in the *New York Times Book Review*, you said that writing was like having a fit or going to war. Besides helping release tensions, it served you as a form of social activism and so in the new book that you're going to subtitle "Peace," will that be your major goal—to achieve peace?

Kingston: Yes, yes—to put out into the world a vision of peaceful living and of how human beings can relate to one another harmoniously and joyfully and how groups of people come together. I feel that peace has hardly been imagined. It is rarely dramatized in the theater, in the movies, even in books.

Seshachari: It's only in fairy tales we say, "and they lived happily ever after."

Kingston: Good. I'm going to take that "happily ever after" and continue it and ask, Well, how did they live next? I am meeting the veterans again in mid-December. I think it's a good time because it's the holidays, it is going to be the end of a year and the beginning of a new year. It's a good time to stop and think about the past and the future.

Seshachari: And there's the winter solstice too.

Kingston: That's right. It's a very good time to be with other people and to take stock, assess where you've been and where you're going.

Seshachari: Changing the subject here, I want you, if you are willing, to talk about that little misunderstanding or rift between you and Frank Chin, et al.

Kingston: Well, you know, I don't think of it as a misunderstanding or a rift or anything that's between him and me. It's always been him with these attacks, and I usually don't answer at all. He calls me terrible names such as race traitor. He even wrote me a letter that he's going to beat me up if he sees me. I don't want to honor him with answers.

Seshachari: Has he met you at all?

Kingston: No, we've never met.

Seshachari: Maybe if you did meet, he would recognize you for the warm-hearted human being you are.

Kingston: Oh, no, no. I think that in order to recognize a warm-hearted human being, you have to be a warm-hearted human being yourself. Actually, I've stopped reading his work, because I think he does not mean me well. I read for inspiration and life and help, and I don't think he wants to help me. What are the real important issues at stake? I have identified two. One of them is the racial and cultural myths. Whom do they belong to? Frank would say they belong to real Chinese such as himself. And they do not belong to, for example, the Caucasians. My feeling is, if somebody goes to a bookstore and buys my book, then they have bought the myths, and they can have the great myths of China by reading them. The only way that myths stay alive is if we pass them on. He has also been saying that there is a true text, including the chant of the Woman Warrior. Now I know that myth is not passed on by text; it's mostly passed on by word of mouth, and every time you tell a story and every time you hear it, it's different. So there isn't one frozen authentic version; there are many, many authentic versions different from person to person.

Seshachari: Feminists especially talk of writing alternate myths, and I think alternate myths, in very simplistic terms, imply there is a view of one myth from the male or patriarchal perspective and there is a view of the same myth from a woman's or feminist perspective. When written from a woman's perspective, the myth takes on different shapes and can be interpreted in opposite ways.

Kingston: That explains, why, as a woman, it's absolutely clear to me that we have the freedom of creating alternate myths, and for Frank Chin, as a male, there is a monolith, one monument of a myth. The other difference—I just discovered this recently and am very surprised at this coincidence—I think he just published his translation of *The Art of War* [Sun Tzu, ca., 500 B.C., ascribed to Sun Wu], one of the traditional Chinese books of war. He's brought this into the world at the same time that I am writing my book of peace. You can see the fundamental difference in values.

Seshachari: Critics think of Tom Wolfe's *The Electric Kool-Aid Acid Test* as the quintessential novel of 1960s; I think you have also written a quintessential novel of the Sixties in *Tripmaster Monkey.*

Kingston: Yes. John Leonard called it the Great American Novel of the Sixties.

Seshachari: I remember that. But you wrote your novel much later. You wrote it in the 1980s. So I am particularly curious about its genesis. How did you think of writing about the Sixties in the late Seventies.

Kingston: I am a very slow, slow writer and thinker and reader—

Seshachari: You are a perfectionist.

Kingston: Actually I think maybe it's the normal course of creation. The journey in the *Odyssey* takes twenty years. It takes twenty years to live an experience, learn its meanings, find the words to tell it. I loved being a young person in the Sixties. There were many, many wonderful adventures.

Seshachari: Did you feel privileged like Wittman?

Kingston: Yes, I thought sitting in a coffee house was being in heaven. One of the wonderful things about the 1960s was language. There was a new language and there were wonderful new ways of describing psychedelic states, spiritual states, trying to find new words for political actions like those of Gandhi and Martin Luther King. What do you call that when you sit at the lunch counter and you don't move and you do it with peace and love?

Seshachari: Sit-ins, be-ins, whatever-ins; perhaps satyagraha?

Kingston: Sit-ins and be-ins, yes, love-ins and psychedelics. And I love the slang of the period. And so, of course, I wanted to write a book about that period, using that language. Also when I was writing *China Men* and

The Woman Warrior, I felt very much like a translator. I was always translating Chinese into English and finding English words for Chinese ways and dialogue. I felt so free when I got to *Tripmaster Monkey*. I could use my language and I could use the language that I loved to listen to.

Seshachari: Its language is inside out. It's as if some new person has written this book. It's great. I was also interested in this Monkey—tell me about the title. You worked it in so well throughout. Wittman's the monkey, and you work it in very clearly.

Kingston: This is the first book that I named by myself. That name came to me even before I started writing. Tripmaster was a word from the 1960s. People could be on acid, and there's a tripmaster who suggests trips for them and who guides them and keeps them from flipping out. I feel that I myself was very good at doing that. Often I would be the one who would not take drugs and the other people would take the drugs. I would make sure they were safe. Very different from Ken Kesey. I wanted to make sure that they did not go to any dangerous places, make sure they went to beautiful places with flowers and music and birds. So that's the "Tripmaster," and as for "Monkey," it's utterly clear to me that the monkey spirit came to America in the 1960s. Monkey was at the Democratic Convention in Chicago, and on the march to the Pentagon. It's the most interesting coincidence that Monkey accompanied Tripitika to India and, isn't that funny—Tripitika and Tripmaster begin in the same T-R-I-P? Isn't that odd?

Seshachari: When I connected Wittman to the Buddhist *Tripitika* Monkey [in the questions sent earlier], I thought, Am I concocting this link by myself or is there something to it?

Kingston: I think that it's one of those language miracles. It's right out there in the universe you know, those coincidences, those true coincidences that come together, that Monkey and . . . here is Monkey mind and he is even pre-human in the scale of evolution. He has to rise in this ladder of humanity and become a Buddhist Bodhisatva. And there's also biological evolution that has to take place. I like the subtitle too, *His Fake Book*.

Seshachari: Why did you call it *His Fake Book*?

Kingston: I'd walk into music stores and look at sheet music and find fake books.

Seshachari: What are they?

Kingston: Jazz musicians often made collections of basic melodies of tunes which they improvised off of. I was thinking that I would write about many trips, suggest many stories. I was turning forty when I was writing it and I was thinking, Oh, I'm going to die and this book is going to be so long and I'll never finish it. It took eight years and at one point it was a thousand pages long. So I thought, maybe if I can just suggest the beginnings of some stories, somebody else will take off on them and finish them.

Seshachari: You published some 300 pages of the 1000 pages. Did the other 700 pages [of *Tripmaster Monkey*] burn with the rest of your belongings?

Kingston: Oh, yes. There's nothing left. But the thousand pages of *Tripmaster Monkey*—mostly I took that [manuscript] and condensed it. So it wasn't as if I cut out sections. But, it's turned out that I will be the one who will finish the story of the Tripmaster Monkey growing older because I did manage to live past forty and fifty. I'm hoping that people will say, They call the monk and monkey "Trip" because they go on a long, long trip.

Seshachari: Had you read Hsuang Tsang's account and Wu Ch'eng-en's novel of the same name . . .
Kingston: Oh, *The Journey to the West*.

Seshachari: *Journey to the West* [Hsi-yu Chi] and Arthur Waley's translation, *Monkey: Hope Novel of China* [NY: Grove, 1958].
Kingston: Yes. I had. I read them when I was younger and reread them when I was older. I read *Journey to the West* when I was writing *Tripmaster Monkey* too because I just wanted to verify to myself, Am I catching the spirit of this monkey person? Am I right in seeing monkey's presence?

Seshachari: Did you read the original Chinese or did you read them in translation?
Kingston: In translation. My Chinese is not good enough to read it. I just wanted to make sure that I was correct in my understanding of monkey mind. I was seeing monkeys all over in the USA in the Sixties, so I read that book to make sure that I was getting the right spirit and also to see whether there were some stories that I had forgotten that I could just grab.

Seshachari: I noticed too that at the time you were writing your *Tripmaster Monkey*, Henry Louis Gates, Jr. was writing his *The Signifying Monkey*.
Kingston: I know, I know. See, so the Monkey was here, and it went inside Henry Louis Gates's mind, and it went inside my mind too.

Seshachari: And he takes it as a kind of trope. He calls it a peculiarly African American rhetorical trope. How would you signify your monkey?

Kingston: I love it whenever I find [something] like the African American Monkey and Chinese Monkey—when I find out that they are both monkeys and they are both here in America, then I feel connected to African American people and again inspired that we are all one human race. I think it's so important for us to find figures like that, so that we can make our human connections. My monkey signifies the way the natural mind and body work—jumping around, undisciplined. Buddhists say "monkey mind" and "horse willpower."

Seshachari: I loved your idea when you said [in the Convocation Address] that you have learned to be Black by reading ethnic literature. We have all learned to be White by learning about pilgrims and pioneers and in that sense I learned to be Chinese by reading *China Men* and *The Woman Warrior*. I think it's a marvelous concept of letting in multicultural ideas through reading and changing oneself into the quintessential American who is multiethnic.

Kingston: Yes, yes. You know when Alex Haley wrote *Roots*—and I think *Roots* came out the same year as *The Woman Warrior*—when I got that book and read it, I felt, yes, those are my roots; they're not just his roots, they're not just Black people's roots, those are my roots. Those are my roots all the way to Africa. And Alex Haley gives them to me as a gift and I receive them by knowing about those roots and by reading that book and by letting all of that awareness into my consciousness and into my heart.

Seshachari: Of the current trends on campuses in teaching ethnic literature, one is called "particularism," where one learns only about one's own culture, like all the African American students taking a Black History course, all the Asian students taking an Asian American Literature course and so on. Then there is the other one called "pluralism," where one takes multiethnic literature all together. Sometimes I'm distrustful of single ethnic courses because students in their youthfulness take that history to be the totality of history.

Kingston: Yes, yes. Also we can enter through any door of this great palace that we have. If we're going to have concentrated Black Studies, Asian American Studies and so on, it would be great for the Blacks to go to the Asian American Studies course and the Asians to go to the Black Studies course or the men to go to Women's Studies and so on.

Seshachari: But that rarely happens.

Kingston: I know it rarely happens. But there's nothing in the rules that says it cannot happen. I mean, it's not institutionally recommended—it's all voluntary. So we do it to ourselves, ghettoize ourselves. But I do believe that if we study any one discipline deeply, it will connect us to everything else.

Seshachari: All minority literature is richly textured, and its literary artistry is always complex because most writers are reinventing themselves or their native culture. In a sense, you are reinventing Chinese mythic culture. It seems to me that those who cannot read original works of their mother culture must face slightly greater problems. Can you elaborate on some of the problems that you faced as you began to write *The Woman Warrior*? What I'm saying is, immigrants of Indian origins send their children to their parents, to their brothers and sisters in India, where the children learn some Indian language and even if they can't read too well, they read well enough to get a flavor of it. I would imagine that because until very recently China was behind the dark curtain and secondly because Chinese ideograms are so numerous that it's a hardship to learn them as a language, it becomes difficult for Chinese immigrants to partake of their culture in its original flavor. So did you ever feel that you were losing something or were you trying harder to understand? What were your responses to the questions you faced as you began to dip into that Chinese mythic consciousness? It's as if the Chinese language was a vast ocean and you didn't know how to swim.

Kingston: Well, I think that I first contended with these questions when I was about 7 years old, and, you know, my first language is Chinese, and I only knew people who spoke Chinese. I talked story and I invented poems and made up songs and I heard stories, but when I began to know the English language and somewhere around 8 years old, I started to write, and the English language was so . . .

Seshachari: Overpowering?

Kingston: No, no. Bright, full of freedom. I felt freedom because the English language is so easy, and I thought, My gosh, everything I hear I can notate it! I can notate Chinese. I can write Chinese in English. I can write English in English and I never had that power when I spoke only Chinese. You speak Chinese and then the written language is completely different. There's no system. It's one word at a time. But all of a sudden, with the 26 letters in the English alphabet you can write anything, so I just felt I had the most powerful tool, and I felt free to express myself.

Seshachari: Have you ever written Chinese words in the Roman script?

Kingston: Oh yes. That was considered cheating when we were in Chinese school. The teachers did not like us to do that, but we would, in pencil, lightly write the Roman script next to the characters and then we would read it out loud. If they found out, they would hit us. But we discovered a method which they use today in teaching Chinese. Now they put Chinese into Roman script for people to study. It's easier to learn that way, and we children were doing it when we were 6 or 7 years old.

Seshachari: Do you think it would be good for China if people learned only the 26 letters of the Roman script?

Kingston: But then we lose that beautiful calligraphy.

Seshachari: Yes, yes.

Kingston: The Chinese are always monkeying around with the language. I don't like it when they simplify the really complex characters because they're so pictorially wonderful. But that's a different art. I heard a talk by Anita Desai and I was so impressed. She said that she chooses to write in English because in English you can replicate the rhythms of any of the hundreds of Indian languages.

Seshachari: I have this other question about ethnic minorities. Central to the communities of minorities is the concept of the "psychic frontier" and the imaginary line which demarcates Us vs. Them. The Whites vs. African Americans, African Americans vs. Asian Americans and so on, and this frontier is a shifting frontier—it has to be. Arnold Krupat defines it as a "shifting space in which two cultures encounter one another." Can you comment on that frontier vis-a-vis the Chinese Americans and the Anglos? How has it changed from the time you were a 7-year-old going to an Anglo school and discovering the English language as a power tool, and now when you are trying to enlarge the area of understanding between different ethnic groups?

Kingston: I must say that I never pictured psychic space like that because the actual way in which people live in my hometown of Stockton was not in well-defined ghettos. People were very much interspersed.

Seshachari: And yet, until you were 7 years old, you didn't have a single Anglo friend, right?

Kingston: I didn't meet any of them until I went to school.

Seshachari: And would you define that psychic space where you really didn't mesh—where although you lived so close, you did not talk with a White friend?

Kingston: Actually, there weren't any White people in our neighborhood. But there were Black people. The next door people were Black, and there were Mexicans and Filipinos, but they were all very interspersed and while we saw them, we didn't go inside one another's houses, that's true. But that time when I didn't have any friends of other colors, that was a very short time. As soon as I started school—and my parents put me into school very early, I think they lied about my age, I must have been only 3 years old. At that age I met all kinds of other people. In Stockton, there isn't a Chinatown where people lived. So I don't quite have that sense of very clear boundaries between one and another.

Seshachari: I have one observation though. European immigrants into the United States appear to lose their ethnicity much faster. Within two or three generations, they get so totally assimilated into the big melting pot mass that we call them typical Anglo Americans whereas, the third and fourth generation Asian American immigrants appear not to be [so totally assimilated] because of their color.

Kingston: Also because we look different. And we have different customs, we have different language, and then also the deliberate prejudices. . . .

Seshachari: And so would you say that people of color on this continent are in a kind of psychic diaspora? For instance, the third and fourth generations of Chinese still think of China as their country of origin. But the third or fourth generation Germans or Norwegians have no ubiquitous consciousness of another home in Europe.

Kingston: There are many constant diasporas from home countries, and when we are here, diasporas throughout the American continents. You know, the average American moves every four and a half years. And yet, the people of color have stronger senses of community than I imagine the average White person has. These can be communities that band together in hardship, the worst ones being gangs. But then there are also religious communities in the churches. There are China Towns, Asia Towns, family associations that were started 200 years ago when people first came here and they still flourish today. So, in one sense there is this falling apart, losing old languages, losing the old ways, but maybe not so much losing of the old values—

Seshachari: And the communal solidarity?
Kingston: Yes, yes.

Seshachari: Bharati Mukherjee once said that every immigrant must feel powerful because he or she can reinvent one's own past. We see this happen all the time—it is a unique opportunity to gain some kind of self-confidence or a better self-image. So in a sense, we are reinventing our own vision and reinventing our past. We're also reinventing our present and our future and our vision—both in mythic and actual terms. And this vision comes to us in terms of what it is now to be an American, because we are now in America.

Kingston: And we made this stuff up, we made this country up.

Seshachari: Yes, exactly. And so, what is your vision of an ideal American in this multiethnic culture? Your vision interests me since you are writing the Peace book.

Kingston: I guess I would start from the very ground. I picture a people living in harmony upon the earth . . .

Seshachari: In that *Mother Jones* article you said, Marry interracially. You gave two or three different ways of how people could be global citizens.

Kingston: When I said Marry interracially, I was thinking, Oh that's fun. Of course, it's already happening. The rate of "out-marriage," as they call it, among the various Asian populations is 75% and the rate of out-marriage among the Jews is 75% and so it seems that number, 75% is the magic number. Everybody is an "other" and here are all these "others," potentially enemies, and it's such an opportunity to learn how to get along with people you don't like, people you don't look like, and so we can learn the most difficult love.

Seshachari: You once said you were claiming America in *China Men*. When I read *The Woman Warrior*, I felt you were claiming womanhood for all of us.

Kingston: Oh, that's wonderful.

Seshachari: In your *Book of Peace*, what would you be claiming?

Kingston: Oh, what would I be claiming this time? What I would like to do is claim evolution—that we can evolve past being a warring species into a peaceful species so that we are not predators anymore, and that we stop being carnivorous. If only we could stop being cannibals—

Seshachari: You recognize that's very difficult, of course. For instance, during The Warring States period in China [481–221 B.C.], Confucius or K'ung-fu-tzu, who hailed from the state of Wu, was crushed because even the ruler of Wu was not amenable to giving him a state job. The poor visionary died never recognizing how he would soon become an idol worshipped in the decades and millennia to follow.

Kingston: It seems that we just continue being a Warring States period.

Seshachari: Jesus could not stop the warring state. Gandhi could not. But I suppose we cannot give up and say it doesn't succeed.

Kingston: No, we just keep trying and we keep using the simple, gentle tools that we have.

Seshachari: You said in the *Mother Jones* article that "the dream of the great American novel is past. We need to write the global novel. Its setting will be the United States, destination of journeys from everywhere." This idea of enlarging the frontier of the novel is wonderful. And in the Kennedy era of the early 1960s, for example, the American frontier—the actual Western frontier—moved into the realm of space. Not having anymore territory to explore or conquer, the United States turned its attention to the conquest of outer space. Today, our very terminology is so entrenched in metaphors and tropes of battles and conquests. We are conquering space, we are conquering something. In *The Woman Warrior* you used another such trope, but of course this had legitimacy in the sense that Fa Mu Lan actually went to war.

Kingston: I tried to change the noun "warrior" by putting that adjective "woman" in front of it. Maybe it softens the word—it's a particular kind of warrior.

Seshachari: Can you think of a usable term that approximates the social notion of conquest and is still rooted in pacifism?

Kingston: Well, I guess Martin Luther King Jr. said "overcome, we shall overcome." That's a lovely word "overcome." It's coming home, and over means going high and flying above. That's very nice. But at a PEN international congress in Toronto and Montreal, I was talking about the global novel. Somebody asked the question, Where are you going to set your novel? When I said the United States, they booed me. The Canadians were saying, Why again your country? Again the United States? So, you know, I was being ethnocentric, and I didn't even mean to be. All I meant was I need to start from where I am, and I happen to be in the United States, but I did realize, Oh, it does not necessarily have to be the United States. I need to write in a bigger way; my own consciousness needs to be larger.

Seshachari: And as you said, since the novel has to reach out into its chaotic boundaries, the global boundaries may become cosmic boundaries?

Kingston: I teach William Carlos Williams in my Reading for Writers course at Berkeley. In the 1920s, he was calling for a book that was worthy of the Americas. He was thinking of a big American novel. He was not confining it to the United States. Williams was thinking of the Americas; he wanted a book that was speaking from the large ground of these two continents.

Seshachari: One could think of Whitman's *Leaves of Grass*. It comes closest to being a global poem.

Kingston: Yes, it's global and it's American. What I love about Whitman is that he never forgot he and she, man and woman. How did we slide so far backwards from Whitman?

Seshachari: And so the novel in prose would have to have that similar reach.

Kingston: Yes, the reach that would include everyone. You know when Wittman [in *Tripmaster Monkey*] produces a play, he invites everybody he knows to be in the play—

Seshachari: I liked that.

Kingston: I want novels like that. Put everything I know and everyone I know in them.

Seshachari: And everyone has a part?

Kingston: Yes, everyone has a starring role. Everyone is a star.

Seshachari: Everyone is also a spectator?

Kingston: You're right.

Seshachari: Both a spectator and a star. That's wonderful. At the end of *Tripmaster Monkey*, you said, Wittman Ah Sing has now learned to bring to the surface his Asian American consciousness, and now his problem is to become a global citizen.

Kingston: Oh, yes, yes.

Seshachari: You were suggesting that we are inwardly ethnocentric and we are who we are, an Asian American or an African American or a Mexican American and so on. And in becoming a global citizen one has to turn one's gaze outward. And you suggested some things like interracial marriages, an education that emphasizes pacifism as a societal value, and involvement in sanctuary-type movements, which also include the idea of the city of refuge. How many average people who are the solid foundation of our society but not necessarily writers or readers have the opportunity to become global citizens? The average American does not read much and does not write at all.

Kingston: I think that if a person doesn't read, maybe they cannot come out of themselves. You know you delineated a . . . I think a growth process of human development . . . first there is an awareness of the ego, the self, and then of another and many others to become a communal person. And we need to go even beyond that—our family, tribe, Chinatown, gang, nation—into a larger selflessness or agape. I think it is a very rare person who will take on public and global responsibilities. They don't even go out to vote, and you only have to do that once in two years. Reading and writing should expand and transform the self.

Seshachari: Average persons are not readers in the best sense. Even students who go to class and get their grades don't always read critically.

Kingston: I just read about scientists who measured the strands of neuropeptides in our brains. They found that in the people who are most educated and who consistently read books, the strands actually get longer. In the brains of the ones who don't read, the neuropeptides get shorter. We physically change because of our reading and thinking, and then I hope we become strong enough to create a good society around us. Reading must be an essential tool for envisioning and making the world.

Seshachari: So it becomes a vision that is likely to be just beyond our reach?

Kingston: I hope not. We're publishing more books than ever—

Seshachari: Some people are reading more books than ever but others are not reading at all.

Kingston: This morning we were looking at the best seller list in *USA Today.* They publish a list of 50 books so that they can list more than the 15 that are in the *New York Times* list. There are hardly any literary books on the list.

Seshachari: Your next publication will be. In your keepsake Bancroft Library book, *Through the Black Curtain*, you say that when you learned to write English, you realized that you had parted the Black Curtain and that you were out.

Kingston: Yes, yes. But it keeps swinging shut. When I write, I am at the theater you know. I look forward to the curtain opening up and seeing what's behind. I keep knowing that when I open it, there are all kinds of gifts and visions. And God is behind there.

Seshachari: At the end of the book, however, when you had also just finished writing *Tripmaster Monkey*, you said "I think I'm drying up."

Kingston: I often feel that way, like the weather. In California, we're into our seventh year of drought.

Seshachari: At the end of *Tripmaster Monkey* too, you say that you felt you had no more books within you.

Kingston: Oh, I did? You know what that comes from? Every time I write I put everything I know into the one work. And then when I get finished with it, I say, Well that's it. I don't know anymore.

Seshachari: And then you reinvent yourself.

EPILOGUE: Extract from a telephone conversation a year later in November 1994.

Seshachari: How do you feel about *The Woman Warrior* and *China Men* being adapted into a play? Are you satisfied with the translation of your books into a new medium?

Kingston: I am amazed at the richness and beauty of the play—the costumes hand sewn in China, the immense stage sets and glorious lights by Ming Cho Lee, the voices of the actors transmitting my stories mouth-to-ear, the fusion of Western and Chinese music, the kung fu acrobatics. Much of what I write came out of talk-story. I put talk-story into text. Now, the play returns text to talk-story, and children and non-readers can appreciate these myths and legends too.

Seshachari: Did you write the script?

Kingston: No, Deborah Rogin is the playwright. Her feat was to find an organizing principle for my complex non-linear books. She has braided three strands together—myth, ancestral history, and the life of a young girl. Watching the play, I kept thinking what an interesting girl I was!

As Truthful as Possible: An Interview with Maxine Hong Kingston

Eric J. Schroeder / 1996

From *Writing on the Edge* 7:2 (Spring 1996), pp. 83–96. Reprinted by permission.

WOE: *The Woman Warrior* opens with your mother saying "You must not tell anyone what I'm about to tell you," and then you proceed to do just that. Why do you begin with this particular scene?

Kingston: There has to be a way into the story. And there are obstacles in the way, including orders from one's own mother not to tell. So I thought if I began the book stating what that order was, I could confront it directly and disobey the order. And in that way I could free myself and my voice to be able to tell the story. Since writing that I've seen that there are other people who use this same technique. Alice Walker begins *The Color Purple*: "You better not never tell nobody but God." Toni Morrison begins *The Bluest Eye*: "Quiet as it's kept"—then proceeds to tell the community's secrets.

WOE: The opening seems to do two things: it introduces the conflict between you and your mother, which is one of the central tensions in the book, and it also introduces the theme of storytelling. It reminds me of what Michael Herr once said about *Dispatches*: he thought it wasn't really a book about Vietnam as much as it was a book about writing a book. Do you see something similar going on in *The Woman Warrior*—on one level it's a chronicle of your family, but on another level it's a book about finding voice?

Kingston: In all my writing I am aware of writing itself, or consciousness, or how to put whatever is going on into words. And I suppose I could leave those musings out because they're just the ruminations of the author. I've decided to leave them in because I want to show the working of the mind and how the mind finds the story, how the mind finds expression and creates itself. And that decision has to do with form. How do we find form? How do we emerge from no form into form? I want to set that process down, even though it's abstract, and many people are not interested in those sorts of questions. Most present-day readers are not interested in abstractions. They want to get right to the action. But I have decided I will put all that thinking in.

WOE: Genre was an issue that obsessed critics when *The Woman Warrior* was first published. Critics asked "What is it?" And the same thing happened with *China Men.* How did you arrive at those forms?

Kingston: I'm aware of what reality is, and I'm also aware there is a whole part of my being that imagines. When I write a character, I want to set down what this person is dreaming about. What is he or she fantasizing about? What are the narratives that people tell as they go about the realities of life? Also I think that having two categories—fiction and nonfiction—is too small. I picture a border between fiction and nonfiction, and I am making that border very wide; fiction is a narrow place on one side and nonfiction is a narrow place on another side, and there's this great big border in the middle, in which real life is taking place and also fantasies and dreams and visions.

WOE: What you're describing seems to characterize much of the literature in the last thirty years or so. E. L. Doctorow said there's no such thing as fiction and nonfiction, there's just narrative.

Kingston: I think fiction is a useful label because it's a positive word that we use to describe imagination, we use to describe storytelling. But nonfiction is not a useful word because it isn't anything. I mean, poetry is nonfiction, isn't it? And so I should think that within the idea of nonfiction there could be all manners of things. Including fiction.

I just write whatever I'm thinking, and I don't categorize as I go along. I'll leave it up to others where they put the book on their shelves. But I notice that these distinctions are not a problem for a lot of people—there's bookstores that can put *The Woman Warrior* on the nonfiction shelves *and* the fiction shelves. It's anthropology *and* sociology *and* feminism *and* Asian American history. I break through categories.

WOE: Were you inventing the form of *The Woman Warrior* as you went along, or from the start did you have an idea what it might look like when it was done?

Kingston: I was inventing it as I went along. And I didn't know where I was going to end up, and I did not have a large shape in mind. I felt that I was making the path as I was going along. I like *Armies of the Night*, Norman Mailer writing the novel as history, history as novel. I teach *Armies of the Night*; I use it to show students how we make history in the same way we write a novel. And as we narrate what's going on, we shape history.

I also like that book a lot because he writes about the responsibility of the writer. Does the writer actually go out in the street and perform politics and then write about it? Henry James and Wallace Stegner both said not to commit experience for the sake of the writing. Mailer questions that injunction and the notion of objectivity. The writer makes up the world out in the streets and at home in the ivory tower writing the story. I suppose we try to be as objective and as truthful as possible ("truthful" is the right word); still, we are affecting the truth.

WOE: You were writing *The Woman Warrior* and *China Men* almost simultaneously. It strikes me, however, that the forms are quite different: *The Woman Warrior* is composed of large portraits that overlap in places and *China Men* has portraits juxtaposed against vignettes. Were you working out those two different forms independently?

Kingston: At one point, all those stories from *The Woman Warrior* and *China Men* were coming to me at the same time. But later, when I had written down a lot of the stories, I saw they actually could be organized into two different books because the history actually takes place at different times and different places. The women were in China and had their own society. The men were sailing or traveling and were in Chinatowns, and that was another society. Their stories just fell into two different books.

The way I use myth in the two different books also makes them different: the women had one way with myth and the men had another kind of myth. Myths played different roles in their lives. That discovery affected the form of those two books. The women's myths were more intertwined and inside their lives. In *The Woman Warrior*, myths and the psyche of the women are integrated. In *China Men* the myths are separate from the men's lives. I'll tell a myth such as a myth about a peacemaker, which is an ancient story. And then that would be juxtaposed with a story about the Vietnam War. The characters in the Vietnam War story are not thinking about the peacemaker myth. I'm asking the reader to read these stories separately, and then to think, "What does this myth have to do with this story? And are these heroes at all affected by this myth? Do they even know about it?" The reader has to struggle with the question of what the ancient myths have to do with our modern lives. People went into the Vietnam War with no remembrance of history and with no understanding of the mythic dimensions of our lives. So in structuring *China Men*, I keep the myth and those present-day stories separate, whereas in *The Woman Warrior*, the myths are inside the women and the women are aware of them and living them out.

WOE: Of course, that was the other criticism people had of your work—you were tampering with myth, showing disrespect to Chinese culture. I don't really understand that particular criticism since myth has always been vibrant; if you look at classical Greek mythology, for instance, you can find different versions of many stories. Why do you think you came in for so much criticism on this point?

Kingston: There's a movement in America today where people are looking for roots that will at last get them to firm ground. Those people want something traditional and static. These are very literal people. They say that there is one version of history, and there is one version of myth. And they can hang on to that one version, so it mustn't change. This is traditionalism, retro-thinking, fundamentalism.

My feeling, of course, is different. I would also use that word you used—vibrant. Myth is vibrant and alive as long as it keeps changing. When people emigrate from China (or from anywhere), they bring myths with them, but they change the myths. And if they don't change those myths, those myths are useless and die. So I'm free with myths. I feel I can give them away. One doesn't have to be Chinese to own the Chinese myths; they belong to all of us who hear them. Just like the Greek myths belong to us.

WOE: Earlier you mentioned the need for writers to be as truthful as possible in their work. But sometimes truth seems to lie beyond facts. For instance, if you had stuck to just the facts you had about "no name woman" in *The Woman Warrior* her story would have been incomplete.

Kingston: Yes, but in the example of "no name woman," I didn't have any facts! I didn't even know her name. I had to depend on some things that are not facts to give her her life.

WOE: Then perhaps a better instance is your father's own story in *China Men*; for instance, why did he go to the gold mountain? He seems to give at least three explanations: because he needed to get away from those horrible schoolchildren? because he craved adventure? because he was going to be drafted?

Kingston: Probably all of those things are true. There's also poverty and famine, he's the youngest of brothers, and the other brothers got all of the land. Since he is a strong silent type, how do I ever find the real reasons? *He* won't say what his motives are! This is where the fiction mind comes in very handy. I also had to misdirect the reader—in case the reader works for the INS and deports my father.

WOE: I've heard you mention that Virginia Woolf's *Orlando* and William Carlos Williams' *In the American Grain* influenced your writing of *The Woman Warrior* and *China Men*. How did they do so?

Kingston: I wanted to see American history the same way that William Carlos Williams saw it. For instance, he says to listen to the ground because out of the ground of the Americas comes soul and voice. America's voice will speak out of you. I wanted to be able to do that. After I finished *In the American Grain*, I thought there was going to be a part two because he ends the book with Abraham Lincoln. So I thought I could go and read the rest of it; surely he must have written up to World War II! But it wasn't there. I just couldn't believe there wasn't a part two! My next thought was "Part two is what I'm going to write." I consider *China Men* as part two.

There's a life force that's in *Orlando*. There's a light shining from that book. When I feel discouraged, I can pick it up and read a paragraph and feel up again. Woolf covers four hundred years of history, and one person lives for four hundred years. And I thought, "Yeah, I can treat time like that." The way Virginia Woolf uses time makes sense to me. And frees me, too. If I want a character to live to a hundred and twenty so that he can live many connecting experiences, so that he can go from one part of history to another, then I just go ahead and do it. We don't know exactly how old my grandmother is, my mother and my father are, because they have all these fake papers and stories, and so I just went ahead and gave them long lives and didn't worry about their ages. *Orlando* gave me permission to make them as old as they needed to be.

I'm influenced by everything I read. I just read *Billy Budd* again today, and I hope I was influenced by Melville.

WOE: Was there any particular reason you picked that up?

Kingston: I was trying to describe a veteran of the Vietnam War, and I kept thinking of him as Billy Budd. I wondered, "Is this a correct comparison?" So I read it again today, and I realized that the book is about war. I didn't think about that before; I just thought it was about somebody good who was on a ship. I didn't remember the war. In those days they weren't drafted, they were impressed. The captain in the book even says, "Use the right word for it, it's impressment." Billy Budd is a draftee. And he goes along with it. The story is about mutiny within the military during wartime.

That's the way I'm influenced by reading; I pick up a book and think, "I want to be influenced."

WOE: Does Billy also make you think of your brother, whom you talk about in the story, "The Brother in Vietnam," who is forced into making a series of compromises?

Kingston: But Billy Budd never compromises because he doesn't know how. He's an angel. I've been thinking about various veterans who didn't compromise. They were often the ones who ended up in the brig. I guess it's because they were idealistic. I don't think I know any real Billy Budds. It amazed me at the end, he was so very simple, he wasn't afraid of death. His face didn't change when he was executed.

WOE: I've heard you say that you regret that central metaphor, the warrior, of *The Woman Warrior*. But in some ways the metaphor seems so fitting. Fa Mu Lan fights for a completely just cause. And when you confront your racist boss we are struck by the rightness of your action.

Kingston: Yes, but "warrior" has in it that word "war." Fighting injustice can be done in various ways, such as speaking up or writing. But the word "war" connotes using a weapon—Fa Mu Lan's sword or a gun. Part of my regret for using that metaphor is that since writing *The Woman Warrior*, I have become more of a pacifist. I keep wishing I could invent a peace language. Instead of a woman warrior with a sword, I could create one with a pen who would be just as dramatic. I learned recently about a critic who argues that everybody—including me—who writes about the Vietnam War keeps using the Homeric paradigm. I think he's misread me; I do constantly say, "How can I be the Woman Warrior in America? There's no problem that I have today that I can solve by getting myself a horse and armor and a sword." I do say that in the book.

WOE: When you published *Tripmaster Monkey*, some critics seemed to be relieved that it wasn't about your family, that it was clearly fiction. Some were struck by how different Wittman was from you. I was actually struck by the ways in which he was similar to you. You set the book in 1963, and at that point both you and Wittman had been out of UC Berkeley for a year and you and he both marry Caucasians that year. But perhaps most importantly, you both share an overriding vision of community that shapes your actions and your art. Do you feel this strong connection to Wittman?

Kingston: I do. He's born out of my imagination, so of course he's me, he's who I would have been if I had been a man. Actually, I feel that way about all the people I write about—that I am like them.

Larry Heinemann has an interesting exercise that he gives to students in his writing workshops: write down characteristics of a person who's completely not yourself. Include all kinds of characteristics and personality traits that are not yours. Then create a character using these traits. Of course, what everyone discovers is that the character is yourself!

I really like this exercise because I think that writing has to do with how to get out of one's own narcissism and solipsism in order to imagine another human being and the rest of the universe. It's also very important to be able to create more than one character, the "I" character; it's necessary to be able to enter into the soul and the skin of another human being. This exercise is just great because it's a way of imagining yourself into an other. And not only any other, but somebody who is unsympathetic. I think it's an exercise in compassion.

WOE: The Sixties are still such a disputed time in our history that it seems like a lot of novelists avoid this period. Was it difficult to set the novel in the Sixties?

Kingston: One difficulty in writing about this period is that there are so many stereotypes of the Sixties. And those stereotypes are a way of denying what happened, of simplifying and reducing what happened in the Sixties. It seemed very natural to write about that time because that was an exciting and interesting time of my youth. Even though there's the difficulty of breaking through readers' stereotypes, I've had a lot of experience with that. In the same way, when I wrote about Chinese American men and women, I had to break through terrible stereotypes that are like walls in readers' minds and critics' minds. Wittman is an American just as I am, too, an American. This shouldn't be surprising.

I hope that the surprise for many readers is also in the language. During the Sixties, there were beautiful experiments and breakthroughs in the American language. There were ways of trying to write about new psychic experiences, psychedelic experiences, drug experiences, spiritual and religious breakthroughs. The civil rights movement made new language. Then there was the war, and there was a new language for writing and talking about war and peace. The fun for me in writing *Tripmaster Monkey* was to be able to use the slang of the Sixties. Using Wittman as the central character allowed me to have the fun of using slang, which is a men's language. I don't think women use slang the way men use slang. The slang of the Sixties was really macho. I liked being able to try that voice.

WOE: You published a short piece in *Mother Jones* magazine a few years ago about what happened to Wittman. He moved from the Bay Area, the vortex of the 1960s, to Hawaii, where he was on the edge of both the Sixties and the United States. What would he be doing today?

Kingston: This is what I'm working on; my next book is that story of Wittman going to Hawaii and his continuing involvement with the peace movement. He's doing pretty much what I'm doing today. He fights within himself a certain sort of intellectualism and inaction. After his Berkeley education he doesn't quite want to be an intellectual. He also keeps wanting to be more of a man of action, but at the same time he's not going to be a soldier. These are a young man's battles. And I hope that by the time he gets to be fifty (I haven't written about this yet), he will be a happy community organizer—somebody who knows how to pull a community together. By the time he's in his fifties, of course, he would be one of the elders of the community.

In this new book I'm trying to find the peace language that I mentioned earlier. I'm trying to find a way to show acts of peace that are as dramatic as acts of war. How can we find the nonviolent language to tell a story about facing up to somebody who wants to fight us? How can we do so in a way that's not like *High Noon* or *Shane*? Can we talk our way out of such a situation? You mentioned that scene about facing up to the employers in *The Woman Warrior*, but it took no more than a paragraph to write that. Can the same scene be done more dramatically? So that when a reader reads it, it stands out more than the story of getting on the horse and riding into battle?

WOE: So this new book will be a sequel to *Tripmaster Monkey*?
Kingston: Yes. I'm calling it *The Fifth Book of Peace*.

WOE: Didn't you have a lot of the *Fourth Book* done? How did you overcome the experience of the fire and begin again?
Kingston: Ralph Ellison had a similar experience with a fire and lost a book he was writing; it was such a terrible blow to him that he never seemed to be able to come back from it. But I don't think I'm like that.

Do you know what else I lost? I lost my ability to read. The same thing happened to my husband Earll—we just couldn't read. It was one of my symptoms of post-traumatic stress disorder. I wasn't able to concentrate. Even the newspaper—I couldn't get past the first paragraph. I would read slowly, and I wouldn't be able to concentrate. That lasted longer than not being able to write.

I did not immediately start writing the book that was lost. I started to write in the same way that I wrote when I was a child. The way I could write again was to begin the way I did when I was a kid, which was to write about what I was feeling. Just about "I." I couldn't write from an omniscient point of view or about somebody else's feelings. I just wanted to write about my own feelings, and they could be as incoherent and ungrammatical as I wanted. I had no thought that this was going to be published or read by another person. It would be writing in the same way that a diary writer would write.

WOE: When you came back to the book, had it changed?

Kingston: I led into that former book. I spent hundreds of pages writing in this other way. And then, after I don't remember how long—a month or a year—then I could start writing about other people and writing fiction again. So this new book is going to be very complicated. I've decided to leave in all the stuff about how to get into the thinking mind, the mind that can write. How do you get into words again? I am going to leave all that in. That's about a third of the book. Next I get into the book that I was writing, which is the fiction about Wittman. Then finally I come out of the fiction. So this book enters a real nonfiction place, then it flies to a fiction place, and then it grounds us again in a nonfiction place. I haven't seen another book like it, nor, once again do I know how people will categorize it. Are they going to call it fiction or nonfiction? It is a nonfiction fiction nonfiction sandwich.

WOE: In calling attention to the process of writing it sounds a bit as if you're doing something that Tim O'Brien does in his work.

Kingston: Yeah, he does a beautiful job of that. I really like the way he writes about writing. He'll write a story, and then he'll write about how he wrote the story. Next he'll get into a story that he imagines. Then he'll hear from the person that he was writing about, and modify the story. He does a beautiful job.

WOE: Wasn't it at the time after the fire when you were trying to get back into writing that Deborah Rogin was working on the adaptation of *The Woman Warrior*? Were you involved with that project at all?

Kingston: Soon after *The Woman Warrior* was published, we began trying to write scripts, but it wasn't until right after the fire that the Berkeley Rep got it together to produce the play. I was involved with it; I talked to various people: the producer, the director, the playwright.

WOE: Did you feel that the theater was a more appropriate medium than film might have been?

Kingston: We still want to make a film. But I think that the theater was a wonderfully appropriate medium because it was a way of getting all of those people on stage, people from all different Asian American backgrounds. It was a breakthrough in nontraditional casting. I think a movie would try to make everybody look the same, like everybody in the family would have to look the same. But in the play, it was really wonderful to have Vietnamese accents, Japanese American accents, Hawaiian accents, a Singaporean accent, and all the different Chinese accents. What they were doing with the music and acting styles was wonderful stuff, the fusion they were doing, using jazz and Chinese opera and masks—I really thought that was a right way to translate what I was doing.

WOE: In the story "The Brother in Vietnam," the account of your brother's initial teaching career seems in some ways to mirror your father's early teaching career.
Kingston: Yeah, that's true.

WOE: Both might be described as nightmarish. I wonder if your own early high school teaching career might also be characterized this way.
Kingston: It was so easy for me to write about my father's teaching and my brother's teaching because I just used their experiences to express my own feelings about teaching. I was trying to teach high school and write *The Woman Warrior*. Sometimes when I taught this course called "The Novel into Film," I would show the students a film, and I would be up in the projection booth writing my book.

I did my student teaching at Oakland Tech and Oakland High, and I taught at Sunset High School in Hayward, California, and then high school in Hawaii. I've taught school at every level: I've taught grammar school, high school, college, business college. I've taught literature, writing, and math. So I've had lots of experiences—I've stopped fights, I've taken weapons away from kids.

WOE: Did you ever reach a point where you thought, "This just isn't worth it"?
Kingston: No, I always thought it was worth it. But I have many times reached the point where I'd think, "I can't do this anymore. I'm just physically and spiritually incapable of going on." I've had burnout maybe three or four times. But then I always went back. You know, taking weapons away from the kids—that's not the worst part. I think the worst part is when you get a group like the football team sitting in the back row and they've got their

arms folded and they won't participate in a discussion. They're not making a lot of noise in class or anything. In fact, they're quiet. But they just aren't listening, aren't engaged. I think, "I'm friendly and I care about them; my lessons are interesting, I know I'm entertaining." No matter what, I just wasn't getting through to them. But then there are times when you do get through.

One reason I keep going back is I have a recurring dream (or nightmare) that my mother—big, middle-aged, at her strongest—says to me, "Have you educated America yet?" Or she says, "Well, what have you done to educate the world lately?" So it's a calling, a challenge, and I have to do it.

WOE: That accounts for why, after you have been successful as a writer, you came back to teach at your alma mater, Berkeley, where you teach writing seminars for graduate and undergraduate students alike. But most recently you've been working with a very different population of writers.

Kingston: I've been on leave of absence from Cal for the last three years teaching war veterans. I've had writing workshops and meditation workshops for war veterans. I think I have a calling to be a teacher in the same way that I have a calling to be a writer. I can't not do it. If I didn't have a job as a teacher, I'd start a class and ask people if they want to come.

I first started thinking about doing the veterans' workshop about six or eight years ago when I attended one of the retreats that Thich Nhat Hanh had for veterans of war. He called these workshops "Healing the Wounds of War." Most of the people who attended were Vietnam veterans from America and from Vietnam. They'd get together for meditation and discussions. At the time I thought, "They need one more component; they need an art. And specifically writing." So I asked to give a writing workshop during one of these Thich Nhat Hanh retreats. I incorporated writing into a Buddhist day of meditation. A few years later, the Lila Wallace Fund gave me a fellowship and asked if I would pick a community project to work on. I decided that what I wanted to do was to give more of those writing workshops—to do them on a regular basis and include veterans of all wars.

WOE: One of the things you did with those workshops was to expand the definition of a veteran—for instance, you had spouses of veterans attend the workshops. How did you find the people who would be in the workshops?

Kingston: Most of them found me. One way they found me was that for years I've been carrying around the letters of veterans who wrote to me, and I didn't know how to answer them. Finally, one way to answer them was to say, "Let's get together and figure out how to express ourselves in art. Let's make an art out of this war that we were all in."

I think the veterans themselves expanded this idea of what a veteran is because they began to see that there are veterans of these wars who were never in uniform. Wars have terrible consequences for all kinds of people: people who were in prison camps, people who watched their families die in front of them. Surely those people are also veterans! And then, most wonderfully, the definition expanded to peace veterans. People who were in the streets, who were in demonstrations, who were in riots. People who went to jail because they refused the draft. We all began to see that they were also veterans of war.

WOE: Could you describe what one of those workshops would be like?

Kingston: Because we thought of ourselves as forming a writing community, we spent lots of time together. When we were together it was the strength and the support of the community that made it possible for us to heal war wounds and also to create art.

We usually tried to meet in a beautiful place, like a farm house, or some other lovely place in nature. We would begin the day with meditation, and then we'd usually have some kind of an exercise or question that we'd all think about; each of us would then talk about ourselves in relation to some question, such as how we felt on Veteran's Day; or how we felt when we just heard that Lewis Puller Jr., who was a Vietnam veteran and award-winning writer, killed himself. I usually give a talk on some aspect of writing, and then everybody goes to some nice corner of the room and we write together. I've also invited other people—Larry Heinemann and George Evans and Grace Paley and Vietnamese writers from Hanoi and Saigon—to give the talk on writing. And, of course, the speakers not only talk about writing but also about what we've all been through. When we're writing together, in community, I like to think that we're not writing alone. We know there's other people who want to hear our stories. Then we eat together (we do a lot of civilized things together). After lunch, I evoke the Bodhisattva of compassionate listening, Kuan Yin, the goddess of mercy. Then we read our work aloud and listen to one another. We all try to listen with compassionate understanding and without judgment. We listen for what is said, but also what's not said. Everyone takes a turn reading, and then we do a walking meditation. Next we give responses to one another's readings, and then we have a meditation again. That's the end of the day. I like to think that we're living together for one whole day.

WOE: I've encountered veterans who didn't want their writing to be seen as therapy; they wanted it to be seen as art. Was this an issue with your group?

Kingston: I think that's so good you could recognize that. The whole time that I've been giving these workshops—especially at the beginning—I wanted to make sure that the veterans didn't see this time as merely therapy. I didn't want them to see me as a therapist trying to fix them. We were writers. And what we were producing was art.

What's really wonderful is that two of the veterans are right now coming out with books, and a whole lot of others have published shorter pieces. One of the veterans, John Mulligan, whose book is being published, also has two plays out at the same time. These veterans are producing professional, published work.

WOE: Many veterans didn't complete high school, let alone college. How were your students able to publish their work so quickly?

Kingston: It's not quickly—it's been three years. Six years counting the workshops with Thich Nhat Hanh.

WOE: But many people complete high school, college, and creative writing M.A. programs and still aren't able to publish their work.

Kingston: I think a lot of the veterans were already writers in the way that I was a storyteller when I was two years old and a writer when I was eight years old. When I first met them I was impressed when a couple of people said, "I think I went to Vietnam so that I could find some stories to write." They were like born writers—they had a calling. They were already writers when they went to Vietnam. Even though they hadn't written anything, some of them already had that inspiration. And then there was another type of person; maybe they weren't thinking like that, but they were full of life experiences and adventures and traumas and feelings and pain. These people just began to think, "Well, what if I wrote it down? Maybe I can use this stuff! Just this garbage that happened, this excitement—maybe it can be used." They are gifted with so much more than what most college students have because there's just a whole lot of life in them. They just need to find a way to set it down.

WOE: What was it about the workshops that helped them to do this?

Kingston: The community of people who wanted to hear the stories. And I wanted to hear the stories. One crucial technique of a teacher is to convince students that "Yes, I do want to hear what you have to say. So just tell it to me or write it to me." It was also important to set aside a lot of time to hear stories. (In our case it was just one day a month, but it was all day.) With their jobs and everything else they were doing in their lives, they had to organize their lives so that there was one whole day that they could devote to this consciousness and this writing.

WOE: This is very different from teaching undergraduates at the university. Does each group of writers have its unique problems?

Kingston: The people that I worked with in the veterans' workshops were older and had more experience (although I often find that certain people at the University have a lot of life experience and are full of eagerness and knowledge). But because I haven't been back to teaching college since the experience of teaching veterans, I'm trying to anticipate whether I'm going to feel differently about college-age people. Offhand, I think they would respond to the same kind of teaching.

I've been wondering what would happen if I began a class at a public university with meditation. Would it really be possible for me to go into a university teaching situation and ignore that we have spiritual lives that need to be written into our stories? I don't want to get up in front of a university class and appear New Age and flaky. But I've been working hard to integrate people's psyches and I know that we cannot separate our spiritual lives from our intellectual and artistic lives. This is the work I've been doing with the veterans—pulling all the pieces of our lives together. By spring I'm going to figure out how to do this in my college class.

Index